The Political Police in Britain

The Political Police in Britain

TONY BUNYAN

WITHDRAWN

ST. MARTIN'S PRESS   NEW YORK

Contents

Preface

The purpose of this book is to trace the development of the agencies of the state whose function is to counter and contain political movements in this country. Existing treatments of the main agencies concerned – the police, the Special Branch, MI5 and the military – tend to consider their activities separately; here they are considered as part of an interdependent matrix. The full import of their practices cannot, however, be adequately understood without also taking into account the role of law (and its application in specifically political situations) together with the techniques of surveillance and infiltration employed by the state and by private industry. Lastly, the wider social and political context within which the state acts and within which it has developed historically must be the starting point if an adequate understanding is to be furthered.

The limitations of this book should also be noted at this point. No attempt is made to treat in depth a number of topics related to the main themes: the continuing conflict in Northern Ireland; public order and police powers; foreign intelligence agencies operating in Britain; and the role of the media. The reasons for this are partly because some of these areas have been dealt with already, and partly because to have done so would have substantially extended an already lengthy book.[1] Nor is the book primarily concerned with the histories and activities of political movements themselves, but rather with the state's reaction to these movements.

The book may serve two functions, according to the political perspective of the reader. On the one hand, it is an historical and contemporary examination of the actions of the state – which casts it in the mould of a critique. To this extent liberals will find much that should make them feel decidedly uncomfortable. On the other hand, by drawing out the historical and on-going confrontation between the

[1] Northern Ireland: John McGuffin, *The Guinea Pigs* (1974) and Eamonn McCann, *War and an Irish Town* (1974). Public order and police powers: Ian Brownlie, *The Law Relating to Public Order* (1968); A. Coote and L. Grant, *The NCCL Guide* (1972); D. Madgwick and T. Smythe, *The Invasion of Privacy* (1974); B. Cox. *Civil Liberties in Britain* (1975).

state and socialist movements in Britain it may aid those engaged in political struggle.

Few people have access to the raw information necessary to an understanding of the basic structures, histories and practices of the state and its agencies. Those who do – the agencies themselves, some politicians, and the media – more often than not act together to mystify rather than to inform. What is recorded here therefore is not only the more newsworthy aspects of their work but also information on precisely those aspects which may lead to an everyday knowledge of their activities and practices.

August 1975   TONY BUNYAN

Acknowledgments

I should like to thank the following organisations for their help in preparing this book: The National Council for Civil Liberties; Hull University Library; The Public Library (King's Cross, London). Many individuals gave invaluable help in gathering source material and commenting on certain parts of the book. In particular I should like to thank Tony Smythe, Larry Grant, Frank Pearce, Phil Kelly and Chaz Ball. For editing Christine King, and for typing Molly Ann Coleman.

Chapter 6, on the private security industry, was contributed by Chris Bunyan.

Introduction

I

The subject of this book is the maintenance of law and order and the continuing internal security of the British state. More precisely the book is concerned with the response to political opposition by the state agencies concerned with these tasks. The liberal-democratic view of the state is part of our 'received history'. This view permeates not just education and politics but also everyday life. Liberal-democratic theory does not, in the main, view the state as a central concept for understanding either the present or the nation's historical past.[1] Where the state is postulated it is seen as operating over and above the different sectional interests within society, acting as it were in the interests of all the people regardless of class or colour.

Most people in Britain would characterise the political system under which they live as a democracy – with universal adult suffrage, freedom of speech, democratic institutions at national and local level, and the protection of individual rights by the law of the land. The tenets of liberal-democracy however extend beyond the right to vote and the right of free speech, embracing a fundamental commitment to the ownership of private property and to a market economy.

Britain, as is well known, does not have a written constitution like other democracies in the West, but the constitutional relationship between its different institutions is nonetheless made explicit by historical practice. Underpinning the various elements of the constitution is the idea of the separation of powers. This asserts the independence of the executive, the legislature and the judiciary from each other. The Civil Service is thus free from political bias, the law from governmental or political influence, and the police from state direction. Indeed the law, the police and the Civil Service retain public

---

[1] See for example: Sir C. K. Allen, *The Queen's Peace* (1953); Walter Bagehot, *The English Constitution* (1963) introduced by Richard Crossman; Sir Ivor Jennings, *The Law and the Constitution* (1959); Sir O. L. Keir, *The Constitutional History of Modern Britain* (1966). Also see Appendix.

1

confidence because they are above sectional interests and in this way are able to act in the name of society as a whole.

An alternative to this interpretation of society and the state is that from within the socialist tradition. This perspective, to which the author subscribes, insists that 'A theory of the state is also a theory of society and of the distribution of power in that society.'[2] The state in this view is not simply an institution common to all societies, to be studied in the search for universalistic features: it can be understood only in an historically specific context, in this case Britain. The development and practices of the institutions of the British state are therefore intimately linked to the rise of capitalism and the classes that grew out of it.

The liberal-democratic belief that the state acts as a neutral arbiter has an important legitimating function since it implies that the state acts for the benefit of society as a whole. Working-class political action is therefore not seen for what it is, a confrontation of capital and labour, but as action against the interests of all. In this way the class nature of democratic institutions and of the state are continually denied as a reality. The crux of this 'confusion' lies in the supposed relationship of the government to state institutions, for it is argued that the democratically elected government controls these institutions. It is often accepted that the term 'government' can be used as a ready substitute for the term 'state'; however, the government is but one of the institutions which make up the state. The executive authority of government itself is limited in respect of the other state institutions, whose policy and practice more often than not lie outside of direct governmental control. The government therefore does not control the state; rather, the institutions making up the state – of which the government is one – act together in commanding state power.

This book is concerned with those state institutions which operate primarily through the actual, or potential, use of coercive sanctions and repression (including physical force). These institutions include the military, the police, the prisons, the courts of law, the government (the exercise of executive power, i.e. PM and Cabinet) and the state administration.[3] Furthermore, these institutions should be seen not as

[2] Ralph Miliband, *The State in Capitalist Society* (1969) p. 2.

[3] The inclusion of the latter may require some explanation: it refers to what is conventionally termed the 'Civil Service'. The departments manned by the Civil Service are state institutions and their personnel, far from being servants of the people as a whole, are state employees.

subservient to government, as the liberal-democratic notion suggests, but rather as interdependent centres of state power.

II

The role of these institutions and the repressive state agencies in liberal-democracies is to ensure the reproduction of the capitalist system.

'A safe and independent life for a nation and its people requires effective defence against the threat of attack from outside. It requires the maintenance of the nation's relations with the rest of the world, and *of its essential economic base*. It requires the preservation of law and order, and the ability to cope with emergencies threatening the essentials of life.'[4]

These agencies thus have a two-fold purpose. Firstly, the maintenance of law and order through the law (and the judiciary) and its enforcers (the police) when society is at 'social peace'. Secondly, for the internal security of the state in those periods when the very foundations of the capitalist system are under attack – in short, when the 'normal' rule of law is insufficient to contain political opposition.

The agencies most involved are only marginally subject to liberal-democratic control through the formal political system. The police are constitutionally answerable to the law of the land and not to democratic institutions (so too, is the Special Branch which is recruited from the ranks of the uniformed police). The military are responsible to the Crown and their actions are governed by Queen's Regulations. Of the intelligence agencies military intelligence (the Defence Intelligence Staff) is formally responsible to the Ministry of Defence, MI5 to the Home Secretary and MI6 to the Foreign Secretary.[5] In reality these agencies operate with a high degree of independence.

[4] Franks Committee Report (HMSO, 1972) Vol. 1, p. 64. My emphasis.
[5] MI5 and MI6 are now officially called DI5 and DI6. However, in order to avoid confusion over the many appellations which have been given to these agencies in the past, MI5 and MI6 are used throughout this book. MI5 is responsible for countering foreign espionage and combating subversion within Great Britain, while MI6 is concerned with intelligence-gathering and spying externally.

Moreover, Ministers of both parties have always resisted detailed questions into the working of the military, police, Special Branch and MI5, on the basis that they are not constitutionally responsible to parliament.

The ways in which each of these agencies historically attained in-dependence within the constitutional framework and the part they have played in sustaining the capitalist structure of British society will become apparent as the origins of their present status and practices are examined in the following chapters.[6]

---

[6] See the Appendix for an historical account of the general relationship between the state, liberal-democracy and capitalism.

1 *The Political Uses of Law*

The British state has available to it the whole of criminal law for use against political opposition: the laws used against political activists embrace those normally used against the criminal and those for maintaining public order.[1] There are, in addition, a number of overtly political laws drawn up to protect and preserve the state in a capitalist society, and it is to these laws that this chapter is directed.

Today there are three Official Secrets Acts in force, those of 1911, 1920 and 1939. The first Act of 1889 was replaced by that of 1911, and the 1911 Act was supplemented by those of 1920 and 1939. Since their inception there have been two inquiries into the workings of the Acts. The first was a Select Committee appointed in 1938/39 which looked at Section 6 of the 1920 Act. The second was the Franks Committee set up by the 1970–74 Heath government after the prosecution in 1970 of the *Sunday Telegraph*.[2]

The Official Secrets Acts

Prior to the first Act of 1889 the only recourse of government when a civil servant or member of the armed forces leaked information was dismissal or the bringing of criminal charges of theft. For most of the nineteenth century such disloyal conduct was regarded as ungentlemanly and unpatriotic and the state could rely on the social milieu of those professions exercising its own restraints. Disclosures of information in the first half of the century usually concerned international questions, as for example when the publication was proposed in 1837 of Lord Wellesley's 1809 papers from Spain and the Foreign Office could only protest ineffectually. Similarly the government was left without sanctions when *The Times* chose to publish Lord

---

[1] For a detailed consideration of the Public Order Acts see Ian Brownlie, *The Laws Relating to Public Order* (1968).

[2] The editor of the *Sunday Telegraph*, Mr B. Roberts and Jonathan Aitken and others were prosecuted after the publication of a confidential report on the war between Nigeria and Biafra. They were charged under Section 2 of the 1911 Official Secrets Act, and were all acquitted at the trial. See Jonathan Aitken, *Officially Secret* (1971).

Castlereagh's letters relating to the Congress of Vienna some thirty years after the event. There was also the case of William Guernsey who, in 1858, stole some papers from the Colonial Office after he was refused a job there. The papers were published by the *Daily News* and embarrassed Mr Gladstone. (At the time, Gladstone was *en route* to the Ionian Islands, whose inhabitants he hoped – unsuccessfully – to dissuade from their ambition to be joined with Greece.) In 1878 a temporary clerk at the Foreign Office, Charles Marvin, leaked details of the Anglo-Russian treaty on the Congress of Berlin to the press. He was charged under the Larceny Act of 1861 but the case was dismissed for insufficient evidence. This case was followed by other disclosures, such as the organisation of the Exchequer and Audit Office; a proposed pay-rise for letter carriers; and, in 1884, General Gordon's proclamation to the press before MPs got their copies.

To counter these irregular practices the Treasury issued three internal circulars in 1873, 1875 and 1884, threatening civil servants with dismissal for 'discrediting the Service', reflecting a reluctance to legislate where a reminder of correct conduct within the Victorian assumption of shared values was thought to suffice. However, by 1887 this was demonstrated to be insufficient. Internal instructions to the Intelligence Department of the Royal Navy appeared in the press, and a dockyard draughtsman sold a set of warship designs to a foreign power. The First Lord of the Admiralty promised that a Bill employing criminal sanctions would be prepared and two years later the first Official Secrets Act was passed. A Bill was presented to parliament in 1888 under the title 'Breach of Official Trust'. It was mainly concerned with civil servants' disclosures to the press and did not cover spying for or by a foreign power. A re-drafted proposal was presented in 1889, renamed the 'Official Secrets Bill'. In the Commons Lord Salisbury's Attorney-General, Sir Richard Webster, moved the second reading with the following words (given here *in toto*):

> 'I wish to say just a word or two with regard to this Bill. It has been prepared under the direction of the Secretary of State for War and the First Lord of the Admiralty in order to punish the offence of obtaining information and communicating it against the interests of the State. The Bill is an exceedingly simple one and I beg to move its second reading.'[3]

The third and final reading occupied a mere seven columns of *Hansard*. The Bill had two sections: the first dealt with spying and the

[3] *Hansard*, 28 March 1889.

second with breaches of official trust by state employees, and, compared with the later 1911 Act, it limited breaches of trust to those which could be shown by the prosecution to be against the public interest. The duality of purpose which runs through all later legislation has its foundation in this 1889 Act, which sought to encompass both the activities of spies on behalf of a foreign power *and* internal disclosures by state employees.

In 1896 and 1908 the government wanted to amend the 1889 Act which in practice had proved ineffectual in stopping leaks from civil servants. Most of the cases brought under the Act were concerned with minor military and naval secrets, and not all prosecutions were successful. A major failing of the 1889 Act was that it did not punish the recipient of information (except proven spies). Hence a civil servant might be charged, but no action could be taken against the journalist and the paper responsible for receiving and publishing the information. This mistake was not to be repeated in 1911.

The primary motive for the 1889 Act, and for the abortive Bills of 1896 and 1908, was to place restrictions on the unauthorised disclosure of information by state employees. Or, put another way, it was to ensure that the inner workings of government and the state agencies remained hidden from public view and potential criticism – a principle that still remains central to the use of the OSAs. Concern over the activities of foreign spies was secondary, indeed 'foreign spies were openly tolerated'.[4] By 1910 however the capitalist nations of Europe were seeking to challenge Britain's dominance, on the continent and elsewhere in the world, and the Kaiser's obvious militaristic ambitions finally impressed upon Britain's rulers the need to take action against foreign spies.

The 1911 Official Secrets Act is the central law governing this field today, yet it passed through parliament in a mere thirty minutes, occupying less than eight columns in *Hansard*. To understand how this came about it is necessary to go back to 1909. It was in this year that the Committee for Imperial Defence decided to set up a small unit (MI5, then known as MO5) under Captain Vernon Kell, to collect information on German spying activities in Britain. Kell found evidence of holidaying German officers gathering information on harbour plans and the like. However, he soon realised that the 1889 OSA was quite insufficient to deal with these German spies and raised the matter with Sir Henry Wilson, the Director of Military Operations. Up until 1910

[4] David Williams, *Not in the Public Interest* (1965), p. 23.

the War Minister, Mr Haldane, had, along with his fellow Ministers (and most MPs) not taken the Kaiser's posturing seriously. Within months Haldane's view changed when he was presented with evidence from Kell of German spying expeditions. Thus Kell provided the initiative for change in this field against a background of growing awareness of Germany's intentions. He realised that the law as it stood placed the responsibility for proving guilt on the state prosecutor (as is usual in English law) and believed this meant many people he 'knew' to be spies could claim an innocent intent when apprehended. Therefore, 'Kell's only chance was to have the law changed', which he duly set about doing.[5]

With Haldane won over, the question was referred to a sub-committee of the Committee for Imperial Defence, which drafted a new Bill with the aid of the various intelligence services, the War Ministry, the Admiralty and the Home Office. This was presented to the House of Lords in July 1911, where Haldane made special mention of the point raised by Kell. He said that if someone was found

'in a place where prima facie his presence is prejudicial to the safety or interests of the State, he has to satisfy the jury that his purpose was a right one. That – as I have said – is not a new point. It is a section taken from the Prevention of Crimes Act. Under that section certain classes of offenders have to justify themselves when their character and conduct raise suspicion.'[6]

No changes were made in the Lords and within a week the Bill was presented to the Commons. The day selected by the government to introduce this controversial Bill was a Friday, 18 August 1911. Fridays were, and still are, notorious for low attendances in the Commons, because most members leave in the morning for their constituencies and to see their families. Bulloch catches the moment well: 'By a brilliant though unscrupulous use of Parliamentary procedure, Colonel Seely, Under-Secretary at the War Office, carried all the stages within thirty minutes in the face of considerable opposition by two or three Members who were quick enough to realise what was going on.'[7] Seely insisted the Bill be passed in all its stages that day, and the Attorney-General, Sir Rufus Isaacs, smoothed the tempers of Opposition members who saw the Bill as a drastic change in the balance of

[5] John Bulloch, *MI*5 (1963), p. 76.
[6] Bulloch, *op. cit.,* pp. 77–78.
[7] Bulloch, *op. cit.,* p. 76.

British justice by assuring them that their 'ancient liberties' would remain intact. The second reading, the Committee stage, and the third
reading, took just a few minutes and with the Royal seal affixed four
days later the 1911 Official Secrets Act became part of the law of the
land. Bulloch's admiration for the management of the Bill is barely
concealed, and he sums up:

> 'Whatever the motives, the handling of the Bill was a masterly
> piece of Parliamentary "gamesmanship", and it was a real
> triumph for Kell – a vindication and acceptance of all the work of
> his department. And in the years to come the Official Secrets Act
> 1911, proved a very potent weapon against spies who came to
> Britain'.[8]

In fact the 1911 Act became not just a means of tackling spies but, more
importantly, a method of preserving government secrecy.

The Act may have been passed with indecent haste, but the long-
term planning by the government for such legislation is not in doubt.
The historical notes in the Franks Committee Report, compiled with
the advantage of access to official papers, make this point:

> 'Nor was the Bill prepared in haste. The Report of the Sub-
> Committee of the Committee of Imperial Defence on Espionage
> was presented . . . (and the) first draft of the Bill found in official
> papers is dated a full year before its introduction. Some of its
> provisions can be traced back to the 1896 Bill. Some of the wor-
> ding of the new Section 2 derives from the 1908 Bill.'[9]

The bland assertion at the time, that the Bill of 1911 was directed at
foreign spies and not at the home population (civil servants, press, etc.)
was supported by the heading to Section 1, namely 'Penalties for
Spying'. This assertion is rejected by the Franks Committee evidence.
They found a clear intention from 1889 to 1971 to operate the Acts as
'a general check against civil service leaks of all kinds . . . and . . . [not]
confined to matters connected with the safety of the State.'[10] And not
only civil servants and foreign spies came within the purview of the
state. The 1911 Act was backed in 1912 by the introduction of the 'Admiralty, War Office and Press Committee' to 'advise' the press on sensitive matters of state. (This is now known as the 'Services, Press and

[8] *Ibid.*, p. 80.
[9] Franks, Vol. 1, p. 123.
[10] *Ibid.*

Broadcasting Committee', or, more popularly, the 'D-Notice Committee'.)

The motives of the government in moving the 1920 Act, which amended the 1911 Act, were several. The traditional historical interpretation lays emphasis on the need to amend the 1911 Act in the light of the experiences of the First World War. In fact the period between 1917 and 1920 was also one of great turmoil and conflict within Britain when the possibility of revolution along the lines of October 1917 were very real. The protection offered by wartime legislation like the Defence of the Realm Act (DORA)[11] was coming to an end and the government wished to avail itself of similar defences in peacetime. The 1920 Official Secrets Act and the 1920 Emergency Powers Act were specifically geared to this need. Kell at MI5 again played an important part in framing the amendments. During the passage of the Bill the Attorney-General, Sir Gordon Hewart, made several memorable references to the effect that the Bill was primarily intended to deal with 'spying and attempts at spying' and not with civil matters. This had clearly not been the practice prior to 1920, and was not the practice thereafter. Fifteen years later, in 1935, a turf accountant who had an accommodation address for his business, was prosecuted under a section of the 1920 Act. The magistrate dismissed the charges. However, the Attorney-General of the day appealed against this decision and the appeal was heard by none other than Lord Chief Justice Hewart who decided in favour of the state.

The Official Secrets Act of 1939 amended Section 6 of the 1920 Act, which had stated that it was the duty of a citizen to reveal the source of his information in matters affected by the Acts. Failure to do so was punishable by up to two years in prison. The amendment occurred because of the threat by the National Government to prosecute the young Duncan Sandys who used information, gained while in the Territorial Army, to frame a series of parliamentary questions on civil defence. As a result a Select Committee was appointed and its recommendation, that this clause be limited to Section 1 (1911 Act), that is, to cases of espionage, was agreed by the Commons. There have been two significant uses of the Acts against the press in recent times. In one, the *Sunday Telegraph* case in 1970–71 the defendants were acquitted, and in the other, Brendan Mulholland, of the *Daily Mail*, and Reginald Foster, of the *Daily Sketch*, were sentenced to six months and three months in prison respectively in the High Court for failing to reveal their sources of information to the Radcliffe tribunal in 1962.

[11] See p. 52.

Together the three Acts of 1911, 1920 and 1939 provide governments with a formidable and all-embracing net with which to catch spies, civil servants, the press and the citizen in the field of official secrecy. The reluctance of governments – of whatever colour – to consider changes in the Acts is not hard to understand, and this will become even more apparent when we examine the provisions of each Act, and the uses which governments have made of them.

The scope of the Official Secrets Acts

To understand the exact nature of the protection afforded to government by the three Acts, their central purpose should be seen primarily as a means of *internal* rather than external restraint. The extent to which the Acts 'deter' agents of foreign countries from continuing their activities is clearly negligible, and the penalties for being caught are accepted as a necessary risk in this kind of work. In internal affairs the very reverse is true: the Acts not only deter mischievous 'leaking of information', but also underpin the traditional secrecy of the workings of the state on the part of the Civil Service. By this means information is so restricted as to guarantee an ill-informed parliament, press and people on the central issues of the day. The Acts also represent a formidable weapon should internal conflict arise within Britain, and the laws could be used most effectively against political opponents of all kinds.

Section 1 of the 1911 Act opens with the statement: 'If any person for any purpose prejudicial to the safety or interests of the State . . . a) approaches or is in the neighbourhood of, or enters any prohibited place . . . b) makes any sketch . . . (or) note calculated to be or [which] might be . . . useful to an enemy . . . c) obtains or communicates to any person any sketch, plan, model, article or note . . . calculated to be or [which] might be . . . useful to an enemy . . ., then it shall be an offence under this Act.' The section goes on: '. . . it shall not be necessary to show that the accused person was guilty of any particular act . . . he may be convicted if, from the circumstances of the case, or his conduct, or his known character as proved, it appears that his purpose was a purpose prejudicial to the safety or interests of the State'. This means that a known political activist seen approaching Her Majesty's Stationery Office in Holborn Viaduct, or 55–57 Drury Lane (a prohibited place under the 1911 Act, Section 1, no. 1482, issued in 1954) could be sent to prison for between three and seven years. The 'known' political actions and beliefs of the person, presented no doubt from intelligence files, would in themselves be sufficient to prove that his purpose was prejudicial to the interests of the State – and in court the onus would be on the defence to prove otherwise: an act 'shall be deemed . . . prejudicial to the safety and interests of the State unless the contrary is proved' (Section 1, para. 2).

The intent needs little explanation. It is the central clause of the three Acts which, although directed ostensibly at espionage, was used in the case of the state against Terry Chandler in 1964 that arose out of the Committee of 100 demonstration at Wethersfield airfield. On appeal against conviction and sentence the House of Lords determined that 'the interests of the State' were defined by the government of the day and not by the courts. In other words if the Attorney-General, who has to consent to every prosecution under the Acts, gives his approval in a decision to prosecute, then this is deemed to express the government's view that the interests of the state have been jeopardised. The all-embracing nature of the section is clear from such terms as 'approaches, or is in the neighbourhood of' and '(might be) useful to an enemy'. Further, while a definition of 'an enemy' may well have been easy in 1911 it is far less so today. For example, suppose Britain became involved in a war in the Middle East on the side of Israel. This would place political activists sympathetic to Palestine or Arab causes in the category of spying under Section 1. What may today be considered perfectly legitimate political action would become illegal overnight, and be punishable by up to fourteen years in prison (1920 Act, Section 8).

Under Section 2 it is an offence for a state employee to retain any sketch, note, plan, article, document or information, or communicate these to an unauthorised person (throughout this chapter reference to 'unauthorised persons' means effectively everyone outside state employment). The receiver of such information, in whatever form, is also guilty of an offence, and both are liable to up to two years in prison and/or a fine. It is this section which the Franks Committee was set up to investigate because it is the provision most frequently used against journalists and newspapers. The term 'official information' is described as anything which 'relates to or is used in a prohibited place' or which is entrusted to a state employee.

Section 3 of the 1911 Act defines a 'prohibited place' as every building which the state chooses to define as such, and the section proscribes not only any action directed against these places, but also any information held about them 'useful to an enemy'.

Section 4 deals with inciting others to commit an offence under the Act (the penalty for which is the same as if the offence had actually been committed by the accused); Sections 5 and 6 allow for a person to be charged with a felony (the more serious charge) or a misdemeanour, as the state sees fit, and for a person 'being about to commit' an offence to be arrested as if he had actually committed it; Section 7 makes it an offence to harbour a person who has committed, or who is about to commit an offence. The latter provision applies to both serious and technical offences under the Acts and is an exception to the normal rule of law. For example, under the Criminal Law Act 1967 it is only an offence if the person harboured *has* committed an arrestable offence, that is, one carrying a sentence of more than five years' imprisonment.

Section 8 states that any proceedings under the Acts must have the consent of the Attorney-General. Finally, Section 9 allows for search warrants to be granted by a JP or, in the case of 'great emergency', by a police superintendent alone.

The 1920 Act amended and strengthened the 1911 Act, and it was drafted and enacted in the period just after the end of the First World War. Section 1 of the 1920 Act created a series of additional offences including the use of false pretences to gain access to a prohibited place (e.g. wearing an official uniform or using a forged pass) and the mere act of giving an official document to another person. The definition of an 'official' document specifically includes 'any passport', thus making a perfectly innocent act capable of being construed as an offence, and no purpose prejudicial to the state or intent to misuse the passport, is required for prosecution. Under Section 2 communication (in whatever form) with a foreign agent is sufficient for prosecution, for it is assumed that a defendant has committed an act prejudicial to the interests of the state. The prosecution does not even have to prove that the defendant has actually been in communication with the foreign agent; it is sufficient if he has, or has had, the name and address of such a person in his possession, or has visited the address of the said person. With this amendment the term 'enemy' in the 1911 Act is extended to 'foreign agent'. An 'enemy' presumes the country to be at war (or about to be), whereas a 'foreign agent' is defined as one who, in the interests of a foreign power, is likely to act against the 'safety or interests of the State'. It is not difficult to imagine the possible uses of this section against political opponents, for if they do not innocently infringe it, the simple 'planting' of an address will suffice.

Section 4 deals with anyone interfering with the police or armed forces in or near a prohibited place. Section 5 says that all private radio messages or telegrams must be produced on demand. Section 6 governs the registration of accommodation addresses, and also requires the production of information to the police on demand. The former part of the Section stems from the use of accommodation addresses by two German spy rings in the First World War, and later this section resulted in the absurd prosecution of the turf accountant.[12] Section 6 was amended by the 1939 Act and its application limited to cases in respect of Section 1 of the 1911 Act, that is, to cases of espionage. However, despite this amendment the Act still requires anyone holding any information in relation to these Acts to tell a police officer or member of the armed forces all he knows on demand – not to do so is punishable by up to two years in prison. The section offers no protection against self-incrimination and is yet another exception to the normal rule of law. In 1920 when Sir Gordon Hewart was challenged on this point he said it was the moral duty of every citizen to offer up information about spying: 'I cannot think it can be regarded as harsh that the Bill should make a statutory duty of that which is already a moral duty . . .' he said.[13] Section 7 makes 'any act preparatory' to committing an offence punishable in exactly the same terms as if the offence had actually been committed, and again the normal rules of evidence are breached, with perfectly innocent acts being liable to interpretation as 'preparatory' by the police and the courts. Section 8 allows for trials under the Acts to be held *in camera* (in secret without any press reporting) at the request of the prosecution. There is not a single recorded case of a judge refusing such a request.

The Official Secrets Act of 1939 was a very short one amending Section 6 of the 1920 Act. This section had originally applied to all the provisions of the 1911 and 1920 Acts, whereby refusal to give information was an offence. Two cases which arose in 1938 led to the amending Act. In the first case a journalist refused to divulge his source of information for an article couched in terms similar to those used in an internal police circular. The circular referred to a man passing fake £5 notes and the journalist considered it in the public good that everyone should be warned of the man's activities. His public-spirited attitude afforded him no protection and he was fined. The second case involved Duncan Sandys.

In the summer of 1938 the House of Commons was enraged to find the Acts invoked against one of their own number – and a respectable Tory at that. Sandys, a serving officer in the Territorial Army and son-in-law of Winston Churchill, sought to bring attention to the lack of anti-aircraft guns available for the defence of the homeland. However, being a discreet MP he first wrote to the War Minister, Mr Hore-

[12] See p. 10.
[13] *Official Secrets Act 1911–1939*, NCCL briefing paper. Undated, p. 8.

Belisha, indicating the area of his concern. After the discussion with the Minister about his proposed parliamentary questions Sandys was summoned by the Attorney-General and threatened with prosecution under Section 6 (1920), for refusing to give the source of his information. Clearly his knowledge had been gained through service in the Territorial Army, and his motives were geared to the protection of the security of the state rather than the reverse. Parliamentary indignation forced the government to grant an inquiry, and the Select Committee on the Official Secrets Acts reported in July 1938 and April 1939. Meanwhile Sandys was summoned to appear, in full dress uniform with sword, before a Military Court of Enquiry set up on the instruction of the War Minister. Sandys ignored this request and the court was dismissed. In November 1939 Section 6 of the 1920 Act was amended to limit the powers of interrogation into sources of information to espionage cases alone. This was not the only effect of Sandys' action. Professor Harold Laski wrote in *Tribune* at that time:

> 'These actions must be linked to the consistent refusal . . . to permit inquiry into the well-sustained charge of inefficiency and maladministration. The resignation of Lord Swinton was prime facie proof that there was substance to these charges.'[14]

The Acts had been used then, as they were to be used in the 1970 *Sunday Telegraph* case,[15] to silence criticism of government ineptitude.

Under the Acts, even though many of the charges carry a maximum of two years in prison (and in some cases only three months) the powers of arrest without a warrant still apply. The Criminal Law Act of 1967 limited this power of arrest without warrant to offences liable to more than five years' imprisonment – limited, that is, with the exception of the OSAs. Under Section 8 (1911) the police are effectively given the right of speculative searches, that is, without any direct evidence of an offence having been committed. The very nature of offences under these Acts means that circumstantial evidence can be gathered and used in court, and the issuing of search warrants can likewise be made on little or no evidence. The power to hear a case *in camera*, allowed under the Acts, is not limited to those where state security is involved. In 1967, for example, proceedings against a postman, who was charged under Section 2 (1911) with communicating information which led to a mail robbery, was held *in camera*.

---

[14] 8 July 1938.
[15] See footnote 2.

The burden of proof lies with the defence, not the prosecution. This would include a case where someone made an innocent visit to a house which happened to be used by a foreign agent. For prosecutions under Section 1 (1911 and 1920 Acts) a person's character and previous convictions may in themselves be used as proof of the alleged offences. Finally, the maximum sentence laid down (by the 1920 Act) is fourteen years' imprisonment, but this can be exceeded – as in the case of George Blake, who got forty-two years, by making sentences on separate counts run consecutively – and this is entirely at the discretion of the judge.

The Official Secrets Acts provide government with a formidable weapon with which to counter real or imagined spies and errant state employees. Restriction of the rights of a defendant under the Acts offends in many ways against conventional rights within the rule of law, and it must be borne in mind that the Acts would become an even more formidable instrument should major civil disorder ever occur over a sustained period.

The use of the Official Secrets Acts

A large number of state employees fall within the terms of these Acts. They include all civil servants, those employed in state contract work in private industry, members of all the armed forces, policemen, postmen, telephone operators, prison officers, employees of nationalised industries and visitors to government departments (in the latter two categories only where access is granted to official information).[16] Most of these people have to sign one declaration on joining state service and another on retirement – an 'official' secret must be kept even to the grave.

So what constitutes an official secret? The 1911 Act defines it as any sketch, note or document, or knowledge which 'relates to or is used in a prohibited place or anything in such a place'. Everything from the number of lavatory rolls used to the idiosyncratic private habits of a Principal Officer is 'officially secret'. Or, as Sir Martin Furnival-Jones, a past head of MI5 told the Franks Committee: 'It is an official secret if it is in an official file.'[17] Given this ludicrous definition hundreds of people break the Official Secrets Acts every day. The civil servant who tells his wife where his work is taking him tomorrow, the Press Officers

[16] The Acts do not apply to local government where the authorities rely on criminal charges to deter potential offenders.
[17] *Franks Report*, Vol. 3, p. 249.

of every department, MPs and journalists briefed by Ministers and senior civil servants, are but a few. What might offend against the interests of the State is determined by the government of the day, so any Minister may himself reveal information about his plans and actions. Equally it is common practice for Ministers to 'leak' advance information of proposed controversial legislation to the Press Lobby of the House of Commons in order to gauge the temperature of public opinion without being formally committed to introducing a Bill. What constitutes an offence is therefore quite arbitrary in practice.

The Acts have been used more to stop the circulation of government information internally than against the activities of foreign spies (and their British-born accomplices). Between 1945 and 1971 there were twenty-one prosecutions under Section 1 (espionage) and twenty of these were against agents of a foreign power. The remaining case was against six members of the Committee of 100 who were jailed for conspiring to enter the Wethersfield airforce base. Under Section 2 there have been twenty-three prosecutions involving thirty-six defendants. Twelve of these cases concerned official information related to defence, but only two concerned foreign agents. Six defendants were acquitted, four were sent to prison and the rest were fined. Under the amended Section 6 two national journalists were sent to prison for refusing to reveal their sources in the Vassall spying case.

The loyalty of the British state employee is not left to chance for in addition to signing an official secrets declaration most employees are vetted by the security services, and promotional prospects exercise a strong restraining influence in the milieu of state service. One of the first recorded peacetime prosecutions under the 1911 Act was in 1919 and concerned the disclosure by a War Office clerk of information about contracts for army officers' clothing to a director of a firm of tailors. They were both prosecuted under Section 2. A magistrate's court dismissed the charge so the Attorney-General prepared a bill of indictment and at the Old Bailey Mr Justice Avory directed the jury on the central question. He agreed there was no danger to state security as in the spirit of the 1911 Act, but he relied on the precise wording of Section 2 to show that the information supplied '. . . was, or might be useful to the person to whom it was communicated.' The jury accepted this and the two defendants were fined.[18] The case – as the government intended – clearly placed all official documents and information under the Acts and served as a warning to all civil servants. In 1932 a sixty-year-

[18] *The Times*, 12 February 1919.

old temporary clerk at Somerset House gave details of the wills of three famous people (Sir John Rutherford, Sir William Pryke and Mr Leo Maxse) to a *Daily Mail* reporter a few hours ahead of the time they were due to be released officially. They were both prosecuted under Section 2; the clerk was given six weeks in jail and the journalist two months. An appeal was lodged partly on the grounds that no pecuniary advantage was gained, that the clerk was seriously ill, and that no harm to the public good had been caused. The government feared that the inflexible rule of secrecy was about to be breached and the Attorney-General, Sir Thomas Inskip, appeared in person at the appeal hearing. He spoke of the 'corruption of civil servants' and the appeal duly failed.

The case of Major Vernon, in 1937, was concerned not simply with the use of the Acts against a civil servant, but with his subsequent dismissal from state service, and the strong suspicion that the whole affair had been instigated by the security services. At the time the case arose Major Vernon was a senior Technical Officer at the Royal Aircraft Establishment in Farnborough, where he had been employed for over twelve years. Prior to this he had gained an impeccable record in the First World War. Since 1921 Vernon had been a socialist and during the term of the National Government he and some other progressive members of staff at Farnborough set up an informal study circle for the discussion of political questions. Vernon was also a member of the local Labour Party, and from 1929 to 1933 helped form Self-Help clubs for the unemployed of the area. As is still the case, Civil Service rules did not preclude members from taking part in political activities of this kind.[19]

After it was hinted, in 1936, that the study circle was disapproved of, it was disbanded, and Vernon concentrated on private study and the occasional attendance at local Labour Party meetings. When he returned from holiday on 22 August 1937, he found his house had been burgled and that the four culprits (in a car bearing a fascist sticker) had been apprehended by the police just twenty miles from the house. The four men had removed all his socialist literature, some papers on technical matters (on which he was working) and some other household articles. On 3 September Vernon was suspended by the Farnborough authorities, who had examined all the documents closely with the help of the security services. When the trial of the four men came up at Kingston Quarter Sessions there occurred a remarkable

---

[19] *The Strange Case of Major Vernon*, NCCL. Undated, p. 14.

shift of emphasis. The central concern of the defence lawyer, Mr Lawton (a fascist parliamentary candidate), and the prosecution lawyer, Mr McClure, became the political views of Vernon himself – who was appearing as a prosecution witness to confirm his ownership of the items stolen.

Vernon's questioning by the defence included repeated assertions that he was a member of the Communist Party. Evidence put forward to support this contention were Vernon's subscription to Claud Cockburn's *The Week*, the possession of Left Book Club editions, a letter in which he referred to 'voting red' (in the context this meant voting Labour), and the fact that he met the key defendant, Ford, in a shop which sold the *Daily Worker*. Ford alleged that Vernon had worked with him when both were in the Army, to encourage troops to desert. Vernon denied this and no action had been taken by the authorities to confirm the point. Ford had last seen Vernon in 1934 – over two-and-a-half years before he committed the burglary. Since 1937 Ford said he had been 'waging a more or less private war on Bolshevism'[20] and claimed that he had planned to take the stolen documents to the authorities in Whitehall.

Q: Where were you taking the stuff?
A: To Whitehall, to the police.
Q: Which government department were you going to see?
A: The Police Department. I'm not sure, but I think it is called Scotland House.
Q: Did you believe that that was the Secret Service Department?
A: Yes.[21]

Another of the defendants told the court: 'I was just about to stop the car to phone Whitehall to say that we were coming there.'[22]

The jury found all four guilty of larceny, but the Chairman of the Sessions took a lenient view when passing sentence as Detective Sergeant Bishop (for the police) gave favourable reports on their past behaviour. He said: 'All four of them appear to have very good characters as far as we know.'[23] The four were bound over for twelve months. In fact Ford had deserted from the Army and was an ex-member of the Irish Republican Army (IRA); another had been fined a

[20] *Op. cit.*, p. 14.
[21] *Op. cit.*, p. 14.
[22] *Op. cit.*, p. 15.
[23] *Op. cit.*, p. 16.

few weeks before for illegally wearing a Blackshirt uniform, and two of
the four were out of work. The National Council for Civil Liberties
(NCCL) commented: 'what would have been the fate of four Communists if they had broken into the house of the Chairman of Quarter
Sessions and justified their conduct on patriotic motives?'

The last act was now played. Major Vernon, in common with hundreds of other civil servants, had taken some of his work home. He
happened to be working on an official handbook of new aircraft. The
notes for this and other documents were among those removed by
Ford and his friends. On 23 October Vernon was fined fifty pounds for
'retaining' information and 'not taking proper care' under the Official
Secrets Acts. Two weeks later he was dismissed from the Civil Service.
The unanswered questions in this series of events were put in an
editorial in the magazine *The Aeroplane*:

> 'Nobody has ever explained why four amiable-looking young
> men led by a self-confessed ex-Irish gunman should have been
> moved to extract these documents . . . that the inspiration should
> have come through the change of heart and reform of soul of an
> ex-gunman . . . is just a little bit too thin even for the average
> reader of a daily newspaper . . . We should so much like to know
> what is behind it, and who instigated these young men. . . .'[24]

In the postwar period there were regular prosecutions under Section 2 which often involved civil servants (postmen, policemen, ser-
vicemen). The case of Miss Barbara Fell in 1962 arose because she
handed some 'confidential' documents on East-West relations to a
member of the Yugoslav Embassy. She was tried under Section 2 (1911)
and sentenced to two years in prison. Miss Fell was an official at the
Central Office of Information and there was no suggestion of the
security of the state being threatened, but on appeal the Lord Chief
Justice said the offence under Section 2 was absolute. Ten years later in
1972 the Legal Adviser to a branch of the Security Service told the
Franks Committee that the said documents were of 'a fairly low
classification'.[25] These four cases show that the application of the Acts
by government has been to ensure predominantly the reliability of the
state's employees, rather than protection against espionage.

If the secrecy of the Civil Service is backed by a multiplicity of sanctions then the armed forces operate under an almost complete
blackout, where the internal procedures leave even less to chance. In

[24] 3 November 1937.
[25] Franks, Vol. 3, p. 252.

1964 a radio supervisor lost his two good service medals at a court martial because he failed to properly supervise the burning of out-dated classified material according to army regulations. In 1935 the proposed sale of the Wellington–Nelson letters of 1815–1930 at Sotheby's was stopped by the authorities under the Acts. In 1973 the Ministry of Defence itself was apparently concerned that secrecy could be carried too far, when it was reported that Naval Intelligence had held details of the Soviet missile ships in operation in 1963, yet did not release them to the Ships Department of the Admiralty for ten years, when they were only of academic use.[26]

An area which creates problems for the authorities is that of ex-servicemen or intelligence officers wanting to write up their wartime exploits. One of the first recorded cases saw Sir Compton MacKenzie facing the full weight of Section 1 (1911) over his book *Gallipoli Memories*.[27] He had been engaged on intelligence duties in Athens in 1916 (thirteen years previously) and had included confidential information in his light-hearted account.[28] The trial was held *in camera* and the jury found him guilty. Such well-known figures however have little to fear. But we can only guess at the number of books which have never gone further than the censor's desk at the Ministry of Defence, for all ex-members of the Armed Forces are required to submit their manuscripts to the MOD before publication. For instance, the war-time exploits of Major Clayton Hutton took five years to reach the public. His book *The Hidden Catch* finally appeared in 1955 ghosted by 'Charles Connell' from the original manuscript.[29] 'Mr X' (Major Hutton in disguise) was apparently an extraordinary freelance entrepreneur in the Second World War who managed to spend hundreds of thousands of pounds producing gadgets for wartime agents.

No such difficulties however were faced by Mr Anthony Nutting when he wrote of the internal machinations of the Eden government over the Suez crisis of 1956. Mr Nutting had been a Privy Councillor and based his account on notes made at the time. The book was submitted to the Cabinet Office at proof stage and they made a number of amendments – removing the names of the civil servants, the subject matter of some meetings, and the means of communication used. The

[26] *Sunday Telegraph* 22 July 1973.
[27] Published in 1929.
[28] MacKenzie got his own back in 1933 when *Water on the Brain* was published. This was a novel based on purportedly fictional characters thus clearing him from any possibility of prosecution.
[29] *New Statesman*, 28 April 1956.

Cabinet Office protected the interests of the Civil Service, but left Eden and Selwyn Lloyd exposed to all kinds of ridicule. Hugh Thomas observed: 'it can be said that the Acts are not made to apply to politicians, providing they accept the strictures of the Civil Service by the channel of the Cabinet Office.'[30] This privilege was not afforded in 1958 to two Oxford students who were sent to jail for three months for using information gained during National Service in an article published by the student magazine *Isis*. The article told of the activities of monitoring stations spying on Russian troops movements and defence arrangements which, given the tender state of East–West relations, might well have provoked some prickly reactions. While the publication of this information was not in the state's interest it was clearly in the public interest that information on such ventures should be publicly known.

The Franks Committee

The Committee, headed by Lord Franks, to look into Section 2 of the 1911 Act was set up in 1971 and its report was published in September 1972. The official press hand-out (from the Home Office) which accompanied the publication of the four-volume Report noted that the Committee had been set up by the Tory government to fulfil an election pledge to eliminate 'unnecessary secrecy' in government. This item in the Tory election manifesto was a response to the Wilson government's handling of the D-Notice affair (involving the *Daily Express* and Chapman Pincher) and the prosecution of the *Sunday Telegraph* over its Biafran revelations. The latter case resulted from an article in the *Sunday Telegraph* on 11 January 1970. Summonses were issued on 11 March and on 20 May the three defendants were committed for trial at the Old Bailey. The General Election of June 1970 returned the Tories to power but this did not end the prosecution, for they inherited a legal obligation to pursue the charges. The trial ended in February 1971 and the Franks Committee was appointed in April of that year.

Even during the life of the first Wilson government, the Fulton Committee on the Civil Service had reported in 1968 that the administrative process was 'surrounded by too much secrecy' and suggested a review of the Acts. Inaction however cannot be laid at the

[30] Thomas, in *Crisis in the Civil Service* (1970) p. 121.

door of any particular party in government, for it must be seen in the context of the practices built up over the past two hundred years by the state's administration. Governments of all colours have been only too happy to hide behind the Acts and oppose any reforms when in power, and to complain of too much secrecy when in opposition. So it was the Tories who, having received the Report of the Franks Committee in 1972, let it be known in December 1973 that there would be no legislation in the next session (the parliamentary year). Nor did the Labour government take any action during 1974.

The Franks Committee detailed seven limitations on the disclosure of information. Paramount among these are the sanctions exercised within the Civil Service where a civil servant 'who tends to overstep the mark, to talk too freely, will not enjoy such a satisfactory career as colleagues with better judgement and greater discretion.'[31] The other limitations are: formal Civil Service disciplinary procedures; recruitment and vetting; security classifications and privacy markings; the D-Notice system; the Public Records Act (which keeps closed public records for thirty, forty or one hundred years at the discretion of the government); and, finally, the three Acts themselves. In order to see how other governments handled the question of official information members of the Franks Committee visited several countries. The French, Americans and the Swedes all operated a more limited law, and a more open system of access to information. The only exception was Canada, an ex-colony whose laws closely resemble our own.

The Franks Report considered three areas, each of which, it was suggested, required a different approach. The first was the field of espionage in relation to an 'unfriendly' government, the second the 'internal' defence of Britain against insurrection, and the third what is commonly known as 'law and order'. Among the departmental evidence to the Committee which is of interest here is that given by the Home Office in relation to information held by the police. The Home Office was represented by Sir Philip Allen (Permanent Under-Secretary) and Mr F. L. T. Graham-Harrison (Deputy Under-Secretary). During their evidence they stressed the anxiety of the police over the need to protect information held by them. Mr Graham-Harrison spelt out the two kinds of information held by government. Firstly, there is that information which people and firms give voluntarily or are required to give by law, and secondly that which governments 'just happen to acquire in the course of business in one

---

[31] Franks, Vol. 1, para. 58, p. 28.

way or another'. He went on to make this point explicit in relation to
the police:

> 'in the nature of things first of all the information is very largely
> going to be unfavourable information about individuals, and
> secondly, a certain amount of it at any rate is going to relate to
> doubts and suspicions and things that are not entirely factual or
> provable . . . most of it I think is not obtained in pursuance of a
> statutory power to require somebody to give it . . .'[32]

Mr Graham-Harrison is clearly referring to the increasing amount of
information being compiled by the police and the Home Office on the
personal histories, social habits, and political activities of thousands of
people, the majority of whom have never been convicted of a criminal
offence. More specifically the Home Office was worried that the information held by the Regional Crime Squads, Criminal Intelligence, the
Special Branch, the National Immigration Intelligence Unit and Drugs
Intelligence Unit would be left unprotected. It is interesting to note
that no statutory legitimacy is presented for holding this information –
for none exists – but the state still seeks to apply sanctions against its
employees who 'leak' this illegitimately-gathered information. The
Committee's Report itself made a distinction in its proposals between
these two kinds of information held by the state. The Report proposed
to afford protection to information given voluntarily or by statutory
obligation, but to leave unprotected information acquired 'in one way
or another'.

In the Report the Committee also proposed the abolition of Section
2 of the 1911 Act and its replacement by a new statute bearing the title
'The Official Information Act'. This new Act would cover information
in the following areas: defence and internal security, foreign relations,
currency and reserves, Cabinet proceedings, maintenance of law and
order, information given by the citizen, and official information used
for gain. In the first three areas, *only* those matters covered by the
classification SECRET and DEFENCE–CONFIDENTIAL would involve an offence, and at the time of a prosecution the classification
would be re-examined to see if it still held – for instance, information
about an event or plan in 1915 might well be de-classified. The Committee saw no reason to go further than the normal rule of law and
specifically excluded the use of several provisions in the three Acts such

[32] Franks, Vol. 2, p. 345.

as those concerning preparatory acts and the power of a superintendent to sign a warrant. Further the receipt of information was only to be an offence if it was *knowingly* communicated to another person. The mere receipt would no longer be an offence.

The Report was explicit in wishing to protect information 'entrusted to the government' by firms or individuals but specifically excluded certain areas from protection:

'Some [information] is provided by third parties, e.g. police or medical reports. Often factual information of this kind is inextricably mixed up with assessments and opinions favourable and unfavourable. A great deal of information of this kind is obtained by Crown servants in the course of carrying out their duties. This information is on an entirely different footing (to that given voluntarily or statutorily), as it is not entrusted to the Government. This does not mean that the Government should not keep such information private, but there is not the same reason for giving it special legal protection.'[33]

This distinction would probably apply at least to information held by the National Immigration Unit, the National Drugs Intelligence Unit and the Department of Health and Social Security (DHSS).

The evidence and recommendations of the Franks Committee were published in September 1972. However, they were not debated in the House of Commons until June 1973, and in December that year the government shelved any likelihood of acting on the findings. The Conservative government's reluctance to act was clear. The Ministries were up in arms, as only highly classified material was to be properly protected, leaving many official documents to be safeguarded solely by internal sanctions and discipline. The government, through the Home Secretary Mr Carr, gave the appearance of accepting the Committee's main recommendations and so fulfilling their election pledge, but an examination of Carr's reservations show critical areas where the Report's findings were rejected. He said that all information held by and about the intelligence and security services (external and internal) should continue to be protected regardless of its classification, as should all that concerned with foreign affairs and monetary policy. The Report had proposed that only information in the SECRET and DEFENCE–CONFIDENTIAL classification should be legally

---

[33] Franks, Vol. 1, para. 195, p. 72.

protected. Then Mr Carr drove a horse and cart through the Report by saying that all information held by government however acquired should come under the sanctions of any future Act:

> 'We believe that, however acquired, personal information about individuals or about private companies and concerns held by a Government department requires protection from improper disclosure, by the criminal law.'[34]

So in the end the central contradiction appears. The government sets up a Committee which suggests the state relinquishes its hold over much official information: this Committee reports back to the government, which then decides what to accept and what to reject.

The October 1974 election manifesto of the Labour Party contained a pledge to amend Section 2 of the 1911 Act. In December 1974 two people, John Russell and Mila Caley, were arrested and charged under Section 2 with the 'unlawful possession' of a photocopy of a 'restricted' MOD document. The document in question was the MOD's manual, 'Land Operations Vol. 3 Counter Revolutionary Operations'.[35] On 2 January 1975 the charges against Russell and Caley were withdrawn at Marylebone court on the decision of the Attorney-General and the DPP not to proceed with the prosecution. Whether this decision was taken because the Labour government intended to announce at some future point a change in Section 2, or for lack of evidence, or because the public disclosure of the document's embarrassing contents would have been inevitable at a full trial is not known – although the latter reason strongly suggests itself.[36]

Summary

The use of three Official Secrets Acts represent the last resort in suppressing public knowledge of the workings of the state. However, there is another method which is occasionally employed – Crown Privilege, which is judge-made law. This gives the Crown (the state) power to withhold documentary evidence from any court. The central ruling on Crown Privilege was given by Lord Simon in the 'Thetis' case (1942). He said it could apply 'where disclosure would be injurious to national defence, or to good diplomatic relations, or where the practice of keeping a class of documents secret is necessary for the proper ad-

[34] House of Commons, 29 June 1973.
[35] See Chapter 7.
[36] *Time Out*, 10 January 1975.

ministration of the public service'.[37] The effect of Crown Privilege is to seal the gaps left by the Acts by excluding the possibility of civil servants being called to give evidence or documents being used in evidence.

Another feature of the Acts is the role of the Attorney-General, whose *fiat* has to be given to all prosecutions after the case is drawn to his attention. He decides whether or not an alleged offence is against the 'safety or interests of the state', and in reaching his decision he may consult with his political masters – the government which appointed him. Similarly, he decides whether to prefer charges for indictment or summary prosecution, the former bringing the likelihood of a bigger sentence. The post of Attorney-General originated in the seventeenth century and his accountability was later transferred to parliament where, after a time, the duality of his role emerged. He is both an MP and a member of the government, appointed by the Prime Minister on the one hand, and a senior officer of the supposedly neutral law on the other. When the 1911 Act was presented to parliament the role of the Attorney-General was envisaged as a safeguard against the arbitrary use of the Act. In practice the only safeguard he fulfils is to ensure that no case is brought which might embarrass the government.

The two central Official Secrets Acts, 1911 and 1920, were both passed in haste by parliament and with the direct intervention of the intelligence and security services. The 1911 Act was passed at the start of the pre-war spy mania which was later to sweep the country in 1914, and the initiative for and drafting of the Act was by MI5 and the Committee for Imperial Defence respectively. The 1920 Act was passed to preserve repressive wartime legislation in the face of ruling-class fears of revolution, strikes, and Irish 'troubles', and again MI5 had a hand in drafting the Bill. In short, the Acts were passed at a time when British imperialism was triumphant and there were, presumably, a number of secrets worth protecting. Those days are long gone; we have no Empire and few secrets worthy of the name.

Even when the formidable walls of secrecy outlined above occasionally break down, it is for the government of the day to determine whether state security is involved. In his book on state secrecy David Williams says: 'The full potential of the Official Secrets Acts is yet to be seen.'[38] The implication, in this context, is that their use against political activists in any situation short of the actual outbreak of civil war could be formidable.

[37] Williams, *Not in the Public Interest* (1965), p. 194.
[38] Williams, *op. cit.*, p. 95.

Incitement and sedition

The provisions of the law have left few avenues free of sanctions when threats are made to the internal security of the state. From the Statute of Treasons of 1351 and the first Riot Act of 1381 (at the time of Wat Tyler's rebellion) the monarchic, and then the bourgeois, state has sought protection for its privileged position against insurrections and disturbances of public order. The ultimate power of the ruling class in a liberal-democracy rests on the loyalty of the repressive agencies of the state, the army, the police and the courts, to that class. Attempts to seduce members of the police and the armed forces from their duty are viewed as being directly subversive to the interests of the state, and the law reflects this.

The passing of the Incitement to Mutiny Act occurred at the time of the French revolution when the ruling class in Britain feared that the spread of democratic ideas might lead to their overthrow. The combination of talk of freedom, economic depression, and the naval mutinies at Spithead and the Nore led to the legislation of 1797. In the same year the Unlawful Oaths Act was passed which forbade the taking of an oath by people with a seditious purpose in mind. Thus it became a powerful weapon against the early trade unions – the Tolpuddle Martyrs were condemned to transportation under this Act in 1834. Both of these Acts are still in existence, for unlike many other measures passed during this period of repressive legislation they were not repealed after the 1832 Reform Act. A young Ivor Jennings commented on this period:

> 'Much legislation of the period 1797 to 1820 was deliberately aimed at the suppression of democratic ideas. With the acceptance of the democratic principle it became a relic of the class domination which had been overthrown . . .'[39]

The Incitement to Mutiny Act was originally passed as a temporary measure and was not made permanent until 1817 when the post-war depression led to widespread demonstrations (which included the massacre at Peterloo in 1819). The Act was directed against anyone who endeavoured to seduce members of His Majesty's forces from 'their duty *and* allegiance to His Majesty' or who incited them to an act of mutiny of any kind. The intention was not just to deter attempts at incitement, it was to guard against the intrusion of democratic notions into the ranks.

[39] W. Ivor Jennings, *The Sedition Bill Explained* (1934) p. 12.

This Act, which had been unused for so long, became an important weapon for the state against the labour movement in the period 1910 to 1930. The first recorded use of the 1797 Act for a hundred years came about when five trade unionists were prosecuted in 1912 (the last occasion being in 1804). The five, including Tom Mann, ran a paper called *The Syndicalist* which reprinted a leaflet entitled 'Open Letter to British Soldiers'. The letter called on soldiers to recognise their working-class origins and to refuse to act against industrial workers.

'When WE go on strike to better OUR lot, which is the lot also of YOUR FATHERS, MOTHERS, BROTHERS and SISTERS, YOU are called upon by your officers to MURDER US. DON'T DO IT. The Idle Rich Class, who own and order you about, own and order us about also ... YOU, like US, are of the SLAVE CLASS. WHEN WE rise, YOU rise; when WE fall, even by your bullets, YOU also fall ... think about things and refuse any longer to MURDER YOUR KINDRED. Help us to win back BRITAIN for the BRITISH, and the WORLD for the WORKERS.'[40]

The original publishers were not prosecuted but the five syndicalists were. All were found guilty and sent to prison although the Home Secretary was forced to reduce the sentences.

After the introduction of conscription in January 1916 several anarchist papers were prosecuted for sedition. In 1918 John Maclean was appointed as Russian Consul in Glasgow by the Bolshevik government and when, in a speech, he called for the end of the war to be hastened by strikes and mutinies he was arrested. At his trial, where he defended himself, he told the jury: 'I am not here as the accused; I am here as the accuser of capitalism dripping with blood from head to foot.'[41] Maclean was sentenced to five years' penal servitude but, after a long hunger strike, he was released six months later.

It was the threatened use of the 1797 Act against five Communists and its subsequent withdrawal of the charges which led to the downfall of the first Labour government in 1924. John Campbell, the acting editor of *Workers Weekly*, the paper of the then small Communist Party, was arrested and charged under the Act on 5 August 1924. The basis of the prosecution was an allegedly seditious article that urged troops not to fire on the working-class: 'Let it be known that, neither in the class war nor in the military war, will you turn your guns on your fellow

[40] *The Syndicalist,* 1912.
[41] *Wildcat,* No. 1, September 1974.

HALT! ATTENTION!!

Open Letter to British Soldiers.

This letter to British soldiers, reprinted from *Sheldrake's Military Gazette* (Aldershot), of March 1st, 1912, is the subject of the charge against Crowsley, Guy Bowman, the Buck brothers, and Tom Mann. Read and judge for yourself. Let the voice of the PEOPLE be heard.

Men! Comrades! Brothers!

You are in the Army

So are WE. You in the Army of Destruction. We in the Industrial, or Army of Construction.

WE work at mine, mill, forge, factory, or dock, producing and transporting all the goods, clothing, stuffs, etc., which make it possible for people to live.

You ARE WORKING MEN'S SONS.

When WE go on Strike to better OUR lot, which is the lot also of YOUR FATHERS, MOTHERS, BROTHERS, and SISTERS, YOU are called upon by your officers to MURDER US.

DON'T DO IT!

You know how it happens always has happened.

We stand out as long as we can. Then one of our (and your) irresponsible Brothers, goaded by the sight and thought of his and his loved ones' misery and hunger, commits a crime on property. Immediately You are ordered to MURDER US, as You did at Mitchelstown, at Featherstone, at Belfast.

Don't You know that when You are out of the colours, and become a "Civy" again, that You, like Us, may be on Strike, and You, like Us, be liable to be MURDERED by other soldiers.

BOYS, DON'T DO IT!

"THOU SHALT NOT KILL," says the Book.

DON'T FORGET THAT!

It does not say, "unless you have a uniform on."

No! MURDER IS MURDER, whether committed in the heat of anger on one who has wronged a loved one, or by pipe-clayed Tommies with a rifle.

BOYS, DON'T DO IT!

ACT THE MAN! ACT THE BROTHER ACT THE HUMAN BEING!

Property can be replaced! Human life, never.

The Idle Rich Class, who own and order you about, own and order us about also. They and their friends own the land and means of life of Britain.

You DON'T. WE DON'T.

When WE kick, they order YOU to MURDER Us.

When You kick, You get courtmartialed and cells.

YOUR fight is OUR fight. Instead of fighting AGAINST each other, WE should be fighting with each other.

Out of OUR loins, OUR lives, OUR homes, You came.

Don't disgrace YOUR PARENTS, YOUR CLASS, by being the willing tools any longer of the MASTER CLASS.

YOU, like US, are of the SLAVE CLASS. WHEN WE rise, YOU rise; when WE fall, even by your bullets, YE fall also.

England with its fertile valleys and dells, its mineral resources, its sea harvests, is the heritage of ages to us.

YOU no doubt joined the Army out of poverty.

WE work long hours for small wages at hard work, because of OUR poverty. And both YOUR poverty and OURS arises from the fact that Britain with its resources belongs to only a few people. These few, owning Britain, own OUR jobs. Owning OUR jobs, they own OUR very LIVES.

Comrades, have WE called in vain? Think things out and refuse any longer to MURDER YOUR KINDRED. Help US to win back BRITAIN for the BRITISH, and the WORLD for the WORKERS.

1. When the *Syndicalist* reproduced this leaflet in 1912 five people were prosecuted and sent to prison including Tom Mann, the paper's editor, and the printer.

workers.'[42] The police sent the article to the Director of Public
Prosecutions (DPP) and the Attorney-General, Sir Patrick Hastings,
agreed to proceedings being taken. Sir Patrick, who was only a recent
convert to the Labour Party, was much taken aback by the ferocity and
indignation of Labour MPs, and the next day charges were withdrawn.
Then the Tories took the field, demanding to know why the charges
had been withdrawn and calling for a parliamentary inquiry. The
MacDonald government refused to bow to this demand and on a censure motion they were defeated by 364 votes to 198.[43] Again in 1925
and 1926 members of the Communist Party were jailed under the Act,
as were a further two members in 1931 after the Navy mutiny at
Invergordon. Under the 1797 Act prosecutions were limited to those
on indictment (trial in the High Court before judge and jury) and so in
the early 1930s the state sought to make offences in this field triable by
magistrates' courts.

The other Act enabling sanctions to be taken against those who seek
to undermine the security of the state, by attempting to seduce
members of the state apparatus from their duty, is the Incitement to
Disaffection Act of 1934. The 1934 Act was described by Ronald Kidd,
the first General-Secretary of the National Council for Civil Liberties,[44] as one which 'constituted the most open attack on liberty of
thought, speech and the Press which had been seen in modern times'.[45]
The purpose of the Act is 'the prevention and punishment of
endeavours to seduce members of His Majesty's forces from his duty *or*
allegiance to His Majesty' (Section 1). By changing one word from the
1797 Act the Law Officers of the Crown extended the earlier Act and
made conviction much easier. They changed the word *and* to *or*, so
whereas the 1797 Act required that a soldier be seduced from a) his
duty *and* b) his allegiance to the Crown, now either will suffice. Any
attempt to get a soldier to disobey a single, possibly trivial, order constitutes an offence. Nor would the National Government accept an
amendment to limit this clause to leaflets and pamphlets intended and

[42] The real author of this 'Open Letter' was Harry Pollitt, a member of the
Communist Party executive committee. See J. Klugmann, *History of the British
Communist Party*, Vol. 1 (1968) p. 342. For an account of the Labour Cabinet
reactions to this affair see *The Campbell Case*, N. D. Siederer, reprint from the
Journal of Contemporary History, Vol. 9, No. 2 (1974).

[43] See p. 158 ff. for the subsequent controversy of the election and the Zinoviev
letter.

[44] NCCL was formed in 1934.

[45] Ronald Kidd, *British Liberty in Danger* (1940) p. 59.

devised for the armed forces. Thus a leaflet prepared for general use by, for example, the Peace Pledge Union could open it to prosecution if it fell into the hands of a soldier. By Section 2(1) the mere *possession* of a seditious document can be an offence, for anyone who

> 'with *intent* to commit or to aid, abet, counsel, or procure the commission of an offence under section one of this Act, has in his possession or *under his control* any document of such a nature that the dissemination of copies thereof among members of His Majesty's forces would constitute such an offence, he shall be guilty of an offence under this Act.'

As originally drafted this clause would have placed the onus on the accused to prove his innocence (as under the Official Secrets Acts); however, this was amended to 'with intent to'. This concession was not as magnanimous as it may seem for 'intent' is always a matter of inference – in law a person's intentions are inferred from the natural and probable consequences of his or her actions. Even actual possession does not have to be proved. If an offending leaflet were found in someone's house (regardless of whether it belonged there or was planted there) this would be sufficient to prove that it was under his or her control. In practice perfectly 'legal' leaflets, pamphlets or books owned by pacifists or political activists could leave them open to charges. When the Bill was introduced in parliament the Attorney-General Sir Thomas Inskip – a man who exhibited those fine qualities of the British ruling class, deafness combined with obstinacy – drew attention to the fifty thousand copies of a paper called *The Soldiers Friend*, produced by the Quakers, which had been distributed to soldiers and sailors over the previous two years. A god-fearing citizen could not hope to hide under the religious gown for, as Sir Thomas told the Commons: 'If a man wants and intends to seduce a member of His Majesty's forces the fact that he quotes from the Bible instead of Communist literature will not prevent him from being convicted.'[46]

The Act makes the very existence of a document which might seduce a serviceman evidence against the author, the publisher, the printer and anyone found in possession. And the penalties can be severe, with two years in prison and/or a two-hundred-pound fine on indictment and four months and/or twenty pounds on a summary charge. Political activists, from the Labour Party to declared revolutionaries, could become targets for the state in times of civil disorder, and this

[46] W. Ivor Jennings, *op. cit.*, p. 15.

1934 Act adds to the already massive battery of laws available for such contingencies.

A further consequence of the Act is to preclude any attempt to educate politically members of the armed forces, causing Ivor Jennings to comment: 'Though he (the soldier) must die for his King and Country if some politicians say so, he may not learn what his King and Country stand for, and why he must die.'[47]

One of the immediate effects of the Act was to make printers very wary of prosecution and several pacifist groups found their literature effectively censored. As with so many laws the threat of the Act was as effective as its actual use. But a case did arise in 1936 which confirmed the worst fears of the opponents of the Act. An eighteen-year-old son of a vicar was sent to prison under Section 1. Hugh Phillips, a student at Leeds University, was sitting in the station restaurant in Leeds and struck up a conversation with a Corporal William Crabtree, an RAF aircraftsman. After a few pleasantries Phillips asked Corporal Crabtree if he was contented with the RAF. Crabtree, leading the young man on, replied that he was not. He then asked Crabtree if it was possible to steal an aircraft and received an affirmative answer. When the time came for Phillips to leave he took Crabtree's address and said he would write. On 1 December 1936, Phillips wrote the following letter from St Peter's Vicarage, Leeds.

'Dear Crabtree,
I will write at length later on. Just a few remarks, however, and don't forget to burn this letter quickly. If you honestly feel properly revolutionary there are two really good lines for you to take. One is to get in touch with the Rev. L. Schiff, 24 Arundel Square, London N7, also get a permit from Madrid to fly over there on the sly some day – which I imagine you could do, and I fancy you could take the fellows with you. They need help. The other, and possibly better alternative, is to keep very silent and make close friends with those beneath you, so that when you come to the time when we can have a revolution, not only you and your bomber can come to help us, but the whole squadron.

At all events be patient. The time is getting very close when world war, and thus revolution, will come. The possibilities of reading must be few in the RAF, but any book or pamphlet can be got at Progress Bookshops, Woodhouse Lane, Leeds. Well, remember the names of the authors – J. Strachey, K. Marx,

[47] W. Ivor Jennings, *op. cit.*, p. 16.

Engels, Lenin, Stalin, P. Dutt, Jackson, Gallagher, Pollitt – and try to get hold of the 'Manifesto of the Communist Party' . . . But don't forget Spain will you? The workers of the world are uniting, and most quickly . . . Yours very sincerely, Hugh Phillips.'

At his trial Hugh Phillips pleaded guilty and his defence counsel suggested his actions were due to youthful impetuosity: 'He studied too well and not wisely the works of such persons as Karl Marx and others.' Mr Justice Singleton, sending Phillips down for twelve months said: 'You have pleaded guilty to an offence which strikes at the very safety of the Realm.'[48] After public protests the Home Secretary reduced the sentence but the conviction stood.

During the Second World War the Defence Regulations issued by the government effectively supplanted many existing laws, especially in relation to sedition and incitement to disaffection. In December 1944 the Special Branch raided Freedom Press and arrested the four editors of *War Commentary* (the wartime title of *Freedom*, the anarchist weekly paper). The four were charged under Defence Regulations 39a with conspiring to cause disaffection and three were sent to prison for nine months. It was not until they arrived in prison that they realised why the state had suddenly acted against them. 'Once we got inside, we found the nicks full to overflowing, not with criminals from the home front but with soldiers sentenced by military courts in France, Italy and Germany, for desertion and subsequent offences.'[49] By late 1944 it appeared that some British soldiers were not quite as enthusiastic as Winston Churchill to die in exacting the final victory.

Some thirty-six years later the 1934 Act was used to send Michael Tobin, a libertarian socialist, to jail for two years. Early in 1972 a court in Liverpool held that a pamphlet, *A Letter from a Soldier of the IRA to the Soldiers of the Royal Greenjackets*, was not of such a nature as to be capable of causing soldiers to desert and a defendant was acquitted of a charge under the 1934 Act. However, this same pamphlet was the basis of the charge against Michael Tobin in Maidstone Crown Court where it was held to be likely to cause disaffection. The Liverpool defendant had admitted that he wrote the pamphlet and Tobin was charged merely with intent to commit an offence as he had copies in his possession. The Appeal Court refused to reduce the sentence of two years, which was the maximum possible. Later, in May 1974 Pat Arrowsmith was

[48] *Yorkshire Evening Post*, 9 March 1937.
[49] Article by Philip Samson (one of those jailed in 1945) in *Wildcat*, No. 1, September 1974.

sentenced to eighteen months' imprisonment under the 1934 Act for distributing leaflets calling for the withdrawal of British troops from Northern Ireland. In November 1974 she was released at the appeal on a legal technicality.

The Incitement to Mutiny and Incitement to Disaffection Acts are not the only statutes guarding against the seduction of the state's forces. There is also the Emergency Powers Act 1920 and the Police Act 1964. Following the Metropolitan Police strikes of 1918 and 1919, the 1919 Police Act made police membership of trade unions illegal and – in the same terms as the later 1934 Act – made it an offence to attempt to cause or to cause disaffection in police ranks. The idea was to isolate the police force from democratic influences and to exclude the chance of a conflict of conscience arising, a move which bore fruit in the 1926 General Strike when the police were loyal to a man in support of the government. The offence was retained in the superseding 1964 Police Act (Section 53). In addition the state can bring a charge of incitement under common law relating to the 'Queen's Peace'. So for example, Sidney Elias, an official of the National Unemployed Workers' Movement, was charged in the early 1930s with inciting his comrades to cause discontent and ill-will between the classes and to create disturbances of the peace. More recently, in 1971, the black defendants in the Mangrove Nine case were charged with inciting a riot, of which they were acquitted.

1900 to 1936 was a period of sustained struggle between the labour movement and the state, when a large part of political action was still of an extra-parliamentary form. There were, for example, the syndicalist and the shop stewards' movement, and later, the National Unemployed Workers Movement. The period immediately after the First World War (1917–1920), the General Strike, and the early 1930s, were times of very real concern to the British ruling class, times when they saw revolution just round the corner. The issues of public order and the loyalty of the state agencies of policing (the police and the army) were central to this concern. The 1919 Police Act, the 1920 Official Secrets Act, the 1920 Emergency Powers Act, the 1934 Incitement to Disaffection Act, and the 1936 Public Order Act, all came out of this period.

The whole of the period is punctuated by the prosecution of leading working-class militants, and the partiality of the state was well illustrated by the failure to prosecute – between 1912 and 1914 – those who prepared to resist the plans to incorporate Ulster into a free Ireland. Sir Edward Carson, Bonar Law and Sir Henry Wilson were three of the better-known plotters. Indeed one of Sir Henry's complaints against the Asquith government was that they were 'contemplating scattering troops all over Ulster, as though it was a Pontypool coal strike'.[50] Quite clearly this was a revolt of Gentlemen and was not to be viewed in the same way as actions of the political militants of the Left.[51]

The use of conspiracy charges

Though the law of conspiracy was used extensively against the emerging labour movement in the nineteenth century, when it was described as 'an impressive illustration of judicial bias',[52] it was not until the early 1960s that it again came into common use against political activists. Before considering the application of conspiracy law in political offences it is necessary to understand the general nature of conspiracy law. The law on conspiracy is not based on parliamentary legislation, but has developed as judge-made law. A conspiracy is a common law offence usually held to be an agreement by two or more people to do an unlawful act or a lawful act by unlawful means. The lines between incitement, an attempted offence and conspiracy are hard to draw, and are usually drawn by the state's prosecutors when deciding what charges to bring. In law these three offences are known as inchoate offences, which means that proof of the offence does not require proof of any actual crime having been committed and allows the state to bring charges for uncompleted crimes at any stage up to the actual act.

The offence first appeared in law during the reign of Edward I, to prevent malicious prosecutions, and was later developed into a legal weapon by the Star Chamber to cover all crimes – both criminal and moral. A judgement in 1663 extended the scope of conspiracy to include an agreement to act against the government or the public as a whole. In the nineteenth century conspiracy law was used against strikers and pickets, and in 1875 the Conspiracy and Protection of Property Act supposedly ameliorated the situation somewhat by distinguishing between peaceful picketing and violent picketing. The breadth of the conspiracy laws, and the difficulties they present for the

---

[50] *That's Sedition – that was!* (1934) p. 4.

[51] The British Army did revolt in this cause at the Curragh Mutiny in March 1914.

[52] A comment made by Cyril Asquith, later a distinguished Lord Justice, in *Trade Union Law for Laymen*, 1927. For a comprehensive review of the use of the conspiracy laws see *Whose Conspiracy* by Geoff Robertson (1974).

defence case, has been shown up by judicial pronouncements over the years. In 1876 an Appeal Court judge said: 'The conspirators may repent and stop, may have no opportunity, or may be prevented or may fail. Nevertheless the crime is complete: it was complete when they agreed.'[53]

The scope of the conspiracy laws took on a new dimension in 1972–73 in the case of Kamara where a group of students from Sierra Leone had been charged with conspiracy to trespass and unlawful assembly when they occupied their country's High Commission building. They were convicted on both counts but appealed on the grounds that there was no such offence as conspiracy to trespass. Lord Justice Lawton delivering the Appeal Court's judgement, said that because a tort (civil wrong) had been held in the past to be an indictable offence it followed that 'an agreement to trespass is an indictable conspiracy, no matter what absurd results can be envisaged if prosecutors and judges do not use common sense',[54] and the appeal failed. Prior to this decision conspiracy was generally held to apply only to criminal offences and not to civil ones, and its new effect was to make the conspiracy to commit an offence punishable much more severely than the actual committing of the criminal act. The Kamara case was taken to the House of Lords, as the final court of appeal, and the then Lord Chancellor, Lord Hailsham, descended from his governmental perch to deliver the judgement.

The judgement Lord Hailsham delivered fell into three parts. 1) Conspiracy to commit any act which could be regarded as criminal is an indictable (serious) offence. He spelt out the meaning of this point for the benefit of the law and order lobby (police and public alike). Such an action could be brought, he said, 'in the vast majority of the squatting cases, the "sit-in" cases or many of the cases in which sports grounds are forcibly occupied or disrupted'.[55] 2) Conspiracy to commit a public mischief is an indictable offence. 3) Conspiracy to trespass is a criminal offence in the following circumstances: where those in the conspiracy 'invade the domain of the public', e.g. embassies, and he specifically extended the 'public domain' to include private property, thus catering for squatters and factory work-ins. Despite the appeal decision given by the House of Lords in the subsequent Withers case to do away with the crime of conspiracy to commit a public mischief that

---

[53] Justice of Appeal Brett in *Aspinall*, 1876.
[54] DPP v. Kamara (Appeal), October 1972.
[55] Appeal hearing in the House of Lords, Kamara v. DPP, 4 January 1973.

of conspiracy to trespass remains firmly entrenched in law.

In fact the decision only confirms the earlier state prosecutions concerned with the Wethersfield Six and the Greek Embassy cases in the 1960s. The Wethersfield Six were all members of the Committee of 100, which had organised a demonstration at the Royal Air Force base at Wethersfield in Sussex on 6 December 1961. The day before the demonstration the six – Ian Dixon, Terry Chandler, Trevor Hatton, Michael Randle, Pat Pottle and Helen Allegranza – were arrested, the Committee's offices were raided by the Special Branch, and the homes of the six were searched. The demonstration still took place and over three thousand civil and military police were mobilised to confront several thousand activists, but there was no invasion of the base. The decision to prosecute the six, despite the fact that the threat to the base had not materialised, rested with the government, in particular with the Attorney-General, for they were charged with conspiracy under Section 1 of the 1911 Act which contained the catch-all clause 'any purpose prejudicial to the safety and interests of the state'. When questioned on his action in Parliament the Attorney-General admitted that this was the first time Section 1 had been used in a case not involving foreign spies, and when asked about the intention of the section replied: 'In considering whether or not to prosecute I must direct my mind to the language and spirit of the Acts and not to what my predecessors said about them many years ago in an entirely different context.'[56] As it was admitted that the prosecution did not involve espionage or the civil service, the application of the Act took on a new meaning, that of curbing political rights. For there is no doubt that at this time the state was facing a serious challenge from CND and the Committee of 100, a challenge which embraced hundreds of thousands of people.[57]

Two other points about this prosecution deserve attention. Firstly, why were the six charged under this Act rather than under the Public Order Act which was more directly relevant? Was it because the Official Secrets Act threw the onus on the defence to prove innocence? Secondly, why were these six selected and not the many others who took part in the Committee's work? In this respect it was a selective prosecution intended to blunt the effectiveness of political opposition. The six were convicted and sent to prison for eighteen months.

In the Greek Embassy case the charge of conspiracy was to play a

[56] A. F. Wilcox, *The Decision to Prosecute* (1970) p. 25.
[57] See p. 125 ff.

minor but significant role. A few days after the military coup in Greece a group of fifty people occupied the Embassy on 28 April 1967. Twenty minutes later a large force of police arrived, broke down the barricaded doors and arrested the demonstrators. Finally only forty-two were charged as some escaped from the police vans.[58] They were charged with threatening behaviour with intent to provoke a breach of the peace and that contrary to common law they unlawfully fought and made an affray. Terry Chandler was additionally charged with assault on a policeman. At the committal proceedings these charges were dropped and two different and more serious charges were substituted: riotous assembly under common law and forcible entry under a statute of 1381. The magistrate threw out the second charge but committed them for trial on the first.

Prior to the trial at the Old Bailey, it is alleged that a series of deals (plea-bargaining) took place between the DPP's office and the defendants. Clearly something happened for the charges entered eventually were different from and more serious than those on which they had been committed for trial. The indictment contained charges of conspiracy to riot and trespass, however, in the court the defendants pleaded not guilty to the conspiracy charge but guilty to unlawful assembly (which was not raised at the committal proceedings). Twenty-eight of the defendants were given conditional discharges for two years, eleven were fined, and three were sent to prison: Terry Chandler for fifteen months, Mike Randle for twelve months, and Del Foley for six months. The importance of this case is to emphasise the power of the state's prosecutors to choose the charges brought against political activists, to change them at the committal and to change them yet again before the actual trial.

The use of conspiracy charges against political activists took on a new dimension in the late 1960s. Against the background of increasing conflict in Northern Ireland four people were charged with conspiracy to possess firearms in 1971 in the Soar Eire case. The purpose of the conspiracy charges (as distinct from that of possession) was to link the four defendants arrested in Hackney with a fifth man detained in Northern Ireland – who had made a seventeen page statement involving the others. The charges against them were withdrawn after four days of the Old Bailey trial when the central role played by a Special Branch agent-provocateur became evident, and the statement by the man from Northern Ireland was shown to have been obtained

---

[58] *The Greek Embassy Case*, a pamphlet by Andy Anderson, 1967.

'under duress'.[59] One of the great advantages of bringing a charge of conspiracy for the police and the state prosecutors is that it enables them to cast a wide net and include, sometimes after the committal, people who are alleged to have only taken part in the conspiracy and not in any of the substantive charges. Of the Stoke Newington Eight four of the defendants were charged only with conspiracy and not with possession of firearms.[60] Another example was the case brought against Roche and Egan in 1971. Roche had thrown a CS gas cannister into the Chamber of the Commons to bring home to MPs the reality of the struggle in Northern Ireland. He was initially charged with possession of a noxious substance (two CS gas cannisters) under the Firearms Act. Then a charge of conspiracy to effect a public mischief was added and Bowes Egan, a known Irish activist, was charged with conspiracy but not with possession of the gas cannisters. Egan, who was nowhere near the Commons at the time of the event, was eventually acquitted.

Yet another case involving conspiracy resulted from the Anti-Internment League (AIL) march to Downing Street on 5 February 1973. The demonstration was to mark the anniversary of Bloody Sunday when the British Army killed thirteen unarmed civilians in Derry. A pitched battle broke out in Whitehall after police provocation, including concerted charges by lines of mounted policemen. Four members of the AIL were afterwards charged with conspiracy to cause threatening behaviour and with riotous behaviour. This was the first time conspiracy had been used in conjunction with Section 5 of the Public Order Act, 1936. The jury found John Gray, the AIL organiser, guilty on both counts, Bowes Egan and Michael O'Kane guilty on the second count only, and acquitted John Flavin. So John Gray was in effect convicted of having conspired with himself – which is a legal impossibility. The jury asked for leniency in the sentence and the three convicted got suspended sentences.

The twenty-four building workers' pickets in the Shrewsbury trial were charged in 1972 under the 1875 Conspiracy and the Protection of Property Act that they 'wrongfully and without legal authority intimidated divers people with a view to compelling these people to abstain from their lawful work.' It was the first use of this Act against trade unionists since it was passed, and what was in question was not merely public order but the direct threat they posed to the productive process by successful picketing. All were convicted, most were bound over or

[59] *Sunday Times*, 18 June 1972.
[60] See p. 41 ff.

fined, three were sent to jail. Two of these, Des Warren and Ricky Tomlinson, received sentences of two and three years respectively. These sentences were upheld in the Court of Appeal in November 1974, despite a nationwide campaign by rank and file trade unionists.

The two Angry Brigade trials, as they were known, followed a series of explosions at the homes of Cabinet Ministers, leading industrialists and at state buildings between August 1970 and the end of 1971.[61] After the bomb at the home of Robert Carr, the Home Secretary, Chief Sup. Roy Habershon (who was at the time of the bombing in charge of Carr's local police station in Barnet) was subsequently appointed the head of the newly-formed Bomb Squad. In June, after the bomb at the home of the Managing Director of Fords, Commander 'X' was appointed to lead the hunt – in fact, this was Commander Ernest Bond who had been involved in the case for some time. Extra guards were placed on the homes of Ministers and the new Home Secretary, Mr Maudling, asked to be kept in touch with the investigation through 'day and night' reports.[62]

[61] *1970*: August 30 – Home of Sir John Waldron, Commissioner of the Metropolitan Police; September 8 – home of Sir Peter Rawlinson, Attorney-General; October 8 – 2nd explosion at Rawlinson's home; November 20 – BBC van at the Miss World contest; December 3 – machine-gunning of Spanish embassy; December 9 – at the DEP; *1971*: January 12 – at the home of Robert Carr, Home Secretary; May 1 – Biba's boutique; May 22 – Tintagel House, HQ of Bomb Squad; June 22 – home of William Batty, Managing Director of Fords; July 31 – home of Mr Davies, Minister of Employment; August 15 – Army recruiting office in North London; October 18 – home of Mr Bryant, chief of building contractors; November 1 – Royal Tank Regiment HQ in London. This is a list of the explosions attributed to the 'Angry Brigade'.

[62] *Guardian*, 2 August 1971.

Chronology of the Angry Brigade trials

1971	
13 February	Jake Prescott charged.
7 March	Ian Purdie charged.
22 April	Committal proceedings for Prescott and Purdie start at Barnet.
13 May	Charge of Miss World bombing against Prescott is dropped after prosecution witness states Prescott was in Edinburgh at the time in question.

20/21 August	Six people arrested at Amhurst Road: Creek, Mendelson, Barker, Greenfield, together with Christie and Bott.
November/ December	Four more people arrested and charged together with the above six: Angela Wier, Kate McLean, Chris Allen and Pauline Conroy.
10 December to 1 December	Trial of Prescott and Purdie at the Old Bailey. Prescott given fifteen years on conspiracy, but acquitted on two bombings. Purdie acquitted.

1972

February	Committal proceedings at Lambeth. Two of those charged are immediately released after charges withdrawn for lack of evidence – Pauline Conroy and Chris Allen. The Stoke Newington Eight are committed for trial at the Old Bailey on charges of conspiracy, possession of arms and explosives (against six of them), and specific bombing charges against two (Mendelson and Greenfield).
June to December	Trial of the Stoke Newington Eight. Four are sentenced to ten years: Creek, Mendelson, Barker and Greenfield. Four are acquitted on all charges: Bott, Christie, Wier and MacLean.

In all, twelve people were arrested and charged in connection with the 'Angry Brigade' bombings:

- *two* had charges against them withdrawn
- *five* were acquitted on all counts
- *five* were convicted and sent to prison on conspiracy charges.

Not a single person was ever convicted for actually committing any of the twenty-seven bombings and shootings attributed to the three-year-long conspiracy.

Jake Prescott and Ian Purdie had been arrested in February and March respectively and committed for trial in April 1971. On 20/21 August six people were arrested at 359 Amhurst Road in Stoke Newington. The house had been raided at 4pm on Friday, 20 August and the four occupants arrested. Two people who visited the house the next morning were also arrested. Those arrested were held at Albany Street police station and it was not until 11pm on the Saturday evening that they saw a solicitor. The newspapers carried reports about a series of raids but did not mention the arrests, and it was not until the following Monday at noon that the six were charged under the 1883 Explosive Substances Act. One of those arrested, Jim Greenfield, alleged at the time that he had been beaten up while at Albany Street station but it was not until a year later – at his trial in August 1972 – that positive evidence of this appeared: Greenfield's pullover had been sent to the Woolwich laboratory for explosives tests which proved negative.

'However, it was then sent to the police laboratory at Holborn and human blood traces were found on the arm and chest areas. Proof of assault, suggests MacDonald? Could be, says Bond. "I am suggesting that this evidence has been deliberately suppressed and withheld for a year," asserts MacDonald. In a flurry of confusion Judge James intervenes and Mathews, the prosecutor, says it was not Bond's fault but his and the DPP's.'[63]

Before those arrested at Amhurst Road came up for committal proceedings at Lambeth in February 1972 the trial of Prescott and Purdie was held at the Old Bailey in November and December 1971.

At the Barnet committal proceedings Jake Prescott was charged with conspiracy to cause explosions between 30 July 1970 and 5 March 1971. He was also charged with the specific bombings at Mr Carr's house, the Department of Employment and the Miss World contest. Ian Purdie was charged with conspiracy. Three key points were to come out of the hearing. Firstly, a representative of an Edinburgh car-hire firm positively identified Prescott and Purdie as having been in that city at 2.30pm on the day of the Miss World contest, and the charge against Prescott for this bombing was immediately withdrawn. Indeed it could be asked what evidence the police had for this charge

[63] *Time Out*, 22 September 1972. MacDonald was one of the defence lawyers.

apart from their own suspicions? Secondly, a key witness against
Prescott, a Mr A, appeared in court. Mr A had shared a cell with
Prescott (while he was being held in custody) and he alleged Prescott
made incriminating remarks about the bombings. Mr A's evidence
together with that of a Mr B, was to form a crucial part of the prosecution case at the Old Bailey. Lastly, there was the attitude of the head of
the Bomb Squad Chief Sup. Roy Habershon. When asked why he
was interested in Purdie as a suspect he replied that Purdie was a 'candidate for the outrage'. He was then asked about Purdie's arrest and
'admitted in cross-examination that he had ordered Ian's arrest for
questioning, which is illegal. He was not cautioned nor was any
warrant made out for his arrest.'[64] The Old Bailey trial opened on 10
November 1971 – the Judge was Justice Melford Stevenson. The
previous weekend the Bomb Squad had carried out a couple of raids
on two places they had raided three times before, and they were
rewarded with front-page headlines in the two London evening
newspapers – 'London Raids by Yard's Bomb Squad'.[65] Both stories
mentioned the trial at the Old Bailey and the Angry Brigade. This 'fortunate' timing and the virtually contemptuous linking of the raids, the
Angry Brigade and the trial of two people as yet unconvicted typified
the partiality of the press in both trials.

It is usually believed that there is no such thing as a 'political' trial in
this country; there are only criminal trials. And yet in both trials it was
suggested that the motive was provided by the political views of the
defendants. Mr Mathews, the state prosecutor, opened with the
remarks: 'two young men, self-styled revolutionaries and anarchists
... (sought with others) to promulgate their ideals in acts of violence.'[66]
The evidence against Prescott was three-fold: the statements made by
Mr A and Mr B, a statement alleged to have been made by Prescott to
Habershon, and handwriting on three envelopes which contained
Angry Brigade communiques. The first two items are what are commonly known as 'verbals',[67] and were strongly rejected by the defence.
Prescott admitted that the writing on the three envelopes was his but
stated he was told the envelopes were for another purpose. The
handwriting on the other communiques was heavily disguised and it

[64] *Time Out*, 10 June 1971.
[65] *Evening Standard* and *Evening News*, 8 November 1971.
[66] *Time Out*, 19 November 1971.
[67] Evidence based on what is alleged to have been said by a defendant to
another person – usually a police officer.

was suggested that if he was knowingly part of the conspiracy surely he
would have done the same?

The prosecution sought to establish when Prescott's political as distinct from his criminal career had started; he had been to prison
several times before. Mr Mathews, however, did not get the answer
he was expecting.

> *Mathews:* Mr Prescott, before you went to Albany Prison, you took
> no part in political activity, did you?
> *Prescott:* Criminally speaking I had.
> *Mathews:* But had you taken part in political activity, I ask you for
> this reason . . .
> *Prescott:* Well, I'd taken part in expropriation, stealing from the
> ruling class.
> *Mathews:* I wasn't going to refer to that quite, as you might term it,
> political activity . . .[68]

Purdie's defence counsel offered no witnesses and Purdie did not go
into the witness box. Counsel said there was no case to answer and
suggested there was 'an edifice of suspicion and prejudice' but nothing
else. And he went on to quote a case where Judge Devlin said the fact
that the defendant did not go into the box should not be taken as a sign
of guilt. The case in question was that of Bodkin Adams, who was
cleared by the jury – the state prosecutor on that occasion was Justice
Melford Stevenson.

The strength of the insinuations of an association between both
defendants and those arrested at Amhurst Road cannot be
underestimated:

> 'The jury was invited by Mathews to find the evidence against the
> Six (arrested at Amhurst Road) "overwhelming", but he said the
> defendants' association with them was not enough to convict,
> (though) "it might make you extremely suspicious". But when
> you consider the politics of Prescott and Purdie in association
> "with others" and whether "Prescott and Purdie held such
> revolutionary beliefs . . . this confirms the other evidence there
> may be of participation." '[69]

In his summing-up speech Justice Melford Stevenson spent a full day
on Prescott and just thirty-five minutes on Purdie. Stevenson first

[68] *Time Out*, 3 December 1971.
[69] *Time Out*, 25 November, 1971.

defined for the jury the nature of a conspiracy, which is an agreement to achieve an unlawful purpose: 'conspiracies are always hatched in whispers . . . it is, or nearly always is, a matter of inference.'[70] Clearly if proof of a conspiracy is founded on 'inference' then the traditional standards of evidence go by the board. As to the motive for the conspiracy, Stevenson asserted: 'In one sense, politics here don't matter . . . there is only one sense in which politics acquire any relevance in this case. That is in so far as you see they provide evidence of motive for what is alleged to be done here.' Later he made reference to the affinity of political ideas. One of the Angry Brigade communiques presented in evidence ended with the words 'Solidarity, revolution and love'. 'And there is also the letter to Prescott in prison signed: Love, solidarity, revolution. A very trivial matter, but that indicates does it not, a community of ideas between these two . . .'

The case against Prescott on the two bombings charges – Carr's house and the Department of Employment and Productivity (DEP) – rested on the evidence of Mr A, Mr B and Chief Sup. Habershon against which the defence produced six alibi witnesses. Stevenson said that 'grave accusations' were being made by the defence 'to the effect that Chief Sup. Habershon himself was a party to a most wicked conspiracy involving Habershon, and Mr A and Mr B to place false evidence against Prescott.'[71] The jury retired for five hours and twenty-six minutes and returned a verdict of not guilty for Purdie, guilty for Prescott on conspiracy but not guilty on the two bombing charges. Prescott was sentenced to fifteen years in prison.[72] In the outcome the jury accepted the defence contention on Purdie's innocence and on the bombing charges against Prescott, while the handwriting on three envelopes probably tipped the balance against the latter on the conspiracy charge.

The press coverage after the trial eulogised the sentence given to Prescott and all but ignored Purdie's acquittal (after nine months' custody in prison). However, if these journalists had bothered to attend the full length of the trial (instead of just the beginning and the end) they might have questioned the basis of Prescott's sentence. The mood of the media was well represented in an *Evening Standard* article which appeared in the week after the trial. It was headlined 'The red

[70] *Time Out*, 10 December 1971.
[71] *Ibid*.
[72] In June 1973 this was reduced to ten years in line with the sentences at the later trial.

badge of revolution that is creeping across Britain' and it defined the 'enemy' thus:

> 'These guerrillas are the violent activists of a revolution comprising workers, students, trade unionists, homosexuals, unemployed and women striving for liberation. They are all angry . . . Whenever you see a demonstration, whenever you see a queue for strike pay, every public library with a good stock of socialist literature . . . anywhere would be a good place to look. In short there is no telling where they are'.[73]

In November and December 1971 four more people were arrested by the Bomb Squad and held in prison custody – Angela Wier, Kate McLean, Chris Allen and Pauline Conroy. However, when the committal proceedings for the second trial started at Lambeth magistrates court in January 1972, the charges against Chris Allen and Pauline Conroy were withdrawn. The state prosecutor said the Attorney-General had not given leave for their prosecution to continue – which in simple language means that the charges were dropped for lack of evidence. The others, known as the Stoke Newington Eight, were committed for trial by jury. The case opened at the Old Bailey in the first week of June 1972. Six of the eight – Anna Mendelson, Hilary Creek, Jim Greenfield, John Barker, Chris Bott and Stuart Christie – were charged with conspiracy to cause explosions and with the possession of arms and explosives (Greenfield was additionally charged with the bombings at the Italian Consulate in Manchester, and – with Anna Mendelson – of that at Paddington police station); Angela Wier and Kate McLean were charged only with conspiracy. The presiding judge was Justice James and the state prosecutor was again Mr Mathews. For the defence, five of the defendants had lawyers and three – Anna Mendelson, Hilary Creek and John Barker – defended themselves with the aid of McKenzie advisers.[74]

The swearing-in of the jury took more than three hours. Nineteen potential jurors withdrew voluntarily because they said they would be biased, and thirty-nine were challenged by the defence lawyers. The court itself had all the usual trappings of the occasion, though the very obvious presence of Bomb Squad officers in the well of the court, in the public gallery, the entrance to the court and outside in the street

[73] Cited in *Time Out*, 15 December 1972.
[74] A McKenzie adviser is someone appointed to assist the defendant in preparing a case.

emphasised the importance of the case to the state. The press benches as usual were full for a couple of days at the beginning and end of the trial.[75]

Again it was asserted that this was not a political trial despite the state's contention that the politics of the defendants provided the motive for the alleged offences. Mr Mathews, the prosecutor, spoke of revolutionary socialists and anarchists who 'sought to attack the democratic structures of this society with whose politics they disagreed.'[76]

The crux of the prosecution case rested on their assertion that there had been a three-year-long conspiracy covering some twenty-seven bombings and shootings, although these had been 'claimed' by a variety of groups – the 1st May Group, Lotta Continua, the Wild Bunch, Butch Cassidy and the Sundance Kid, and the Angry Brigade. The prosecution alleged that there was a 'common source', the con-spiracy, for the nineteen explosions, six attempted bombings, and two shootings which were presented to the jury on a long schedule. Police explosives experts testified that there had been 123 known attacks on property during the period March 1968 to August 1971. Seventeen of the 123 attacks were against 'foreign buildings' but only ten of these were attributed to the conspiracy, and fourteen devices were said to have used alarm clocks in the timing mechanisms though only six were said to be part of the conspiracy. The defence questioned at every point the basis on which the associated set of twenty-five devices could be said to emanate from a common source. Similar questions arose when Det. Chief Superintendant John Chaffe, head of Scotland Yard's fingerprint department, produced a list of 137 suspects prepared by the Bomb Squad. Only the Judge saw the list but he did confirm that none of the eight on trial were on it. This enormous number of suspects lent weight to the defence contention that the Bomb Squad really had little idea who committed the 'Angry Brigade' bombings. The prize exhibit for the state was the 'arsenal' found at Amhurst

[75] Before the full trial opened two of the defendants, Hilary Creek and Anna Mendelson, applied for bail again and as usual there were objections to this from the police. Creek offered an address in London to stay at during the trial, and Mr Habershon uttered another of his unforgettable observations: *Judge:* Is there any objection to this address? *Habershon:* Yes, my Lord. I have noticed that the address is in N.1, and during our investigations into this case we have discovered that there are many people of a similar ideology living in Islington. *Time Out*, 7 July 1972.
[76] *Time Out*, 9 June 1972.

Road where four of the defendants lived. The jury were shown a sub-machine gun, a pistol, sticks of explosives, and detonators.

The defence case took two months and attacked that presented by the state on every point. Particular care was taken to ensure that the jury understood what was happening; MacDonald (defending Greenfield) said in his opening speech:

> 'Everything when you come into court seems to revolve around the judge. He is the person who gives directions as to procedure. He is the person who when he comes into court we all stand up. When he sits down we sit down. It may feel that all power in the court is centred on him, sitting there in an elevated position half-way up the wall. You may feel that you are not the people who have the power . . . You probably realise that the whole British establishment awaits your verdict with bated breath. And you and the defendants, when you really consider it, are the only unpredictable factors in this whole scenario.'[77]

The investigations, suggested the defence, were conducted during a time of mass working-class opposition to the Industrial Relations Act introduced by an increasingly unpopular Tory government. Where the prosecution had sought to show the 'violent' revolutionary beliefs of those on trial, the defence counterposed the institutionalised violence of the state and capitalist society – in the factory, in the community, and in Northern Ireland.

The central point of the defence case rested on their contention that the arms found at Amhurst Road were planted by the Bomb Squad. John Barker and Hilary Creek put it to police officers in cross-examination that they were both taken out of the flat for several minutes for no apparent reason – only to be returned and confronted with the arms and explosives.[78]

> 'MacDonald said he sought to establish that all four, when arrested, were taken into the hallway at the bottom of the house. He then suggested that Doyle (of the Bomb Squad) was hiding, with the guns and explosives packed into two holdalls, in the bathroom on the middle floor, "until the coast was clear, waiting for the right moment to go up, once the upstairs had been cleared".'[79]

[77] *Time Out*, 13 October 1972.
[78] *Time Out*, 8 September 1972.
[79] *Time Out*, 17 November 1972.

Furthermore, a police fingerprint officer told the court there were no fingerprints on the guns and other items discovered.

None of those living at Amhurst Road denied their contact with people who said they were the Angry Brigade but this was very different to participation and conspiracy. Anna Mendelson told the jury in her closing speech:

> 'we didn't feel and don't feel there is any room or need for bomb attacks on Cabinet Ministers, although we might understand the feelings behind them, because our politics are certainly not the politics of bombing. Bombing a Cabinet Minister is not going to get rid of the capitalist system because there is always somebody to step into his place, unless the situation and the conditions are right.'[80]

The case against the four defendants who did not live at Amhurst Road rested on other evidence. Angela Wier's counsel called seven witnesses to testify that she was attending a Gay Liberation Front demonstration at the time the police alleged she was in France collecting explosives. Kate McLean was alleged to have written the communiques signed by 'Butch Cassidy and the Sundance Kid' but conflict arose over handwriting evidence. While Stuart Christie was – in addition to conspiracy – charged with having detonators in his car boot, defence counsel held these too were planted by the police. Chris Bott faced only the conspiracy charge – that relating to possession of explosives having been withdrawn on the Judge's direction in October.

In his closing speech Justice James extended the definition of a conspiracy from that given by Stevenson. Now the jury was told: 'Conspiracy can be effected by a wink or a nod without a word being spoken.'[81] So after six months and the longest trial on record the jury retired for two and a half days before giving their verdict. After a day they returned to ask a question and indicated they were split 7–5 in favour of conviction. When they returned the verdicts showed them to be very divided. Firstly, four of the defendants were acquitted on all charges – Kate McLean, Angela Wier, Chris Bott and Stuart Christie. Secondly, for the four they found guilty by ten to two of conspiracy and possession of explosives (Jim Greenfield, John Barker, Hilary Creek

[80] *Time Out*, 24 November 1972.
[81] *Time Out*, 1 December 1972.

and Anna Mendelson) they asked the judge to be lenient in his sentence. Jim Greenfield and Anna Mendelson were both acquitted on the specific bombing charges. The sentence was 10 years in prison.

At a press conference after the trial Commander Bond and Det. Chief Sup. Habershon posed for photographers and reporters and left them in little doubt as to their opinions. Commander Bond said: 'Stuart Christie is a member of the Angry Brigade. Those eight people charged were militant members of the Angry Brigade.'[82] This contempt for the verdict of the jury was really part of a face-saving exercise. Of the twelve people arrested and charged by the Bomb Squad in the course of the Angry Brigade investigation five were acquitted on all counts, two had charges against them withdrawn and five were convicted. Moreover, the seven spent many months in prison custody before coming to trial – only to be acquitted. The police would no doubt say this casts doubt on the jury system, while many others will say it casts doubt on the police themselves.[83]

The increased use of conspiracy charges in recent times raises the whole question of judge-made law or judicial legislation. A charge of conspiracy can now be added, at the discretion of the state's prosecutors, to crimes of public order, public morals and political conflict. In July 1972, the Lord Chancellor, Lord Hailsham, told the House of Lords, in reference to two appeals, Knuller and Shaw, heard by their Lordships: 'Of course it is true that the majority of the House of Lords in both cases decided that there was a residual right of the criminal courts of this country to extend the boundaries of conspiracy in an unidentified number of cases.'[84] The use and extension of the law of conspiracy which has been determined by the judiciary, and not by parliament, serves as a good indication of its determined partiality in favour of the established order.

The Emergency Powers Acts

Public consciousness of Britain's Emergency Powers Acts was

[82] *Time Out*, 15 December 1972.

[83] Commander Bond was later promoted to Deputy Assistant Commissioner at Scotland Yard. Det. Chief Sup. Habershon was made a Commander and seconded to the Home Office's Research and Planning Office in 1973. In June 1974 he headed the police investigation into the killing of Kevin Gateley, the twenty-year-old Warwick University student, in Red Lion Square on 5 June 1974. In April 1975 Commander Habershon was appointed head of the Bomb Squad, replacing Robert Huntley. (*Guardian*, 2 April 1975).

[84] House of Lords, 24 July 1972.

heightened when in November 1973 the Tory government declared its fifth state of emergency in just three years of office – more than any other British government in history. The specific conditions which lent themselves to this situation are discussed elsewhere,[85] however the precise nature of the powers taken by government under these Acts needs to be understood because they have not, as yet, ever been fully employed.

The reasons for the passing of the first Emergency Powers Act in 1920 arose some years earlier during the First World War. When war broke out a 'state of national emergency' was declared, the first since the Napoleonic wars a hundred years before. Within days of the outbreak of war parliament passed the 1914 Defence of the Realm Act (popularly known as DORA). The Act had one central clause giving the government power to make regulations for 'securing the public safety and the defence of the realm'. Immediately a series of Regulations were issued. Some were patently ludicrous, for example Regulation 9DD prohibiting dog-shows and Regulation 40B regulating the supply of cocaine to actresses. Others included Regulation 27 which provided for six months in prison for spreading false rumours, and Regulation 14B, for the detention of people of alleged 'hostile origin or association'. For the most part people obeyed the Regulations and attempts to challenge them in the courts were generally successfully resisted. One of the few exceptions was in 1918 when the Shipping Controller tried to requisition not just the ships but also the personnel of the China Mutual Steam Navigation Company, and the courts upheld the objection.

The Regulations made under DORA were due to lapse when hostilities were officially declared to have ended; however, the government and various state agencies were keen to retain the key powers afforded by DORA for more permanent use. The period immediately after the war was a testing time for the ruling class, and in 1919 the first draft of a national emergency plan was prepared for the supply and transport system by Sir Eric Geddes.[86] Before DORA expired in 1921, the Emergency Powers Act was brought in, which was to 'make exceptional provisions for the protection of the community in case of emergency'. The government was empowering itself with special sanctions in cases of major strikes, civil disorders and pre-revolutionary situations. Under the Act a state of emergency can be declared by the

[85] See p. 266 ff.
[86] See p. 258 ff.

monarch if at any time it *appears* 'to the government that the essential services of the country are threatened'. The government (in effect, the Cabinet) is then empowered to draw up a set of Regulations and can 'assume such powers and duties as His Majesty may deem necessary' to restore order and maintain supplies, or 'for any other purposes'. The Regulations once drawn up have to be passed by parliament (a mere formality in practice) and must be renewed by them every month. In effect power resides totally with the executive and all pretence of parliamentary control is forsaken. The totalitarian nature of this Act becomes apparent when it is realised that the executive has the power to suspend or amend *all* laws, the only restrictions under the 1920 Act being: 1) no Regulation shall introduce compulsory military service or industrial conscription – this requires the declaration of a state of war; 2) it shall not be an offence to take part in a strike; and 3) existing *procedures* in criminal cases shall not be altered. But what constitutes a 'crime' can alter fundamentally. The Act, in short, can 'suspend practically all our civil liberties and weight the scales heavily against those who may be in active opposition to the government of the day.'[87] Nor was the Act the only one to be born of DORA's wartime applications; other Acts were passed on the restriction of licensing hours, dangerous drugs, firearms, the sale of tea, and official secrets.

The 1920 Act was first invoked in 1921. The mine-owners had announced sweeping wage-cuts and posted lock-out notices at many pits, and the Triple Alliance – the TUC's predecessor comprising miners, railwaymen and transport workers – called a strike. The Lloyd George government declared a state of emergency and dispatched troops to working-class areas. Three days later the militant miners – not for the last time – were sold out by the right-wing leadership of the Triple Alliance (the day of the sell-out, 21 April 1921, became known as 'Black Friday'). The first sustained use of the 1920 Act was in the General Strike in 1926 when it was in force for eight months, though the strike itself lasted only a few days – and again the trade union leadership capitulated and left the miners to fight on alone.

In the next forty years there were only four declarations of a state of emergency, in the dock strike of 1948 and 1949 (by the Labour government), during the 1955 rail strike (by the Tories), and in the 1966 seamen's strike (by Labour). Sir Alec Douglas-Home's brief period as Tory Prime Minister saw the passing of the Emergency Powers Act 1964 which amended the 1920 Act in two ways. Firstly, it

[87] Kidd, *British Liberty in Danger* (1940) p. 51.

widened the causes which could justify the declaration of an emergency with the words 'There have occurred, or are about to occur, events of such a nature' as to disrupt the life of the community. Secondly, it made permanent the provision from the Defence (Armed Forces) Regulations 1939 to allow the use of the armed forces in direct employment in 'agricultural work or in other work, being urgent work of national importance.' The declaration of emergency by the Tory government in October 1973 lasted for four months and was the longest since that of the General Strike. Previously there were two in 1970 (in July over the dock strike, and December over the electricity strike) and two in 1972 (in February over the miners, and August over the docks again). Since the passing of the 1920 Act only eleven states of emergency have been declared, five of which were during the period of Heath's government.

In November 1974, in response to the extensive IRA bombing campaign in England, parliament rushed through – in one day – the Prevention of Terrorism (Temporary Provisions) Act 1974.[88] The basis of the Act had been drawn up as part of the Home Office contingency planning after the Old Bailey explosion in March 1973, and the Bill introduced by the Labour Home Secretary, Roy Jenkins, was substantially the same as that provided for by the previous Tory government.[89] Introducing the Bill in the Commons Mr Jenkins admitted that 'These powers are draconian. In combination they are unprecedented in peacetime . . .'[90]

The Act contained three Parts. Part I proscribed the IRA in Britain and provided for up to 5 years in prison for members of the organisation. Part II gave the Home Secretary the power to exclude people from Britain he considered – on police evidence – to be involved in the 'commission, preparation, or instigation of acts of terrorism' (Section 3:3). Exemption from expulsion was only granted to those permanently resident in Britain for the previous twenty years. The right of appeal to an 'adviser' was provided for, but his advice to the Home Secretary is not binding and may be ignored by the latter. The procedure laid down for expulsion (or exclusion if entry to the country was being sought) was closely modelled on Schedule 2 of the Immigra-

[88] This Act is similar in most respects to the 1939 Prevention of Violence (Temporary Provisions) Act. See Chapter 3.

[89] *Sunday Times*, 8 December 1974.

[90] *Hansard*, 29 November 1974. In May 1975 the Act was extended for a further six months.

tion Act 1971. Part III extended the powers of arrest and detention of the police by allowing them to hold a person for questioning for 48 hours, and for a further five days on the issuing of a Detention Order by the Home Secretary. In addition, the police were empowered to search premises on a warrant issued by a police Inspector (or above) and not, as is usual, on the authority of a magistrate.

In practice the Act fully justified the description 'draconian'. In the first four months of the Act's operation, between November 1974 and April 1975, three people were charged under Part I, two subsequently having the charges against them dropped; forty-five Exclusion Orders were issued and only five of the eleven appeals were successful; 489 people were detained under the Act at police stations but only sixteen were later charged with criminal offences. The predominant use of Part III of the Act – to search, arrest and detain – has, in effect, been to expand the intelligence-gathering of the police and the Special Branch rather than to catch those involved in bombings.

The NCCL rightly observed that the police already had sufficient powers to combat the IRA: 'police powers in practice are far wider than in theory . . . the new law, therefore, legitimises and extends past abuses.'[91] The issuing of Exclusion Orders (i.e. deportation) was open to even greater abuse. For, in effect, Orders were issued by the Home Secretary against those whom the police lacked sufficient evidence to bring before a court of law. Kidd's comment relating to the similar 1939 Act could be equally applied to this Act: 'if the evidence against them was not such as would satisfy a court of law it was clearly dangerous that powers should be given to the executive by which it can determine a man's "guilt" while he is denied access to the courts.'[92]

Finally, there was the Emergency Powers (Defence) Act, 1939, which related to the declaration of a 'state of war' (external or internal). Regulations issued under the Act were termed Defence Regulations and came into force automatically. They did not require parliamentary approval. This Act also allowed that 'Any Act of Parliament may be amended, suspended or applied with or without modification.' Though the Act was repealed in 1959 it stands as a model for future legislation should the threat of war – whether external or internal – arise again. This is not the place to give a full account of the treatment in the Second World War of conscientious objectors, pacifists, and political activists of all parties to the left of the Tories. Some idea of the

[91] NCCL Annual Report 1974/5, p. 10.
[92] R. Kidd, *op. cit.*, p. 77.

wartime restrictions on political freedom is conveyed in a letter from the Middlesbrough Police to the NCCL. The NCCL had protested at the treatment of four members of the Young Communist League. The Chief Constable replied that he had told the four young men: 'that free speech was still allowed in this Country, provided a person chose rather carefully what he said.'[93]

The central piece of legislation in this field, the Emergency Powers Act 1920, was the product of a period of great uncertainty in the ranks of the ruling class. This same mood seemed to prevail during the 1970–74 Heath government and may account for its tendency to reach for drastic powers at the slightest challenge.[94] The line between a permanent state of emergency and the declaration of a war situation is very fine, as we have seen in Northern Ireland. To date, few of the eleven states of emergency have progressed beyond the declaration of emergency itself, while in one or two cases troops have been deployed and a few erring individuals warned of infringing minor provisions. In each case one side or the other has stepped back from the brink of outright confrontation whether because of cautious trade union leadership, respect for the rule of law, or the economic rather than political nature of the labour movement's challenge. Whatever the reasons, the Emergency Powers Acts have been and, more importantly, remain a powerful weapon against any widespread opposition.

The four fields of law considered here were all designed to preserve and perpetuate the status quo of the British state. The Official Secrets Acts guard its plans, thoughts and actions; the incitement laws ensure the loyalty of the repressive agencies of the state; the conspiracy laws ensnare the 'leaders' of militant political groups; and the Emergency Powers Acts seek to pre-empt civil disorder and revolution. Each Act offends commonly accepted democratic rights under the normal rule of law. By their very nature these Acts are overtly political in their implications and in their use (which is not to say they are the only political laws), and the partiality of the judiciary in giving interpretive judgements is perhaps nowhere better illustrated. Clearly the actual and the potential use of the Acts must be distinguished. Their actual or threatened use has been most effective in guarding state secrets, leaving the mass of the people in almost total ignorance of the state's actions. In effect they have bequeathed to the country a Civil Service so

[93] Letter, 21 August 1940. For a detailed account of wartime legislation see Kidd *op. cit.*

[94] See p. 266 ff.

loyal and tight-lipped as to be almost inhuman. Indeed in other Western liberal-democracies no government is guaranteed such a blanket of secrecy as that in Britain. Further, the use of these laws against emerging movements of political opposition has proved an important adjunct to other forms of harrassment. Their potential use in the Britain of the late 1970s and 1980s depends on the developing situation. It is clear, though, from history that political movements have not been deterred from acting by the draconian potential of British law.

2 The Uniformed Police

The police in this country are the instruments for enforcing the rule of law; they are the means by which civilised society maintains order, that people may live safely in their homes and go freely about their lawful business. Basically their task is the maintenance of the Queen's Peace – that is, the preservation of law and order. Without this there would be anarchy.[1]

This statement exemplifies the dominant attitude towards the police today and also provides a basis for explaining their historical development in Britain. Conventional police histories pose the anarchy of pre-police times against a progression towards a civilised way of life. They argue that this can be explained through the recognition by all the people of the need to respect the rule of law and its enforcers, the police. Underpinning this respect is the independence of the law and the police from sectarian or class interests so that by protecting the rights of all, the liberty of the individual is guaranteed. An alternative history must seek to explain the interests that the police were formed to protect, and the way in which the system gained general acceptance.[2]

The historical development of the police can be divided into four periods: 1) prior to 1829, the system of 'old policing', as it is known; 2) 1829–1870, the formation of the 'new police' in London, and by the 1860s, their extension to all parts of the country; 3) 1870–1920, a period of internal reforms and consolidation; 4) 1920–1964, the amalgamation of forces and the initial application of technology to policing.

Prior to 1829 – the 'old policing' system

For some six hundred years prior to the formation of the Metropolitan police in 1829 the system of 'old policing' effectively maintained law and order throughout the land. Only in the latter part of this period,

---

[1] *Report of the Royal Commission on the Police* (1962) p. 21.
[2] See Appendix for the political and economic context.

with the rise of capitalism, did this system begin to break down. Since Anglo-Saxon times the enforcement of the King's Peace was the collective responsibility of each town and hamlet. Each township was charged with apprehending and punishing an offender, and could be fined for neglecting to carry out its duty. In Norman times it became the practice for a township to appoint one of its members to be responsible for its collective role, and this person gained the name (from the French) of 'constable'. The most usual form of apprehending an offender was to raise the 'hue and cry' in which all the townspeople had to take part. The 'hue and cry' was later replaced by the issuing of warrants by magistrates.

Until 1829 there were only two statutes governing law enforcement, the Statute of Winchester, 1285, and the Justices of the Peace Act, 1361. The Statute of Winchester recognised the practice as it existed and added to this by calling for the appointment of watchmen to aid the constable. It also laid an obligation on the citizen to aid the constable in the hue and cry or to face a fine, and for the constable to bring the offender to the court for punishment. From the reign of Richard I certain knights had been appointed to ensure the King's Peace and they later became known as Keepers of the Peace. In the fourteenth century the Keepers of the Peace were all drawn from the feudal aristocracy, and the Justices of the Peace Act, 1361, formalised the practice and gave them the name Justices of the Peace (JPs). Like the knights before them they were appointed by the Crown. The constables, who were originally chosen by the local community, now began to lose the initiative and became 'the mere subordinates of local Ministers of the Crown.'[3] The magistrates (JPs) combined three functions. They were responsible for law and order, the judicial and administrative authority in the locality, and they were charged with maintaining the Peace of the Crown, whence they derived their authority.

From the sixteenth century onwards, with the beginnings of capitalism, the duties of the JPs extended to dealing with vagrants and paupers, and with the regulation of wages and working hours. During the next two hundred years, with the movement from the land to the towns, the growth in population, and the advent of large numbers of people living in poverty, crime increased. The ruling class responded first by seeking to extend the old system of policing and then later by the formation of regular police forces.

[3] Quoted in the Royal Commission, p. 11, from Simpson, 'The Office of Constable', *English Historical Review*, 1895.

There were several attempts to make the old system work in the late eighteenth century. The number of offences which were liable to capital punishment were doubled. The home-based army, increasingly used to combat the 'mob' both in London and the provinces, was supplemented by the militia and the yeomanry; magistrates encouraged the use of informers by extensive use of rewards for a conviction (blood money); and the middle class formed voluntary protection societies.[4] But by the end of the eighteenth century the only part of the country to have anything like an adequate system of policing was the City of London. By an Act of 1663 it was empowered to employ up to one thousand nightwatchmen who guarded the ships and warehouses of dockland. London was then the world's biggest port, through which half the world's produce moved. By far the largest users of the port were the West Indies merchants whose sugar was the product of slave-based agriculture.

Patrick Colquhoun, a London magistrate, who was appointed the overseeing JP for the City in 1798, set about reforming this policing system. Within a year of Colquhoun taking up his post fifty full-time constables were employed for the first time. In 1800 he wrote *Treatise on the Commerce and Police of the River Thames* in which he estimated that more than ten thousand thieves and footpads were at work in the area of the docks. But, more importantly, Colquhoun estimated that 'nine-tenths of all crimes in the port were committed, not by professional offenders, but by persons whose presence in the area was essential or at least fully justified, such as port workers, watchmen, sailors and revenue officers.'[5]

Colquhoun's police force was given official status under the Thames River Police Act (1800), and the superintending magistrates were made directly responsible to the Home Secretary. The first 'new' police force was formed. Its formation was, however, significant for another reason. It led to the establishment of the money wage in the docks. The theft of goods from the docks represented not just a criminal act, it was a substantial threat to the profits of the merchants. Nor was this problem confined to the docks; similar crimes were committed throughout manufacturing and industry. At this time workers in many jobs were paid partly in money wages and partly in kind. The

[4] Radzinowicz (1956/1968), rewards: Vol. 2 pp. 83–127; informants: Vol. 2, p. 414 and Vol. 3, pp. 176–178; protection societies: Vol. 3, pp. 100–103 and Vol. 4, pp. 218–219.
[5] Radzinowicz, *op. cit.*, Vol. 2, p. 359.

farmworker got part of the harvest, the coalman part of the coal he handled, the carpenter got odd bits of wood and chippings, and in the docks the ship's mates were entitled to any spilled sugar. For the dock labourer this often formed his total wage; according to Colquhoun they 'would on every occasion agree to work without wages, and even solicit their employers to be preferred on these terms, trusting to a general licence to plunder for their remuneration.'[6] The emergence of the river police quickly eliminated this form of wage and, in doing so, effectively tied this section of the working class to the money wage. 'From the very outset, therefore, there was nothing impartial about the police. They were created to preserve for a colonial merchant and an industrial class the collective product of West Indian slavery and London wage labour.'[7] It was to be twenty-one years before the rest of London was to get a police force. Outside the City the powers of the magistrates were extended, those at Bow Street employing a number of Bow Street runners. By the late 1820s London, a city with nearly one and a half million people, was policed by four hundred and fifty constables attached to magistrates' courts and some four thousand watchmen.

Policing was (and still is) concerned with two areas – public order and crime. The maintenance of public order was essential to frustrate the nation-wide struggles by the new working class. Luddism, which emerged in 1811, represented the first tentative moves by the working class to organise itself against the emerging industrial capitalism.[8] While the violence of the workers was against property, that used in response by the state through the army, militia and yeomanry was against people. The massacre at Peterloo in 1819, when eleven men and women were murdered and hundreds injured by the army, was among the more ignominious actions perpetrated in the name of law and order. Public order was maintained by the extensive use of force. Crime on the other hand largely concerned individual acts against the propertied classes, such as stealing from factories, pick-pocketing, assault and robbery, and burglary.

Crime was perceived by the ruling class to be inextricably bound up with poverty, the poverty of the new urban poor and the low wage-earning farm workers. The JPs, in addition to administering the con-

[6] Radzinowicz, *op. cit.*, Vol. 3, p. 166.
[7] Ian MacDonald, from a paper to the Towards Racial Justice Conference, September 1973.
[8] See E. P. Thomson, *The Makings of the English Working Class* (1968).

stabulary and dispensing justice, had also been responsible for the moral health of vagrants, tramps and the unemployed since the sixteenth century. A plethora of charitable organisations existed for the relief of poverty and the combatting of crime. The repressive nature of the welfare schemes as administered by the magistrates and later by the Poor Law Guardians is often underestimated as a mechanism of maintaining law and order.[9]

The ruling class sought security for their property (home and factory) and in their everyday lives. The creation of a stable society could not be guaranteed in the long-term, however, by continually resorting to the use of outright force by the army.

> 'Once the class begins to organise, to agitate, to demonstrate, you need a force which has all the appearance of independence, which cannot be seen to be visibly taking sides in the class struggle, but which is merely there to enforce the law. The genius of the British ruling class is that they realised the need to have such a force and set about creating it.'[10]

This process did not come about overnight. Nearly seventy years passed after the creation of the London force before it could be said that the police were alone able to tackle crime and public order over the whole country.

1829–1870 The formation of the 'new' police

The legislation leading to the 'new police' was the 1829 Police Act which set up the Metropolitan force in London. This was proposed by Robert Peel, the Home Secretary, with the enthusiastic support of the army chief, the Duke of Wellington. Wellington had seen from experience that no lasting peace could result from the continual use of the army. The army had been engaged on domestic duties since the end of the Napoleonic wars without successfully imposing a peace. Sir Charles Napier, who was in charge of the army in the North during the Chartist period, observed afterwards that an organised body of police should be the first line of defence and the army the last.

The new London force placed much emphasis on patrolling the beat, and this began to afford some protection in the middle-class areas of London from vagabonds, footpads and gangs. Magistrates continued to play a major role in directing police work. At the behest

[9] Cloward and Piven, *Regulating the Poor* (1972) Ch. 1.
[10] Ian MacDonald, *Race Today*, December 1973.

of an important personage magistrates could order the police to patrol specific areas of London, place a guard on a house, or send a special detachment to watch for pickpockets at Ascot and Epsom. The importance of patrolling was also clear for the apprehension of criminals, because unless caught on the spot or already known to the police there was little chance of their being caught at all, as no records were kept of crimes committed. To enforce public order the police, rather than the army, were used increasingly to break up political meetings in London and to spy on working-class movements. One such movement was the National Political Union of the Working Classes. In May 1833 they held a demonstration at Cold Bath Fields, which the police broke up with baton charges. One person was killed, a policeman, and the coroner's jury returned a verdict of justifiable homicide. The government appealed to a higher court and succeeded in getting the decision annulled (the culprit was never caught). In the same year a Select Committee of the House of Commons was set up to investigate the infiltration of a police spy into the meetings of one of the NPU's branches. For over a year a policeman in plain-clothes, William Popay, had taken part in discussion meetings in Camberwell and Walworth and had been to several demonstrations. He was discovered only when one of the men saw him in a police station. The NPU members were indignant that they were 'compelled to pay for the maintenance of spies, under the pretence of their being persons employed for the preservation of the peace, and the protection of their property and their lives.'[11]

Popay, it transpired, had been working under the direct instructions of his superior, Superintendent McLean, who in turn was working on the unwritten orders of the two Commissioners of Police at Scotland Yard – Colonel Rowan and Richard Mayne. Popay's reports had been forwarded to Rowan and Mayne and most had been passed on directly to the Home Secretary. Much of the Select Committee's indignation was directed at the notes taken at a meeting of a speech by David Hume MP, that were passed to the Home Secretary (Lord Melbourne). The sole outcome of the inquiry was the vilification of Popay and not of his bosses, whose instructions he had been obeying.

In London the success of the new police was partly in combating crime and political opposition and partly in convincing the bourgeoisie that, unlike the French police whose arbitrary powers were feared, the London police did not threaten their liberty. The only

[11] Select Committee Report, in British Parliamentary Papers, Crime & Punishment, Police, Vol. 5, p. 5 (1968).

people whose liberty was curtailed were those who broke the law; that is, largely members of the working class who offended against the property and person of the bourgeois class. The Municipal Corporations Act, 1835, required borough councils in the cities to appoint Watch Committees who, in turn, were to be responsible for maintaining local police forces. However, as the decision to implement this law lay with the reluctant local councils (who had to bear the costs), only a handful responded. In 1839 the County Police Act was rushed through parliament as one means of combating Chartism. This Act permitted the counties to form police forces but it was not obligatory. The old system of policing however did not disappear for many years. By the early 1850s only half the fifty-odd counties had 'new' police forces and most major towns had none. The Chartists were largely put down by the army with some help from the militia, yeomanry and special constables. Local prosecution societies, formed by members of the propertied classes and offering rewards for information leading to a conviction, were said to number over five hundred in 1840.

Only by the County and Borough Police Act of 1856 was the recruitment of a regular police force made obligatory. By 1860 there were 259 separate forces and their size varied considerably. Each one was under local control (with JPs playing a large part) and there was little or no co-operation between them. Record-keeping was limited to noting prosecutions and convictions – reported crimes were not recorded. Moreover, many of the police, like the class they were drawn from, could not read or write. But the biggest problem for the Metropolitan Commissioners and the local watch committees was to maintain a stable force. In the first thirty years of the Metropolitan Police, of the total number employed one-third was dismissed and the same number resigned voluntarily, and this pattern was repeated outside London.

The passing of the 1856 Police Act did not result simply from a recognition of the value of police forces: a major factor was the ending of transportation overseas as a form of punishment. Several statutes had allowed for this alternative to capital punishment; for example, the Vagrancy Act of 1744 singled out 'incorrigible rogues' as deserving of transportation ('incorrigible rogues' were those who escaped from prison or repeated a serious offence – today known as 'hardened criminals'). America was the destination of those transported until the War of Independence and then, after a few years, Australia became the recipient country. By the 1850s, however, Australia was becoming too valuable a colony to allow increasing numbers of criminals to populate it (most did not return to England on their release), and the cost of providing sea passages, jails and wardens was becoming prohibitive. Lord Grey used the savings to justify a Treasury grant towards part of the cost of provincial forces (as an incentive to reluctant boroughs and counties). More generally it was recognised that if these 'hardened criminals' were to be imprisoned in Britain and finally released back into society, the system of policing had to cover the whole country.[12]

1870–1920 Internal reforms and consolidation

The next period in the development of the police, from 1870 to 1920, saw three major changes. There was the extension of police activity into working-class areas; internal reforms like record-keeping, improvements in conditions of work and pay; and the start of detection after the event, with the formation of the Criminal Investigation Department (CID) at Scotland Yard.

The duality in the role of the policeman which is clearly apparent today – the friendly, helpful bobby and the use of coercive force – dates from this period. The process by which police activities gradually extended into working-class areas and a respect for the rule of law was gained was a complex one. Both before and after the formation of police forces the new bourgeois class had shown itself much less enthusiastic than the landed aristocracy and the local gentry (small farmers) to take up arms every time disorder broke out in the neighbourhood. They demanded in effect a force capable of action as a shield between them and the militant sections of the working class. Moreover, several contemporary writers observed that the use of the militia (raised and led by the landowners) and the yeomanry (local gentry) served to exacerbate not diminish class violence.[13] No permanent peace could prevail if its maintenance depended on the continual and direct confrontation of master and wage-labourer. The new police forces removed this contradiction, for all the lower ranks were drawn exclusively from the working class. Once established these permanent forces were numerically far stronger than the combination of the 'old' constables and watchmen. The first of the new policemen were invested with the full authority of the law and instilled with a value system antithetical to their class origins. And through frequent parades, inspections, and drilling they were slowly turned into a disciplined and obedient force.

[12] See Radzinowicz, *op. cit.*, Vol. 4, p. 300–301.
[13] See essay by Allan Silver, 'The Demand for Order in Civil Society', *The Police*, ed. J. Bordua (1967).

Because the 'criminal class' came predominantly from the proletariat, detection was possible only through a first-hand
knowledge of the matrix of working-class life. To apprehend these
criminals meant that the communities had to be patrolled, bringing a
very real intrusion into everyday life. Despite their class origins, the
way in which the police came to act as a legitimate instrument of coer-
cion was by no means a peaceful one. Policemen were individually attacked or set upon by outraged groups attempting to frustrate an
arrest, and many policemen resigned because of this. But by patrolling
working-class communities the police also came to act on behalf of individual working people. For the first time working-class people
gained some protection from attack, robbery on the streets, and
burglary at home. Moreover, the need to give some security for the
working man and his family was essential if they were to accept that
policing was in their interests.

The violence against individual members of the working class used
by the state (through the police and judiciary) in this process was
without precedent in British history. How can the cumulative effect of
thousands of arrests, trials, fines and imprisonments over many
decades be adequately described? It was, in short, a process of attrition. The class was also under ideological attack. The hardworking and
law-abiding were praised while the poor and unemployed were attacked. Ironically, this development has been described by an
orthodox police historian, T. A. Critchley, as follows: 'To the police fell
the unenviable task of appearing to oppress the working people from
whom most had come.'[14]

Prior to the 1870s the only records kept by the police – and these
were often incomplete – were details of prosecutions and of convictions. These records were not centralised, each station in London
operating independently. At Scotland Yard details of only the more in-
famous criminals were kept and co-operation in catching others was
largely *ad hoc*. From the 1870s documentation was made of all reported
crimes and this led to the establishment of a new department of the
Metropolitan Police at Scotland Yard in 1878, the Criminal Investigation Department. Parliamentary concern at the time of the formation
of the police in 1829 centred on the question of policemen working in
plainclothes. Memories of the French Revolution had raised the
spectre of spying by police on unsuspecting citizens. However, in practice police started operating in plainclothes almost immediately after

---

[14] T. A. Critchley, *A History of the Police* (1967) p. 163.

their formation on the instructions of the Home Secretary and the two Commissioners.[15] It had been quickly realised that patrolling uniformed men only warned pickpockets and burglars, so two or three constables out of each station were usually temporarily seconded to plainclothes duties. Plainclothes policemen were also used to spy on political meetings and to infiltrate organisations. After a few years this activity became an accepted practice, for the ruling class learned it had little to fear from police activity. Two inspectors and six sergeants were officially assigned in 1842 to detective duties at Scotland Yard; by 1867 their numbers had extended to fifteen. But in 1877 three of these officers were convicted on charges of corruption and a Home Office inquiry was set up. As a result of the inquiry the Criminal Investigation Department (CID) was created with over two hundred and fifty men under the command of Howard Vincent. The CID quickly expanded and by 1886 it had eight hundred staff.[16]

Now the police had two arms, those in uniform and those in plainclothes. The primary duty of the uniformed police was to patrol the street, to apprehend offenders on the spot, and to act as a general deterrent by their very presence. The job of the new detectives was to take over once a crime had been reported and to devote whatever time was necessary to tracking down the offender. This distinction between the two jobs remains the practice today. The beginnings of detection led to the introduction of scientific methods to police work, and in particular to finger-printing as a means of identification. The idea of using finger-prints was successfully presented to a Home Office Committee in 1893 by Sir Francis Galton and put into practice in 1894.[17] However, while Galton could prove the uniqueness of a finger-print he knew of no means of classification so their use proved to be very time-consuming. A system of classification was provided in 1899 by Sir Edward Henry, who later became Commissioner of the Metropolitan Police. Sir Edward perfected his system while Inspector-General of Police of the Lower Provinces in India, from where he returned to write a book on the subject and to the appointment of Assistant Commissioner in charge of CID. The first conviction gained through

[15] British Parliamentary Papers, *op. cit.*, p. 175–182.

[16] Not until the late 1890s did most provincial forces start detective branches.

[17] Galton, an early psychologist and founding father of the intelligence test, was a great believer in the hereditary ability of the ruling class to rule, and of the superiority of the white races over the 'childish, stupid and simpletonlike' negroes (see his book *Hereditary Genius*).

finger-print evidence was in 1902; prior to this, although used internally by the CID, it had not been admissible as evidence in court.

The Commissioners of the Metropolitan Police during its first hundred years were drawn almost exclusively from those with a background of military or colonial experience. The first two Commissioners were Colonel Charles Rowan, a retired veteran of Waterloo and Richard Mayne, a barrister. When Rowan retired in 1850 Mayne continued alone and thereafter there was only one Commissioner. Mayne died in the job and was succeeded in 1869 by Colonel (later Sir) Edmund Henderson, who had been in charge of the army Convict Department. Henderson resigned in 1886 in the wake of a demonstration of the unemployed in Trafalgar Square. Part of the demonstration went on the rampage through St James – smashing the windows of several well-known clubs. However, the police reserves were sent by mistake to the Mall. Henderson was succeeded by General Sir Charles Warren, who was summoned from his African command. Warren objected to civilian control of the Home Office and his annual reports to parliament 'omitted all reference to crime in London, though space was given to the question of boots and saddles.'[18] He too went after failing to control marches of the unemployed in the first Jubilee year, 1887. James Monro, an ex-Inspector General of the Bengal Police, took over until 1890 when Sir Edward Bradford, a distinguished Indian Army officer, succeeded him. Immediately prior to his appointment Bradford had been in charge of the political intelligence department at the India Office. In 1903 Bradford gave way to Sir Edward Henry, who, as previously mentioned, brought a finger-print classification system back with him from twenty-five years' service in the Indian Police. Sir Edward lasted through the First World War until the police strike of 1918, when General Sir Nevil Macready – who was then at the War Office – was persuaded by Lloyd George personally to take the post. Macready stayed around to break the police strike of 1919 and in April 1920 he was given the command of the sixty thousand troops in Ireland. In the development of the police force in London their command was largely entrusted to army officers – no doubt the peoples of Bengal and Stepney had certain experiences in common.

The police force did not remain totally isolated from the struggles it was involved in suppressing, for in 1872 and 1890 the London police went on strike for better pay and conditions. In fact the police were the

---

[18] Basil Thompson, *The Story of Scotland Yard* (1935) p. 175.

first in the public sector to organise a union. The first nationwide strike came just before the end of the First World War. The Commissioner sacked one of the leaders of the Police Union and the government refused to negotiate directly with the men. Lord Wittenham, in a speech to the House of Lords, expressed the reaction of those in power: 'If you want to get at the head and source, the *fons et origo mali* of these strikes, put your heel upon the head of Bolshevism. There are healthy strikes and there are unhealthy strikes. These have been unhealthy strikes.'[19] A temporary wage settlement pending a full review lulled the men into thinking they had gained a victory. Meanwhile Lloyd George brought in Macready as Commissioner, for as he later explained: 'This country was nearer to Bolshevism that day than at any other time since.'[20]

When discontent arose again in 1919 the defences were well-prepared. The strike was only patchily supported and the 2,364 strikers were immediately sacked; despite many attempts they were never reinstated. A pay rise, from £1.50 to £3.50 a week, was rushed out of the Desborough Committee which had been set up in 1918 to look into all aspects of policing, the news of which effectively undermined support for the strikers. With the strike broken and its leaders dismissed the government banned the organising of a trade union in the police, and the Police Act of 1919 laid down heavy penalties for any who sought to raise disaffection in their ranks. At a stroke the organisation of a police union was declared unlawful. In 1920 a further recommendation of the Desborough Committee was to set up the Police Federation, which was expressly forbidden to affiliate to the TUC.

Another feature of this period was the relationship between the army and the police in handling outbreaks of disorder. In 1908 a Select Committee was set up on 'The Employment of the Military in Cases of Disturbances'. They reported that in the thirty years between 1878 and 1908 troops had been called on to aid the police on twenty-four occasions, and in two cases had been ordered to fire on demonstrators. In the following forty years troops were called out on fewer occasions, notably in Tonypandy (1910), Liverpool (1919 police strike), the miners' strike in 1921, during the General Strike in 1926, and after the Second World War on no less than nine occasions by the Attlee government. When the miners of the Rhondda Valley took to the

[19] Quoted in G. R. Williams, *The Hidden World of Scotland Yard* (1972) p. 45.
[20] Reynolds and Judge, *The Night the Police Went On Strike* (1968) p. 5.

streets in November 1910 the local magistrates quickly applied for troops. Winston Churchill, the Home Secretary, sent Major-General Macready with five hundred troops. However, he also sent seven hundred London policemen and one hundred mounted police with instructions for these to be used, employing 'vigorous baton charges', before calling on the army. This tactic was successfully employed and the power of the police to handle major disorders amply demonstrated.

In the First World War police duties were extended under the emergency regulations. Their duties already included the prevention and detection of crime and the maintenance of public order; now they assumed a nationwide responsibility for internal security. This was not a totally new role. The maintenance of public order in peacetime necessitated the monitoring of local political groups and trade unions, and the numerical strength and the nationwide presence of the police meant they had been (and still are) the only force capable of fulfilling this responsibility.[21]

1920–1964 Centralisation and technological changes

Between the two World Wars the police consolidated their internal procedures and practices. The outcome of the changes made after the police strikes guaranteed the loyalty of the police in the confrontations of the 1920s and 1930s. During the 1926 General Strike they were loyal to a man. It is interesting to note that during the Depression, when the police were called on to break up marches by the unemployed, the pay of the police was 50 per cent higher than the average industrial wage. The important internal changes in this period were mainly due to the application of science and technology to policing and the increased influence of the Home Office and Scotland Yard in other parts of the country.[22]

Since the 1856 Police Act the Exchequer had been making a contribution to the cost of provincial police forces. The Desborough

[21] The Special Branch at this time was still very small and its activities limited to London. Their inquiries outside London were usually carried out on their behalf by the provincial CID.

[22] The era of the motorcar was born in 1896 when an Act of Parliament raised the speed limit from 4 to 14 mph; however, the London police were not to get their first four cars until 1922. Not until 1934 did Lord Trenchard, the Commissioner for the Metropolis, announce that London was to be patrolled by fifty-two patrol cars in radio communication with Scotland Yard. *Daily Herald*, 12 June 1934.

Committee in 1920 recommended that half the cost of the police should be paid for by central government.[23] The long-term effect of these developments gave the Home Office the impetus to increase its direction of local forces outside London. Scotland Yard had created a rudimentary criminal records office in 1871, where the particulars of convicted criminals were recorded and made available to London police stations. This information was sent out in the weekly *Police Gazette*, which in time came to include supplements for wanted people, stolen cars, and army deserters. Metropolitan Police stations also received urgent messages known as 'Printed Informations' with details of reported crime. From 1914 the *Gazette* was circulated twice a week, three times a week from 1920, and took its current daily form in 1927. During the First World War many other forces increasingly began to use the *Gazette* and in the 1920s it became a common source of information throughout the country. But the first attempt to get some uniform method of training, recording of information, and scientific methods in all forces came only after a Home Office committee report in 1938.

The duties of the police during the Second World War again included internal security, which is to say 'they performed various quasi-military functions'. More specifically,

> 'they acted throughout the war as a kind of intelligence service, reporting . . . on the state of public order and civilian morale . . . the effect of enemy propaganda, and signs of industrial unrest. Mingling with the ordinary population, they were uniquely placed to report on matters of this kind.'[24]

In wartime and in peacetime the uniformed police are the first line force of internal security in the community. It is often forgotten that the police have always to be prepared to undertake duties of this kind at short notice and to this day selected members are specially trained in wartime duties.

Prior to the 1940s an important distinction must be made between the practices of Scotland Yard and the Metropolitan Police, and those of the provincial forces. Apart from being formed nearly thirty years before many other forces, Scotland Yard, the HQ of the Metropolitan Police, has always had a special relationship with the Home Office. The Commissioner of the Metropolis is the only police chief directly

---

[23] The Police Department of the Home Office was set up in the same year.
[24] T. A. Critchley, *A History of the Police* (1967) p. 232–233.

appointed by and responsible to the Home Secretary. In almost every field Scotland Yard was the pioneer of new ideas on detection and scientific innovations. However, although practices like the keeping of criminal records was started in the 1870s by Scotland Yard, it was many years before the forces outside London followed suit. After 1945, in the immediate post-war period, the gap between Scotland Yard and the other forces lessened due to the amalgamation of forces into larger units, the high costs of developing new scientific techniques (largely dependent on central government funds) and the increasing Home Office influence over local forces; since the 1920s circulars with information and advice to provincial forces were sent out daily.

The last major reform of the police in England and Wales stemmed from the Royal Commission on the Police which was set up in 1960 and whose report was issued in 1962; this was followed by the 1964 Police Act.[25] The Commission's Report dealt with a number of central questions: the number of forces, the power of Chief Constables, the scope of local control and accountability generally. Between 1857 and 1962 the number of police forces was cut from 239 to 117, and by 1964 there were only 49. This reduction not only went alongside increasing Home Office direction; the sheer size of the new police areas and the powers assumed by the Chief Constables militated against any local control. Whereas the original Chief Constables were accountable to the JPs, the 1962 Report recognised that this had 'fallen into disuse'.[26] The Commission and the 1964 Police Act made no change in the practice which gave the Chief Constables freedom to determine day-to-day policies unfettered by the restraints of democratic accountability. The watch committees in the boroughs and county areas had by the 1930s lost out to the Chief Constables who were increasingly looking to London for guidance. Moreover, this process occurred during the same period that the majority of the working class were given the vote and Labour Party councillors were beginning to form the majority party on councils.[27] The old watch committees were renamed 'police authorities' after 1964 and their duties were limited to what had become the practice in the years before. Two-thirds of the police authority was drawn from the local council and one-third from magistrates. The police authority was to receive an annual report from

[25] The Secretary to the Royal Commission was T. A. Critchley from the Home Office Staff.
[26] *Report of the Royal Commission on the Police* (1962) para. 80.
[27] See Appendix for the background to this development.

the Chief Constable and its function was to be limited to the provision of adequate staff, accommodation and equipment (thus excluding discussion of policy and practice). Much earlier than this a member of a local Watch Committee summed up the situation: 'The police is not a local service. Every force in the country is controlled from beginning to end by the Home Office. It is a local force in that we are permitted to pay half the cost.'[28]

Several other aspects of policing in this period deserve comment. The first relates to staffing. A little-noticed feature of the makeup of the police workforce is the number of civilians employed; between 1949 and 1959 they increased from 3,881 to 8,082 and by 1966 to about 16,000. This increase represented the replacement of trained policemen by civilians in the collection and retrieval of information and communications, and from 1964 by the introduction of the traffic warden system. Secondly, the Police Act 1964 recognised the importance of the police cadet scheme and recommended that the intake of cadets should be between 30–40 per cent of total recruitment. Within two years there were 3,600 cadets and by 1972 some 4,600 cadets in the country. In earlier times police recruits had inevitably spent several years out at work because they left school at thirteen or fourteen years old and did not qualify for the minimum age limit. With the change of attitude after 1964 recruits were drawn straight from school at the age of sixteen and seventeen. A Home Office working party recognised the problems of subjecting a young man to a police environment from this early age and suggested he should receive training to 'make him a good citizen'.[29] Police cadets, like all unmarried policemen and policewomen, usually live in a station-house. The difficulties in trying to train a good citizen when these cadets are brought up in the rarefied social milieu of police life may go some way to account for the attitudes and extra-legal actions of young policemen today.

To summarise, the modern police were formed at a time when the old system of policing, which had worked quite effectively for more than five hundred years, broke down with the onset of industrial capitalism. The rank and file of the police were recruited exclusively from the working class and came to provide protection primarily for bourgeois persons and property in the name of an 'independent' agency and through an 'independent' system of law. With the beginnings of liberal democracy, in the latter part of the nineteenth century,

---

[28] Quoted in J. Hart, *The British Police* (1951) p. 69.
[29] T. A. Critchley, *op. cit.*, p. 307.

this protection under law was extended to working-class communities and respect for the rule of law was exacted from this class. The liberal-democratic phase also heralded the removal of local and parliamentary control of the police. By 1962 the Royal Commission could assert in relation to the enforcement of law (to investigate, arrest and prosecute): 'We entirely accept that it is in the public interest that a chief constable, in dealing with these quasi-judicial matters, should be free from the conventional processes of democratic control and influence.'[30]

This all too short history of the origins and development of the police will, I hope, enable the reader to more clearly understand the role of the modern policeman. The last ten years have seen yet a further development in the role of the police, one determined only partially by the police themselves.

PART II 1964–1974 – THE ORGANISATIONAL STRUCTURE
OF THE POLICE

There are now forty-three police forces in England and Wales including the Metropolitan and City of London Police.[31] The Metropolitan Police come under the command of the Commissioner of the Metropolis (the City of London Police is also run by a Commissioner). The forty-one provincial forces are run by Chief Constables. The Commissioner of the Metropolitan Police is directly responsible to the Home Secretary, and like the other forces, half of his force's costs are borne by the local rates. Outside London the Chief Constables of provincial forces have, in theory, two masters – the local police authority and the Home Secretary. The powers of the former, as has been mentioned, do not extend to matters of policy and practice. The provincial police are also responsible to the Home Secretary through the Inspectors of Constabulary – all forces outside London are referred to as 'the Constabulary'. These inspectors receive yearly reports from the regional forces on behalf of the Home Office and go on periodic tours of inspection.

In 1974 the forty-one provincial forces had a total strength of 80,644

[30] *Report of the Royal Commission on the Police* (1962) para. 87.
[31] The estimated cost of the police in 1974–75 was £620 million. Scotland, as from May 1975, has eight police forces, and Northern Ireland one.

men and women.[32] The size of these individual forces varies greatly. In all the major cities, where most of the working class live, the ratio of population to police is lower – Liverpool 275:1, Manchester 278:1, Birmingham 348:1, Leeds 383:1 and Bradford 383:1.[33] In the rural county areas the ratio is around 550:1. The full-time civilian staff employed was 19,426 in 1974, compared to 8,700 in 1963. The structure of each constabulary force is fairly uniform throughout the country. Each force has a regional Headquarters where Administration, Criminal Records Office, Traffic Department and a Communications Division are based. Here too is centred the regional Special Branch Department. Below the level of Headquarters the region is divided into Divisions, each of which has in turn an Administrative Department, CID, and Prosecution Section. The Division is commanded by a Chief Superintendent. Then the Division itself is sub-divided into two or three 'areas' (each under a Superintendent) with its own CID departments. Finally, each area has within it a number of police stations run by an Inspector.

This structure has been supplemented by the creation of Regional Crime Squads; started in 1964 as an 'experiment' they were fully operational in all areas of the country the following year. England and Wales are policed by the nine Regional Crime Squads. The Headquarters of the Squads is in London, at Tintagel House on the Albert Embankment, where the National Co-ordinator works. A Squad is under the command of a Regional Co-ordinator and serves between three and seven police forces. The Co-ordinator is responsible to a committee of Chief Constables from the region. In 1973 a total of 839 detectives was seconded to this work from CID, with an average of 93 in each Squad. The primary role of a Squad is to tackle criminals engaged in major crime (e.g. bank robberies). 'In addition to their primary role of directing their operations against good class criminals, the squads are available to assist Forces in the investigation of serious crimes such as murder and also have an important intelligence gathering role.'[34] The police forces of the Constabulary can also call on many services provided by the Home Office and the Metropolitan Police through Scotland Yard.

The organisation of the Metropolitan Police is similar. The police

[32] *Report of Her Majesty's Chief Inspector of Constabulary for the Year 1974*, HMSO, July 1975.

[33] The ratio in London is 309:1.

[34] *Police Review*, 19 October 1973.

The Structure of the Metropolitan Police*

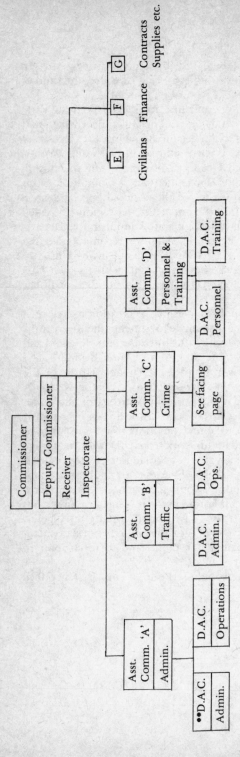

A4 Firearms and explosives
A6 Special constabulary
A7 Community and race relations
A8 Public order and special patrol group
A10 Complaints investigation branch

Work includes traffic management and legislation; traffic wardens.

D7 Cadet training
D9 Detective training
D11 Police War Duties; home defences; firearms training

* Not all the functions of Departments have been noted, only those with structural or political overtones.

** Deputy Assistant Commissioner.

'C' Department (Crime)

```
                          ┌──────────────┐
                          │  Asst. Comm. │
                          └──────────────┘
```

D.A.C. Admin.	D.A.C. Support Services	D.A.C. Operations	D.A.C. Fraud	D.A.C. Sp. Branch

D.A.C. Admin.

Overall policy and efficiency, inc.

C_5 (2) Complaints against CID

C_5 (3) Crime legislation

C_5 (4) Intelligence Statistical Unit

D.A.C. Support Services

C_2 All correspondence *except* Criminal Records Office and Special Branch

C_3 Fingerprints

C_4 Criminal Records office (national)

C_7 Technical support, inc. explosives officers at Cannon Row

C_{11} Criminal Intelligence inc. Drugs Intelligence and Illegal Immigration Unit; International liaison

Also compensation

D.A.C. Operations

C_1 Serious Crime Squads inc. Murder Squad, Bomb Squad (staffed by C11, Criminal Intelligence and Special Branch jointly) and the reserve squad

C_8 Flying Squad, Robbery, Regional Crime Squads (London)

C_{12} Regional Crime Squads, under National Co-ordinator

C_{13} (branch created July, 1973) Special Crime, with 5 sections

  a) currency, cheques and credit card offences

  b) Dangerous Drugs Act enforcement

  c) Hijacking, extradition and illegal immigration

  d) Liaison with US Embassy; charities and lotteries; bribery and corruption; industrial espionage

  e) Post Office offences

region covers a radius of fifteen miles from Charing Cross and is
divided into twenty-four Divisions with 189 police stations. Each Division is denoted by a letter, A to Z (excluding I and O), which is on every
policeman's shoulder with his personal number. The only other
designations are 'CO' (Commissioner's Office) used by the Special
Patrol Group, 'SC' for Special Constables, 'TD' for Traffic Division;
and 'AD' for Airports Division.[35] A total of 21,000 policemen and
policewomen were available for duty in London in 1974 (and there
were in addition 9,903 civilian staff, excluding traffic wardens, cadets
and special constables).

The organisational structure of the Metropolitan Police at its
Scotland Yard Headquarters in Victoria Street is outlined in the chart
on page 76. At the top is the Commissioner (currently Sir Robert
Mark), beneath him are the Deputy Commissioner, and the Receiver
(the administrative head of the civilian staff). Beneath them the
organisation is divided into Departments, each headed by an Assistant
Commissioner. 'A' Department deals with general administration and
includes the Special Constabulary for London, community and race
relations, public order, the Special Patrol Group, firearms and
explosives, and complaints against the police. 'B' Department looks
after traffic management and traffic wardens. 'C' Department
(Criminal Investigation)[36] is the backbone of Scotland Yard. In July
1973 the work of 'C' Department was re-organised, and the workload
is now divided among five Deputy Assistant Commissioners (DAC).
The five areas covered are: Administration, Support Services,
Operations, Fraud and Special Branch (the assignation of the Special
Branch to 'C' Department is more or less notional as it operates independently). Under the re-organisation the Special Branch added to
its duties the investigation of election offences. (The other
Departments are: 'D' – Personnel and Training; 'E' – Civilian staff;
'F' – Finance; 'G' – Contracts and supplies).

[35] The Metropolitan Police assumed responsibility for the policing of
Heathrow airport in November 1974 under the provisions of the Policing of
Airports Act 1974. Officers of the British Airports Authority Constabulary were
integrated into the new force. Similar measures transferring responsibility from
airport police to local forces has now been undertaken for all Britain's major
airports.

[36] Usually referred to as CID, although it should be noted that each of the
Divisions in the Metropolitan Police has its own local CID.

Criminal records and pre-emptive policing

The first question that might be asked is how does policing today differ from that in the past? In the short outline of police history several distinctive stages were brought out. From their formation the uniformed police concentrated on patrolling, and it was only from 1870 that separate detective branches began to be formed. The distinction between their respective roles is described by Howe in his book, *The Story of Scotland Yard*:

> 'The Uniform Branch works alongside the *public*, dealing with traffic control, patrol activities and crime in the streets. The CID on the other hand works alongside the *criminal*. When a crime is reported it (CID) takes over from the Uniform Branch, its sole job being to track down the criminal.'[37]

From the late 1930s increasing attention was paid to the application of science to policing as an aid to detection. But it was not until the 1950s that a concerted effort was made to rationalise the storage of information about crime and criminals. The first regional criminal records offices, which brought together information from several neighbouring forces, were not started until the early 1950s. Until the mid-1960s emphasis on this aspect of policing was concerned with achieving consistent methods of record-keeping and on ensuring quicker access to the man on the beat or in a car. Moreover, the information recorded in the regions and at Scotland Yard was almost exclusively concerned with the convicted criminal

What distinguishes the period since the mid-1960s is the introduction of pre-emptive policing. This involves two assumptions – firstly, that those convicted of a crime are likely to commit another criminal act and, secondly, that the police have to keep themselves informed about those people who are likely to commit certain crimes even though they have as yet committed no criminal offence. It is of course true that such assumptions have for years been present in the everyday practice of the uniformed policeman and the CID at the local level. Indeed it has been seen as a necessary attribute for any successful police officer to be able to make such assumptions. However, this practice had been largely informal, which is to say that the information existed either solely in the head of the officer concerned or perhaps as a notation in a file at a local police station. It is the formalisation and centralisation of information of this kind which marks a qualitatively

[37] Sir Ronald Howe, *The Story of Scotland Yard* (1965) p. 171.

new aspect of policing. A concomitant development has been the formation of special CID squads, like the Regional Crime Squads and the National Drugs Intelligence Unit, to gather specialist intelligence and to act against those sections of society singled out for particular attention. Whether it is someone from the 'criminal class' or a drug-user, the same principle operates – there is a presumption of guilt on the part of the police.[38] The computerisation of records in the Police National Computer Unit adds the final dimension for effective pre-emptive policing, and by 1977 the British police will have the most comprehensive system of computerised information in the world.

Apart from the work of local CIDs an attempt was made after the Second World War to set up a special squad at Scotland Yard to infiltrate the London underworld. This was known as the Ghost Squad and was created in 1946. Fifty men were chosen from the CID and told to go underground, to mix with criminals, and to contact the Yard by telephone only. In 1958, quietly and without ceremony, the Squad was broken up because the CID men were becoming indistinguishable from the criminals – some were even caught 'on the job' by the Flying Squad.[39] With the start of the Regional Crime Squads in 1964 a new approach was tried. Each of these Squads was to concentrate its attention on a select number of suspected professional criminals, many of whom had never been caught. At Scotland Yard the Criminal Intelligence section (C11) operates on the same principle as the RCSs, except that it tackles the national syndicates and gangs. Criminal Intelligence has a small staff of about fifty men and women and is divided into several teams. Their main index files carry the names of over eight thousand proven and suspected big-time criminals each of whom has a fat personal file. The file includes extensive information about personal lives of these individuals – their friends, haunts and habits. This information is regularly updated by the use of informers, by information forwarded from the Divisional collators, and by the periodic surveillance of the suspect by C11 staff. The assumption of guilt which underlies the activities of Criminal Intelligence and the Regional Crime Squads clearly offends against the normal rule of law that presupposes innocence until guilt is proven.

The national centre of police information is the Criminal Records Office (CRO) at Scotland Yard which holds over three and a half

[38] See pp. 89 and 90 for Sir Robert Mark's comments on the presumptions of the present legal system.
[39] P. Laurie, *Scotland Yard* (1970), p. 255.

million files – that is, roughly one for every fourteen adults. The Yard's CRO holds a duplicate of all the records held by the regional criminal records offices plus those generated by the Metropolitan Police and the Yard's own special squads. Each file is numbered according to the number of files opened that year and the year in which it was opened (for example, file number 135,687/1974). It will contain details of arrest, charges, sentences, aliases, description, a photo, and a 'previous history' sheet prepared for court appearances with general information on behaviour, employment, friends etc. National and regional CROs can be consulted either by the policeman on the beat via his radio, or from the station after a person has been arrested.

The critical question in relation to this mass of files is just who has access to them? The answer is, firstly, that anyone who wants to know if someone has a criminal record (such as potential employee) can find out either by approaching the police directly or by paying a small sum to one of the private tracing agencies. Secondly, for certain types of work the police themselves inform an employer of any wrong-doing. In the first case requests for information can come directly from a school or bank and these are usually answered – despite official denials to the contrary. More usually employers use the private tracing agencies to get this information. These agencies employ ex-policemen who are used to making requests to CROs and who – given the demands on the CRO telephones – experience little difficulty because it is impossible to verify each call. James Rule, who was granted official access to Scotland Yard and several regional offices, states in his book, *Private Lives and Public Surveillance*, states this to be a common practice:

> 'The vulnerability of these offices (CROs) is especially great to former members of the police, who are invariably well versed in the techniques of making such requests. Industrial firms employ retired policemen in large numbers as security officers, precisely because of their familiarity with police routines in these and other matters. In many cases too, the personal ties between these private security officers and their former colleagues make it possible for them to obtain services which would be denied to others.'[40]

Rule further found that the Special Branch had 'full and unquestioned access to all criminal record files' as did the police forces of 'friendly' countries.

In the second case there are those professions where convictions

---

[40] J. Rule, *Private Lives and Public Surveillance* (1973) p. 82.

(other than straightforward motoring offences) are automatically notified to a person's employer by the police. These include JPs (to the Lord Chancellor's Office), solicitors (The Law Society), teachers (Home Office), doctors (General Medical Council), bus conductors, postmen, and those in the police constabularies of the armed forces. The responsibility for making these reports rests with the Chief Constables and a Home Office circular (No. 77/1955) absolves them from any legal liability. It states:

> 'An undertaking has been obtained from Government Departments and all other authorities concerned to indemnify the police against any liability which may be incurred by the police authority or by any individual police officer as a result of the submission of a report.'[41]

In June 1973 the Home Secretary reported to the House of Commons that the procedure for reporting offences had been reviewed and in future only convictions, not suspicions, would be reported. This followed the revelation that a senior officer of the North-East Yorkshire police force had reported in derogatory terms to the Central Midwives' Board a nurse who had not been convicted of any offence. Mr Carr, the Home Secretary, assured the Commons this would not happen again and reiterated that information on criminal records would not be transmitted unless it fell into one of the stated professional categories. Two events later in the same year illustrated the inadequacy of these assurances.

In November 1973 evidence was given to the National Council for Civil Liberties that Air France at Heathrow was clearing its new employees through the Scotland Yard Criminal Records Office. Special forms had been printed by Air France which they submitted to the British Airports Authority Police, who in turn have access to the CRO. The Air France general manager commented: 'We thought this was logical, to prevent undesirable elements infiltrating into key sectors of our organisation. We will now have to consider carefully other methods of ensuring maximum security.'[42] Another instance was a request by an Oxford University research team for the criminal records files of 259 unemployed men. The project was sponsored by the Department for Health and Social Security and the Home Office forwarded photocopies of the men's files to the research team. When

[41] Quoted by Rule, *op. cit.*, p. 81.
[42] *Guardian*, 19 November 1973.

questioned the Home Office admitted this was an unusual move particularly as the men could be identified by their files.[43] In the very same week a pile of police records were found on a rubbish dump in North Devon and among the files were some on men who had no criminal record but who were listed as 'worth watching'. The Home Office commented: 'It is entirely up to them (the local police) to keep up their own records. They must be forewarned. They would be at fault for having no information about a person if he was arrested at a later date.'[44] Such a view would justify keeping files on almost everyone.

Access to criminal records files is thus available to a wide range of employers – both state institutions and private industry. The dangers inherent in such practices are clear. If a person is already in employment when he commits an offence then there is a good chance he will face double punishment, first in the courts and second in his future work prospects. For the person seeking employment the passing of such information is equally invidious for he may never know the grounds on which his application is rejected. Furthermore this widespread practice offends the much-lauded principle of criminal law that, having served a sentence or paid a fine, the 'criminal' should be allowed to start afresh without a blemish on his character. A criminal record file once opened is not normally destroyed until the subject has reached an age when his or her criminal potential is at an end (usually sixty-five). It is the extension of police practice to cover those 'suspected' of offences which constitutes the pre-emptive element and, potentially, a massive intrusion into people's lives.

Technology and policing

Two units set up in 1972 extended the principles of the Regional Crime Squads and Criminal Intelligence from concentrating on a selected number of suspects to providing a means of mass surveillance of selected groups. In October of that year the Home Office announced that a special unit (based at Tintagel House) had been established jointly by the Home Office and Scotland Yard to co-ordinate information on drugs and immigration. By March 1973 the two units – the National Drugs Intelligence Unit and the National Immigration Intelligence Unit – were operative. The Home Office press notice announcing the two units explicitly recognised their pre-emptive function. The purpose of the units, it said, 'would be to receive, collate,

[43] *Guardian*, 15 August 1973.
[44] *Workers Press*, 11 August 1973.

evaluate and disseminate information relating to known or *suspected* offenders.'[45]

The Drugs Intelligence Unit started out with the 18,000 names on the files of the Metropolitan Drug Squad and by the end of 1973 held the names of over 250,000 known and suspected offenders on its files. The innate suspicion of local forces who were loath to pass over information to any central agency has been overcome, and the Unit's collection of files now constitutes a national record of suspected drug-users, and is growing in size all the time. The main source of their information is from drugs raids where address books are removed for indexing and the names of all those present are noted. A secondary source is from informers who are usually under threat of arrest. The Unit's job is then to establish a hierarchy, based on the incidence of names and friendships, of users, pushers, and major dealers. The first co-ordinated series of raids took place in Devon and Cornwall in June 1973 and many of the names were provided by the London Unit. Three hundred policemen took part and sixty-nine people were arrested.[46] 'Co-operation with the Home Office, H.M. Customs and Excise Investigation Branch and the Immigration Service is now of the highest order and the future of the new unit looks most promising.'[47]

When it was proposed in the 1971 Tory Immigration Bill that immigrants and aliens would have to register with the local police, parliamentary opposition successfully gained the deletion of the clause referring to black immigrants. This victory was short-lived for within a year the Home Office set up the Immigration Intelligence Unit – without reference to parliament. Establishing who is a legal or an illegal immigrant is one of the problems the Unit faced. However, it should be remembered that the Home Office also includes the Aliens Department and the Immigration Department, who between them deal with entry at airports and ports, and with naturalisation. Therefore these two Departments know who is legally entitled to be here.

Several observations can be made on these two Units. Both were set up on the initiative of the Home Secretary and the Home Office without reference to parliament. When their formation was raised in the Commons, Mr Carlisle, Minister of State at the Home Office

[45] Home Office press release 4 October 1972. (My emphasis.)

[46] Interpol handles the European co-ordination of intelligence on drugs, and the head of their drugs unit appointed in 1972 was a British Special Branch officer seconded from the Yard.

[47] *Report of the Commissioner of Police of the Metropolis, 1973* (June 1974) p. 12.

replied: 'The operational activities of the police are a matter for the Chief Constables concerned; they are not normally subject to Parliamentary control and it would therefore be most unusual for Parliament to have discussed the setting up of the units.'[48]

Both are concerned with two sections of our society in which the police and the Home Office have a special interest. The link between young people who use drugs and those politically active on the Left is well recognised by the police and the Special Branch. The full potential of the National Drugs Intelligence Unit and the National Immigration Intelligence Unit as means of mass surveillance will probably not become evident for a few years, as the integration of the Units' records into the National Police Computer is not planned until 1976.

At present there are at least two limitations on the information available to the patrolling policeman when he radios in for a check on a 'suspect' he has accosted in the streets. Firstly, any inquiry to Scotland Yard CRO can take twenty minutes or more to be processed, and secondly, information stored at the CRO is limited to those with criminal records. The new Police National Computer Unit (PNCU) based at Hendon promises to change this situation. A study of the feasibility of centralising police records in a national computer system was started in 1964 and in 1969 the Labour government announced that the plans were to go ahead. The computers ordered, three Burroughs 6700s, have the capacity to hold up to forty million records – one for every member of the adult population. Each of the eight hundred police stations in England and Wales are linked to the computer by a Visual Display Unit (VDU), a teleprinter, and, in emergency, there is the standby facility to dial into the computer via the local exchange. The system started operating at the end of 1974, and is able to provide an answer in just ten seconds to local police stations – in a few more seconds this information can be with the man on the beat or in the patrol car. Furthermore, the capacity of the Hendon unit is enormous, it is able to handle fifty messages a second. The main indexes being compiled are stolen property and vehicles (registration number and engine number); finger-prints; wanted and missing persons; those on suspended sentences; criminal names (that is, the CRO records of the Yard); all vehicles (including disqualified drivers).

Several features of the system merit particular attention. The criminal names index will include not only those convicted of a criminal offence but also those suspected of having committed an

[48] *South London Press*, 29 August 1973.

offence – instead of the date and place of arrest and designation 'first came to notice' will be used. However, the major mode of surveillance in the immediate future is going to be via the Vehicle Index. Information collected and stored on computer by the National Licensing Centre at Swansea (run by the Department of the Environment) is regularly being transferred onto a parallel Index on the police computer.[49] Each vehicle entry on the computer includes the registration number, the engine number, make, class, colour, and the name, address and date of birth of the owner. In addition there is space for up to one hundred and twenty words of descriptive text for each vehicle – this will obviously include data relating to disqualifications or whether a vehicle is stolen, but it could also include other, more 'political' information starting with a criminal record and ending with a Special Branch notation. Within the Vehicle Index certain breakdowns of information are already in operation, for example, there is a file for stolen and suspect vehicles. Of even more interest are the following three files:

(SUS) – temporary suspicion of being used in a crime[50]
(POL) – being used for police purposes
(INT) – of long-term interest to the police

The first two categories are self-explanatory. The last category is justified on the grounds that would include a note of those active in some form of local public service, i.e. the police chief (and his children?), magistrates, and doctors – even this inclusion begs the question of why these people should presumably receive deferential treatment. Of more interest would be to know what other groups – not on the side of law and order – would qualify as being of 'long-term interest to the police'.

It is estimated that by 1979 the computer will hold on file some 36,325,000 names/entries. These will include amongst others: Vehicles 26,000,000; Fingerprints 3,250,000; Suspended sentences 110,000; Criminal names 6,700,000. The security of criminal records is mentioned elsewhere but it should be noted in this respect that the points of access to this centralised body of information will greatly increase. In the past access has been via one of the nine Regional CROs, now access is possible through over eight hundred stations.

[49] One factor which slows down this operation is that Swansea is on tape while Hendon is on disc.
[50] Information placed on the computer must be confirmed or retracted within forty-eight hours by the submission of form CRO 150, or it is automatically deleted.

When this system is fully operational in 1977 it will be possible for the man on the beat to get information within a few minutes (some estimates put it at ninety seconds). The discretion available to the policeman who is holding a suspect will thus be greatly influenced by the information he receives from the centre. A person with a record or in whom the police have some interest (like drugs or political activity) is more likely to be detained for further questioning.

The next stage in the application of computerisation is already under way. The PNCU answers many of the police demands but an experiment in the Thames Valley police area announced in July 1974 promises to encompass even more information. At the beginning of that year the NCCL received information about a new computer based near Oxford and in March they approached the Home Office for more details. After expressing astonishment that anyone knew of the new computer the Home Office agreed to a meeting – this was held but no details were forthcoming. At the beginning of July,

> 'a Home Office spokesman informed the NCCL that the contract had been awarded, but to maximise commercial advantage to the firm, they did not wish to disclose particulars until the company chose to do so.'[51]

A couple of weeks later the company, Honeywell, announced that they had been awarded a £500,000 contract for a series 6000 computer to serve the Thames Valley police. Honeywell said the system was a '. . . collator project . . . to help in evaluating methods of handling the considerable volume of information about crime which is collated and assessed by the police.'[52]

The post of 'collator' has only been introduced into local police stations in the last few years. Information previously brought together in an *ad hoc* way, say by relying on the good memory of the desk sergeant, is now logged and pieced together by the police collator. This information, which is not related to a specific investigation, has two distinctive features. Firstly, it is termed by the police themselves as 'intelligence', and is of a 'criminal' and 'political' nature. Secondly, it is often related to facts about a person innocent of any offence. Information about anyone the police, or local CID are 'interested in' is passed over to the collator who tries to see patterns, links, or new

[51] Dr Edward Harriman, 'Computerising the police notebook', *New Scientist*, 1 August 1974.
[52] *Ibid.*

angles. The Thames Valley computer, which will be permanently recording and coding this information, represents a major step forward in the extension of pre-emptive policing to regional level.

When the PNCU's programming was under way the *Police Review* remarked that 'It is to be far more comprehensive than any other computerised intelligence service in the world,' and the same editorial went on:

> 'Police intelligence is now forward-looking, anticipating who is going to commit what, when and where, and because it is so purposeful it is also frequently libellous . . . Much of the information is personal details of a suspect, his family associates, way of life, and although it may seem to trespass on the freedom of the individual it is the bread and butter of successful policemanship.'[53]

At present, while the old methods of policing continue, the totalitarian potential of the police computer system seems like very alarmist talk. However, the five years from 1969 to 1974, from the original decision to its implementation, has been a period of interregnum. It will be during the next five to ten years that the effects of this will be seen. The significance of this development to political activity should not be underestimated. Many political activists have acquired a 'criminal record', for the law makes no distinction between a political and a criminal offence, and all those arrested for public order offences (at demonstrations, sit-ins, etc.), or in the normal course of the harassment of political activists (on the street, on raids), or for social practices (like drug-taking) are already incorporated into the system. And those who are not may well be covered by Special Branch records. Moreover if, as many predict, we are heading for times of greater social and economic unrest, the potential for individual or collective harassment of all those opposed to the state is increased a hundredfold by easy access to a national intelligence centre.

Portrait of a police chief

One new aspect of modern policing is the growing assertiveness of the police as an institution. Throughout their history nearly all the demands for changes in their actions and powers have come, not from the police themselves, but from those outside like JPs, MPs, local councillors and the press. In 1967 Critchley noted: 'a questing spirit is

[53] *Police Review*, 5 May 1972.

abroad that is unlikely to be stifled'.[54] Since then the speeches of police chiefs up and down the country for changes in the law as well as for more money and men have become a regular occurrence. Most prominent amongst these voices is inevitably that of the Commissioner of the Metropolitan Police, Sir Robert Mark. Mark started on the beat in 1937 and by 1972 he had risen through the ranks to the highest police post in the land. He was the product of a grammar-school education; his father ran a small clothes-manufacturing firm in Manchester; the religious leanings of the family were to evangelical Protestantism – a touch of which may still be seen today in his pronouncements. By 1957 Mark was Chief Constable of Leicester and was making a name for himself as a good clean cop with progressive ideas. In 1966 however he was faced with the prospect of being out of a job – the amalgamation of police forces at this time brought the integration of the city and county and Mark lost out in the local politicking.

> 'Mark almost despaired. He even calculated his pension, applied for a Churchill Fellowship to America, and toyed with the idea of leaving the force for a firm of London solicitors. A Labour councillor in Leicester made soundings in London, and finally, at the end of a long line of friendly contacts that wanted to keep him in the force, was Roy Jenkins, the Home Secretary, who brought him to Scotland Yard.'[55]

But it was Maudling who was to eventually appoint him Commissioner in 1972.

As early as 1965 Mark was making his views on the system of criminal law known. In the *Police Journal* he wrote: 'The criminal trial is less a test of guilt or innocence than a competition . . . a kind of show-jumping contest in which the rider for the prosecution must clear every obstacle to succeed.'[56] Interestingly, a year later Roy Jenkins was asked his view of changing the rules of evidence against the accused, and he replied: 'I think it may be that some of the rules of evidence now go too far in the other direction, treat the matter too much as a game and not as a war.'[57] What Mark was saying in 1965 became refined by 1971 and honed into a dangerous weapon by 1973. In his notorious Dimbleby lecture Mark returned to his old hobby-horses – he attacked the jury

[54] T. A. Critchley, *op. cit.*, p. 321.
[55] *Observer*, 11 November 1973.
[56] *Sunday Telegraph*, 7 March 1971.
[57] *Sunday Times*, 24 April 1966.

system and the rules of evidence. His message was simply stated: 'Unwillingness to make the law more effective will inevitably provoke demands for harsher punishments and will increase the pressures on the police to use more arbitrary methods'.[58] Here Mark is implying that unless the law is changed as he wants then he can give no assurance that his men will not continue to bend the rules to achieve convictions. Essentially his case for change has rested on two arguments. Firstly, that the police would not bring people to court unless certain of their guilt, and secondly, by saying that the present jury system too often allows the acquittal of the relatively few 'hardened criminals', Mark seeks to change the rules of law for all who came before the courts. His contempt for the system of law is well illustrated by an essay he wrote in 1973:

> 'The procedural safeguards for the suspected or accused in our system of criminal justice are such that committal for trial, involving the participation of lawyers and bench, is itself an indication of strong probability of guilt. Acquittal is therefore unlikely to mean that the accused is innocent in the true sense of the word . . .'[59]

Mark's point is tantamount to saying that all those prosecuted should be regarded as guilty and that even an acquittal should not be taken as an indication of innocence. He also ignores the fact that the majority of cases are heard in a magistrate's court and never go to trial by jury, and that in these cases well over two-thirds of the defendants plead guilty. More specifically, in cases where there is a committal from a magistrate's court to a higher court (with judge and jury) he ignores the fact that the committal is based *solely* on the presentation of prosecution evidence – the defence case being reserved for the trial proper.

Mark's contempt for juries – namely, the adjudication by ordinary men and women in cases holding out long prison sentences – was never more clearly stated than in an interview given in 1975. Juries, he said, 'perform the duty rarely, know little of the law, are occasionally stupid, prejudiced, barely literate and often incapable of applying the law as public opinion is led to suppose they do.'[60] In response Lord Wigoder, QC, vice-chairman of the Criminal Bar Association,

---

[58] *The Listener*, 8 October 1973.
[59] 'Social Violence', essay by Mark in *The Police we Deserve* (1973) p. 16.
[60] *Observer*, 16 March 1975.

observed that in general 'The policeman is usually as convinced of the defendant's guilt as the defendant's mother is of his innocence. Neither is a reliable guide.' Lord Wigoder went on to point out that contrary to Mark's view research into the operation of juries had shown 'in almost every case a rational and sensible decision.'[61]

The police and the press

One of the key presumptions of our system of law is that justice must not only be done but be seen to be done. Over the past couple of years the Metropolitan Police have successfully begun to restrict the right of the press to report on certain important trials. They have also limited access to certain information to selected journalists. Until comparatively recently a journalist had only to produce his National Union of Journalists press card (which specifically states that it is recognised by the Association of Chief Police Officers of England and Wales) to gain access to courts, including the Old Bailey. Over the last two years journalists of 'left-wing' inclinations or from non-Fleet Street papers and magazines have been turned away from the Old Bailey because they do not have a special police press pass – the Metropolitan and City Police Press Card. These police passes are not new; however, until recently they were freely available on application and some eight thousand were issued to the media. Now only two thousand are issued to Fleet Street, radio and television, and the foreign press. Editors are told how many passes their paper is to be given, usually four per paper, and the names of the journalists they nominate are forwarded to Scotland Yard. Journalists 'approved' in this manner are the ones who must cover certain trials, large demonstrations, and the visits of foreign dignitaries – they are also afforded special briefings by the police. In August 1973, after protests by several journalists, representatives of the National Union of Journalists met with Mark to discuss the question. Assurances were duly

[61] *Ibid.* A little-recognised change in the composition of juries came through rating revaluation in the 1960s. With increased home ownership and council housing many more people qualified for jury service. Moreover, since January 1973 the property qualification has been removed and all those on the electoral register are now qualified. Thus the attack on the jury system which has been gathering steam since the late 1960s comes at a time when more and more working class people are able to serve on juries.

given that no discrimination would be made between holders of the NUJ card and those with the additional police press passes. Some time after this meeting, however, Mark issued a circular to the Metropolitan Police divisions on police/press relations expressly stating that preferential treatment was to continue to be given to holders of the police passes. It said:

> 'It is crucial . . . that in future holders of the (police) press identification card should find it of real value in day-to-day dealings with the Metropolitan Police, carrying a significance which is readily recognised and accepted by all members of the Force . . . in normal circumstances card-holders are to be provided with all such information and opportunities for access as can be made available . . . special facilities cannot be accorded to non-holders of Metropolitan and City Police press cards . . .'[62]

Writing in his 1974 Annual Report Mark notes that 'many more responsibly written articles and well-researched features about the Metropolitan Police are now being seen by the public.'[63] And he goes on to say that the new restricted system has led 'to a readier appreciation on the part of police officers of the identity and purpose of card-holders.' At the moment the editors of Fleet Street are happily using these special police passes; one wonders if they will still be happy if and when it is not they who nominate the journalists who are to have passes, but Scotland Yard who will 'let it be known' who is approved of? In 1973 Mr Leslie Boyd, the Old Bailey Court Administrator, replying to a letter protesting at the police practice to reject the NUJ card as a means of press identification, said it was because 'it is issued by someone over whom the authorities have no control'.[64] Precisely.

The police and firearms

The greatest asset of the British policeman is that, from the inception of the modern police force, law and order has been maintained without resort to the use of firearms. But during 1973 two events in London drew public attention to the arming of the police: the shooting of a bank robber in Kensington by a policeman armed for embassy protection duty and the death of two young Pakistanis who were shot down by

---

[62] *Report of the Commissioner of Police for the Metropolis for the Year 1973*, HMSO, June 1974. Appendix.
[63] *Op. cit.*, p. 21.
[64] *Time Out*, 24 May 1974.

the Special Patrol Group at India House in the Aldwych. In the wake of these events further information came to light. Firstly, that there had been a marked increase in the issuing of guns to the police, and secondly, that the police were being rearmed with new, and more deadly weapons.

The story really starts two years earlier. In the winter of 1971 the new Tory Home Secretary, Mr Carr, set up a Home Office working party to look into the question of what arms the police should have. This working group was made up of representatives of the police, the Home Office Police Department, the army, and arms experts (from the arms manufacturing industry). The army nominees outnumbered those from the police side. The group reported at the end of 1972 and orders were put in hand for the recommended weapons. In place of the old weapons – the ·303 Lee Enfield and the ·38 Webley pistol – the police are now being re-equipped with the L39A1 high velocity rifle and the Smith and Wesson Model 10. The L39A1 rifle was rejected by the New York police as being too dangerous for use in cities, as its bullets are capable of penetrating several walls and injuring innocent bystanders. The International Red Cross has also condemned it because its bullets have the same effect as dum-dum bullets – the sheer impact can lead to death. While a spokesman for the manufacturers of the old police revolver said that their pistol could stop a man at thirty yards, 'the new combination of the Smith and Wesson and the ·38 special cartridge would enable the police to shoot a man through a door or from the other side of a car.'[65]

In March, 1973 the Home Secretary admitted to the House of Commons that the number of times guns had been issued to the police had risen substantially. The figures given were: 1970, arms issued on 1,072 occasions (803 in London); 1971 on 1,935 occasions (1,344 in London); and in 1972 on 2,237 occasions (1,717 in London). The figures had doubled in two years. It should be pointed out that in the three years 1970–73, the police only used the guns on five occasions. Additionally, evidence gleaned from the annual reports of Chief Constables throughout the country shows that between 10 per cent and 15 per cent of most police forces received firearms training in 1972 (about 1 in 10 of the latter also undertook training in the use of CS gas).

New guns are not the only new equipment being made available to the police. In October 1973 the Home Office announced that the Police Scientific Development Branch was to provide a 'small technical equipment unit' at Durham, for an experimental period of six months. The

---

[65] *Sunday Times*, 21 January 1973.

equipment made available to thirteen forces in the North included 'items such as metal detectors for finding hidden objects, infra-red equipment for detecting the movements of criminals at night . . .'[66] In July of the same year a joint police-army exercise was held on the South Coast to test infra-red 'people' sensors. The exercise, which was reportedly a great success, was officially directed at smuggling and illegal immigration.

The weaponry now available for future civil disorders, strikes, or major demonstrations has largely been tried and tested in Northern Ireland by the British Army. It is said that when the army went into Northern Ireland to deal with increasing opposition to the continued rule of the Protestant majority, their equipment consisted of a few mesh shields and batons inherited from Cyprus. Since 1969 over three hundred different items of equipment have been introduced into the army's technology for riot control, and the growing police-military interface suggests that these weapons will be used in Britain if the need arises.[67]

The Special Patrol Group and the Special Constabulary

The ability of the police to cope with disorders, short of outright civil war, depends not only on intelligence and weaponry but also on manpower. In the context of the police two groups are especially relevant – the Special Patrol Group, for short-term, isolated outbreaks, and the Special Constabulary for mass demonstrations and strikes. Only in 1972 was it generally realised that the Metropolitan Police Special Patrol Group (SPG) had in fact been in existence since 1965. Since then most regional police forces have formed similar groups – the Commando Squad in Lincolnshire, the Special Squad in Lancashire, Special Services Squad in Bristol and the Special Patrol Group in Birmingham. The SPG started with one hundred men organised in three units. Each unit had Bedford vans marked on the side with 'Special Patrol Group', and on the shoulder of each man's uniform is the designation 'CO' (Commissioner's Office) showing them to be a central force run from Scotland Yard. Today, they drive around in Ford Transits (see picture on page 96) not often noticed – the name was dropped from the side of the vans for greater anonymity. In addition they use a number of unmarked cars. Today, there are six SPG units with a permanent force

[66] Home Office Press Release, 1 October 1973.
[67] For a discussion of the police-military connection see chapter 7. For an excellent summary of these new weapons see *The New Technology of Repression – Lessons from Ireland* (Paper No. 2), British Society for Social Responsibility in Science (1974).

of two hundred men and women. They are all volunteers drawn from London's police, and receive special training in riot control and gun and CS gas handling.[68] Each unit consists of twenty-eight male constables, one female constable, three sergeants and an inspector, and each unit has three transits. A transit can carry twelve officers, including the driver and the radio operator. The radio operator monitors two channels, one for the SPG units and one for the normal London police channel. The annual cost of the SPGs is over £1 million a year.

Attention turned to the SPGs after the killing of two Pakistanis at India House by two armed members of the Group in February 1973. It was then learned that members of the SPG carry arms as a matter of course – two officers in each transit. Yet parliamentary indignation centred on the sale of toy pistols – which the two Pakistanis carried. The critical question however was never really asked – what would have happened if armed policemen had not been instantly available, as would have been the case a few years ago? Presumably the streets would have been cleared and entreaties made to the 'gunmen' to give themselves up. Given that these 'dangerous gunmen' were in fact two young and frightened men, who can doubt they might have emerged unhurt? But no attempt was made to talk to them, to discover they were not 'guerrilla terrorists' – there was no time. In just four minutes they were dead. Mr Carr, the Home Secretary, spoke to the Commons in terms which reflect the consensus reaction: 'I believe prompt action by the police, demonstrating that anyone who attempts this sort of thing at Embassies or High Commissions in London is caught and dealt with, is perhaps the best deterrent and the best way to allay people's fears.'[69]

In November 1974 the SPG's responsibility for guarding embassies in central London was transferred to the newly-formed Diplomatic Protection Group. The Diplomatic Protection Group provides permanent surveillance of embassies and private residences with mobile patrols and is comprised of volunteers who serve for periods of six months. About a third of the Group are permanently armed. Most of the SPG's work is centred in areas of high crime incidence, that is, working-class areas like Lambeth and the East End. Apart from helping the local police in the areas on a specific crime much of their time is spent giving the locality the 'once-over'. Roadblocks are set up, and systematic searches of people are made in the streets. The particular

[68] From 1973 a positive initiative was taken to encourage short term service in the SPG in order that more London police could get special riot training.
[69] House of Commons, 21 February 1973.

2. One of the transit vans used by the Special Patrol Group of the Metropolitan Police Force.

role of the SPG needs to be understood. Firstly, they have no commitment to the locality, so unlike the local police they have no need to maintain a positive relationship with the community. Secondly, their tactics are different. During 1974 the SPG officers stopped and searched 13,001 people in the streets and 28,303 in cars.[70] In the street most people stopped are young people or blacks, usually under the drug laws. And unlike the local police the SPG nearly always search those stopped. Lastly, because they have been trained for riot situations their 'normal' manner tends to be more aggressive than is usual for policemen. This leads to a higher incidence of force which, because it evokes a response from the recipient, leads to a high rate of arrest for assault, obstruction, and threatening behaviour. The modern tendency for all the police cars on call to 'bundle in' when trouble is reported is now usual; but the SPG are specialists at it. After an SPG sortie into Brixton their activities were described at a meeting of local community groups as those of 'organised thugs', a description which many who have chanced to encounter them would endorse.[71]

[70] *Report from the Commissioner of Police for 1974*, Cmnd. 6068, June 1975, p. 47.
[71] For additional complaints about SPG activity in Brixton see, *South London Press*, 23 February 1973; *Race Today*, January 1973.

The SPGs are the specialist riot police for London. However, should mass conflict arise, the ranks of the ordinary police are likely to be supplemented by additional volunteer forces. The body which has played this role in British history is the Special Constabulary. Since the fourteenth century local JPs have been empowered to swear in members of the local community as Special Constables, bound to uphold law and order. Prior to the emergence of the working class in the eighteenth century this method of raising law-enforcers worked relatively smoothly. In the early part of the nineteenth century there grew a marked reluctance in many areas for people to come forward – for example in Hull in 1831, one thousand Special Constables were sworn in but only seven turned up to suppress a political demonstration. This tendency was partly due to sympathy with the emerging political movements and partly because the bourgeoisie were reluctant to risk personal danger. What had prior to this time been presumed to be the duty of every 'law-abiding citizen' was therefore enshrined in law. The 1831 Special Constables Act gave JPs the power to swear in Specials *prior* to the outbreak of disorder and introduced a £5 fine for refusing to serve. With the formation of the police less reliance was placed on the Specials but on the occasion of mass demonstrations thousands were sworn in and held in reserve. When war broke out in 1914 it was realised that the 1831 Act referred only to circumstances of disorder, so the law was changed and the 1914 Special Constables Act regularised their enrolment.[72] During the 1918 and 1919 police strikes, the use of Specials was a clear example of strike-breaking.

Up until this time the enrolment of Specials had taken place only in response to specific threats of disorder and for very limited periods. After the First World War, when the ruling class clearly perceived the danger of Bolshevism taking hold with the militancy of the returning and disillusioned soldiers, the Home Secretary sent out a circular to all local police forces. It urged them to 'reconstitute and strengthen the Special Constabulary organisation established during the war and maintain it as a permanent Police Reserve.'[73] Some forces responded enthusiastically but others were worried about the legality of setting up a permanent force. So in 1923 another Special Constables Act was passed which removed from the 1914 Act the words 'during the present war'. Simple but effective. By the time of the General Strike there were

[72] When volunteers were called for in Ramsgate in 1914 none came forward and the local magistrates, mindful of local pride, nominated and swore in five hundred local citizens.

[73] R. Seth, *The Specials* (1961) p. 120.

permanent groups of Specials attached to every police force. These were supplemented by volunteers after an appeal and the state entered the strike with 226,000 Specials enrolled. In the 1930s there were 100,000 Specials on the police books, but by 1964 there were only 51,000 (the authorised establishment was 100,000). By 1972 the numbers had dropped even further with only 27,440 in the whole country. With the approach of the miners' strike in 1973 special efforts were made by many local forces to increase the numbers of Specials. In London, although the authorised establishment was 10,000 only 2,090 were enrolled in 1974 despite an intensive advertising campaign in 1973. To enrol as a Special one has to be between 18 and 50, British and of good appearance. In return one received training, a police warrant card, a police uniform (with the letters 'SC' on the shoulder) and four hours' patrol work a week. And to ensure that only the upright are allowed to enter applications 'will be searchingly scrutinised by Scotland Yard.'[74]

Over the last one-hundred-and-fifty years the Specials have changed from a volunteer force drawn from the whole community for limited periods to a smaller, permanent and loyal body recruited largely from the petit-bourgeoisie. If and when major civil disorder threatens to break out an appeal for volunteers to join the Specials will no doubt be issued and, as in the General Strike, will provide a rallying point for those committed to perpetuating the prevailing order.

The Home Office

Finally it is necessary to consider briefly the relationship between the Home Office and the police. Since the seventeenth century the Home Office has been responsible for the maintenance of law and order and the internal security of the state. The police forces, which for most of the last century were under the direct control of JPs, are today independent of effective democratic control of their policies and actions. The local police authorities, who meet only once a month, are specifically excluded from considering questions of policy and action, while the Home Secretary is able to dodge parliamentary questioning on the premise of not wishing to impinge on local autonomy: 'the present solution is a classic piece of British humbug, in which the Home Secretary's officials can and do interfere with a large range of police questions, but can still shelter behind the appearance of local autonomy.'[75]

[74] Seth, *op. cit.*, p. 213.
[75] A. Sampson, *The Anatomy of Britain* (1971) p. 368.

In the aftermath of the 1918 and 1919 police strikes the Desborough Committee, which had initially dealt with police pay and police unionisation, moved on to make other recommendations that were to provide to the basis for centralising state control of the police. The first decision was to increase from a quarter to a half the contribution from the central government to the cost of maintaining local police forces. Secondly, they recommended the creation of a Police Department in the Home Office. Thus from the 1920s the future pattern of Home Office influence over local forces became established. This influence rested partly on the daily circulars which emanated from the Police Department to local forces and partly, via finance, on the provision of services and scientific methods beyond the capabilities of a single force. Critchley described the effect of these daily Home Office circulars at the end of the 1930s: '. . . the prolific "advice" and "guidance" contained in Home Office circulars on all manner of subjects became a euphemism for "direction".'[76] The provision of services by the Home Office today includes recruiting publicity, science laboratories, wireless equipment, the Police College and other training centres. On another level there are regular conferences of Chief Constables with the Home Office on matters of common interest, while the Inspectors of Constabulary are the chairmen of the regional committees of Chief Constables.

Beneath the Permanent Under-Secretary in the Home Office hierarchy there are five Deputy Under-Secretaries; one of these is in charge of the Police Department. Under him in the Department are four Assistant Under-Secretaries and eight Assistant Secretaries. Each of the latter is in charge of one of the eight sections of the Department. Their responsibilities include:

F1   Pay and conditions; special constables and 'first police reserve'.

F2   Police powers and procedure; CROs; Regional Crime Squads; detective work; complaints.

F3   Road traffic legislation.

F4   Amalgamation; public order; security liaison; subversive activities; relations between police and blacks; firearms.

F5   Equipment; uniforms; training.

F6   Co-ordination of action in civil emergencies; police war-planning.

[76] T. A. Critchley, *op. cit.*, p. 219.

F7   Police use of computers.
F8   Co-ordination of scientific and technical support services.[77]

That the Home Office should have an interest in all these areas cannot come as any surprise. However, it is interesting to note that the more contentious areas are all of recent origin; for example, security liaison, subversive activities and police/black relations (F4), and the co-ordination of action in civil emergencies and police war-planning (F6). On a general level it is clear that these subjects now constitute a recognised and admitted interest of the Home Office. The staffs of these sections are independently engaged in gathering and evaluating reports from the police throughout the country and from the Special Branch for both the Ministry and their political counterparts.

Conclusion

The first hundred years of policing (in the modern sense) is marked by two features. On the one hand the slow transition from 'old' to 'new' policing which was only completed in the early part of this century, and on the other hand, the establishing of a high degree of independence for the local police forces from democratic accountability. The period which followed the police strikes and the Desborough Committee reports until the early 1960s was substantially one of consolidation. It was after the Royal Commission Report in 1962 and the subsequent Police Act 1964 that qualitatively new directions in policing became evident.

These changes contrasted starkly with the previous fifty years in several respects. Firstly, there was the increasing application of technology, and the full import of current developments will only become evident in the late 1970s as the computerisation programme becomes part of everyday policing. Secondly, the pre-emptive emphasis of policing which was at first directed towards the professional criminal soon extended to more political and social areas like immigration and drug-taking. Lastly, the uniformed police have become increasingly engaged in combating political activity. Although

[77] In addition there are four other Home Office organisations concerned with the police: The Police Scientific Development Branch, the Police Research Services Branch, The Directorate of Communications, and the Forensic Science Laboratories.

their role in this respect goes back through the whole of their history the contemporary social and political context has seen the police prepared to counter all kinds of emergencies – and the increasing co-operation with the military is only one development.[78]

[78] See chapter 7.

3   The Special Branch

One of the problems in examining the Special Branch is that no history of it has yet been written. Passing references are made to it in books on the police, but little else. The first part of this chapter, therefore, attempts to bring together what is known about the Branch, and about its activities against political groups from its formation in 1883 up to the present. The second part of the chapter looks at the structure and operations of the Branch today.

Intelligence gathering before 1883

One of the popular myths put forward by orthodox police histories is the notion that no political police existed before the formation of the Special Branch in 1883. In fact, prior to this date an efficient intelligence-gathering agency was run from the Home Office under the personal supervision of the Home Secretary. Before the sustained political struggles of the 1880s onwards, there were two particular occasions when the working class organised in opposition to the state and industrial capitalism. The first, immediately after the Napoleonic wars, involved the Luddites and the early socialists, who engaged in political self-education and insurrection. These movements of the nascent working class were vigorously opposed by the army and the landed gentry with outright force, persecution and infiltration.[1] The second period was between 1838 and 1848 when the Chartist movement presented its nation-wide challenge. Provincial England relied on a motley combination of forces to maintain order – the army, the yeomanry, Special Constables and self-protection associations formed by the middle class. The impact of Chartism 'made it seem to some the prelude to a general uprising of the working classes, a threat of revolution'.[2]

To combat the Chartists the Home Office had a number of sources of intelligence. The Lord Lieutenants in the counties and the magistrates in the towns were the natural class allies of the central

[1] See E. P. Thomson's *The Makings of the English Working Class* (1968).
[2] Radzinowicz, Vol. 4, p. 232–233 (1968).

government, and were in practice 'the confidential agents of the Secretary of State in their localities'.[3] They sent regular reports to London based on their own experiences and on information provided by spies under their control. Then there were the local military commanders. General Napier, who commanded the troops in the North, had a particularly effective system. He sent a confidential circular to all of his officers asking them to give their opinion 'as to the feelings of the labouring classes in your neighbourhood', and suggested the source should be 'the most intelligent of your soldiers'. As many of the soldiers were billeted with the local people and drank in the local pubs, a most efficient system ensued. 'Thus', said Napier, 'I make spies of them despite themselves.'[4]

The next level of intelligence also involved one of the state agencies – the Post Office. Reports on unusual occurrences were forwarded by local postmasters directly to the Home Secretary. Under the provisions of the 1833 Factory Act, four Factory Inspectors, who had under them a number of Superintendents, were appointed. These Inspectors also provided first-hand reports on the mood and activities of the working class. The few 'new' police forces, which had been formed by this time, rather than employing spies, sent policemen in plainclothes to political meetings and pubs. Finally, there were several occasions when Home Office agents were dispatched from London to prepare independent reports on the situation in an area.

In addition there were less formal sources. Public-spirited citizens – worried members of the bourgeoisie – frequently wrote to the Home Secretary with tales or complaints of inaction by local magistrates. One of the more important sources were press reporters, who provided verbatim reports of speeches by Chartist leaders and these were the basis of several prosecutions. Reporters were generally used away from their own localities as they feared reprisals. Another means of gathering information was through the time-honoured practice of opening the mail. As is currently the procedure, two kinds of warrants were issued by the Home Secretary – those for criminal cases and those for internal security. Unlike the system today, however, most warrants issued in the 1830s contained more than one name, usually six or seven. Between 1838 and 1842 some sixty-nine warrants were issued. Although this method had been common Home Office practice for the previous hundred years, it was not until 1844 that it was publicly

[3] See T. C. Mather, *Public Order in the Age of the Chartists* (1959) p. 183.
[4] *Op. cit.,* p. 165.

known that the mail of political activists was being intercepted.[5]

What stands out from this period was the informal nature of the intelligence structure and the personal role played by the Home Secretary. Later this system was to become institutionalised – and removed from parliamentary control. The Special Branch therefore did not herald a new departure; it was the formalisation and extension of previous practices.

The formation of the Special Branch

The Special Branch was officially formed in 1883 to combat Fenian bombings in London; however, the work of Scotland Yard in dealing with militant Irish nationalism began earlier, in 1867. Before 1883 this work was undertaken by the CID at Scotland Yard, from which the Special Branch developed.

In 1883 the Irish question was again brought to the attention of the English by a series of thirteen dynamite bombings in the course of two years. The bombings started on 1 March 1883 and ended on 31 January 1885. The first bomb went off outside *The Times* building causing little damage, and the second in the Local Government Office in Whitehall. Seven months later in October there were three explosions in the Underground.

The state reacted swiftly. Under the Explosive Substances Act 1883, which was rushed through parliament, the police were given wider powers of arrest for offences in this field. Late in 1883 the Special Irish Branch was formed from members of the Yard's CID. The small squad of about a dozen men were all of Irish birth although their chief, Inspector Littlechild, was a Scotsman.[6] The work of the newly-formed Branch was to keep political militants of the Irish movements under observation, to make inquiries for the Irish government, and to supervise the guarding of the Queen and her Ministers. In this latter task it was assisted by police temporarily seconded from the uniformed branch to this duty.

The headquarters of the Branch was established on the east side of Old Scotland Yard. Several months later, on 30t May 1884, the Fenians planned two bombings. The first was to blow up Nelson's Column, but the sixteen sticks of dynamite were discovered and defused. The second was much more successful – this was the bombing of the Special

---

[5] See p. 197.

[6] In fact the Special Irish Branch was first named the 'Political Branch' of the CID, but this was thought to be too contentious and it was altered.

Irish Branch headquarters. The head of the CID (of which the Branch was part) had received a threatening letter and a constable was instructed to patrol outside and to search for suspicious objects. Although he inspected the public lavatory attached to the police building he did not find the bomb hidden there. Early in the evening the bomb went off, blowing up the offices of the Branch – ironically the bulk of the documents destroyed related to the Fenians. Neither of the two officers on duty that night – Inspector Robson and Sergeant Sweeney – were in the building at the time of the explosion, having left some fifteen minutes earlier.

Trying to prevent Fenian bombings did not constitute the only Irish duties of the Branch. After Gladstone's resignation in 1886 Branch officers arrested five Irish MPs who were wanted by the Royal Irish Constabulary for incitement to sedition. The five MPs – Mr Jasper Pyne, Mr Gilhooly, Mr J. B. Cox, Mr J. O'Kelly and Dr Tanner – were all arrested when they came to England to vote in the Commons. Each of the MPs had managed to evade capture in Ireland and two of them had evolved imaginative methods of avoiding capture. Mr Pyne erected a hydraulic swing in Pyne Castle and every time the police came to carry out the arrest he would swing himself out of reach and remain aloft for many days, while Dr Tanner often spoke from a boat which he would row to the opposite shore after the end of the meeting. All five were eventually arrested in England, handed over to the Royal Ulster Constabulary, and served terms of imprisonment.

When these bombings stopped the Special Branch was retained as a separate squad within the Yard's CID. 'Once the Special Branch had been established, there was no lack of work for it.'[7] Ever since this time the Branch has had a special responsibility for the surveillance of Irish political groups and a permanent section has always been assigned to this task. By 1888 it became clear that the interests of the Branch were not to be limited to the Irish and the word 'Irish' was dropped from its title.

The area of political activity to come to the Branch's attention next was that of foreign immigrant groups, in particular, the anarchists. Many of the politically active immigrant groups at this time were political refugees from repressive European states, especially Russia, France and Germany.[8] Small anarchist groups had been in London

[7] Sir John Moylan, *Scotland Yard* (1934) p. 219.
[8] See chapter 4 for the agent provocateur activities carried out by agencies of these governments.

since the 1840s, centred in political clubs, bars, and discussion groups. From the 1880s the persecution of anarchist movements in Europe and Russia intensified and many, including several famous anarchists came to England. In 1881 Johann Most, writing in *Die Frieheit* (one of the first anarchist papers in England) offended the establishment by an editorial enthusing over the assassination of the Czar, and he was sent to prison for eighteen months.[9]

'The comrades he left in charge of *Die Frieheit* had no desire to appear less courageous than their leader, and when the Irish rebels assassinated Lord Cavendish in Phoenix Park they loudly proclaimed their solidarity with the killers.'[10]

The paper was raided and put out of business.

Others to arrive were Peter Kropotkin (1886) and Rudolf Rocker (1895). Rocker later became a major organiser of the anarchist Jewish movement in the East End of London and worked for a successful strike by sweatshop workers in 1912.[11] A few anarchists tried to emulate their French comrades and one or two bomb factories were discovered by the police and the Branch. What is difficult to determine in this period (up to 1910) is the respective roles played by the anarchists and the agent-provocateurs of European governments (particularly the Russian) who were keen to have them deported and outlawed.[12] For example, in 1892 six anarchists were arrested in Walsall and London after the discovery of a small bomb factory (two were acquitted for lack of evidence), but the French agent-provocateur who encouraged their activities and tipped off the police was never produced in court. The spy was not required to give evidence as the judge did not think this would serve the public interest. In his book, *At Scotland Yard*, Sweeney confirms the role of the spy in this case.[13]

Two cases which occurred in the 1890s illustrate the Branch's work then and today. Both cases involved Inspector Sweeney. The first concerned a group working for social reform and the second the arrest and trial of an alleged 'dynamiter'. The former was centred on the Legitimation League, which had been formed in 1895 in Leeds and

[9] Most later went to America where he became a leading anarchist writer.
[10] George Woodcock, *Anarchism* (1962) p. 416.
[11] See Rocker, *The London Years* (1956). The book includes several instances of Czarist agents at work and details of Rocker's work in the East End.
[12] See also chapter 4 on the siege of Sydney Street.
[13] Sweeney (1904) p. 225.

was effectively destroyed as a result of Branch infiltration and the use of law by 1898. Among the central aims of the organisation was the granting of full rights to illegitimate children, presumably a lawful objective. The League began to gain adherents in 1896 after they successfully campaigned for the release of a Miss Edith Lancester, who had been committed to a lunatic asylum. The committing doctor's grounds were Miss Lancester's belief in the aims of the Legitimation League. In the same year the League moved to London and opened an office with a young clergyman's son, George Bedborough, as the organiser. Many people contributed to the League and its paper, *The Adult*, ranging from high-society liberals to avowed anarchists. It was the participation of the anarchists, and the fact that their advocacy of free love and the abolition of the marriage laws gained ground in the League, that enraged upright citizens and brought its activities under the surveillance of the Branch. Within months of the new office being opened in London, Inspector Sweeney joined the League, attended its meetings and gained the full confidence of George Bedborough. In Sweeney's words: 'I was instructed to obtain a closer view of Mr. Bedborough, and I easily gained access to his intimacy.'[14]

Sweeney sent his reports, together with copious supplies of the League's literature, to the Public Prosecutor's office. However, they could find no legal grounds on which to prosecute so Sweeney continued his undercover work and waited for the right moment. The campaign against the League intensified after a clergyman attended one of their meetings, and a letter, printed in most national papers signed by many high-sounding names, urged that 'the strong hand of the law should crush a teaching which would turn Society into a group of harlots.'[15]

Such was the success of Sweeney's access to George Bedborough that when Lillian Harman, a well-known American anarchist and president of the League, came to England Sweeney was invited to attend a select dinner party of some eighteen people.[16] Soon after this dinner in 1898 came the publication of a book called *Studies in the Psychology of Sex* by Dr Villiers, who ran a firm called University Press Limited. The book appeared under the name of Dr Havelock Ellis, though in fact he had only co-authored it and was later to disown it. One of the outlets

[14] *Op. cit.*, p. 180.
[15] 20 December 1897.
[16] Lillian Harman had been sent to prison in America for living with her child's father without being married.

for the book, which was obscene according to the values of the time, was the office of the Legitimation League. This gave the authorities the chance they had been waiting for:

> 'we applied for a warrant for his (Bedborough's) arrest, convinced that we should at one blow kill a growing evil in the shape of a vigorous campaign of free love and Anarchism, and at the same time, discover the means by which the country was being flooded with books of the "Psychology" type.'[17]

Bedborough was duly arrested by Sweeney (who until this point he had not suspected) and was bound over to come up for judgement if the offence was repeated. Bedborough's position at the trial was hindered because Havelock Ellis had publicly disowned the book, although the intercession of an influential relative assured him of a light sentence.

The object of the exercise was, however, achieved, for Bedborough and other influential names withdrew their support and within months the League effectively ceased to function. Two years of diligent infiltration by Inspector Sweeney had finally paid dividends and the propagation of sexual freedom was efficiently thwarted. It was at no time alleged that Bedborough was himself an anarchist; indeed he was recognised to be a fervent liberal reformer (as were most of the League's supporters), but the views of the League offended prevailing Victorian morality and the full force of the Branch and the law was used against it.

The second case involved an alleged 'dynamiter', and the grounds on which the Branch acted, together with the presentation of the evidence, is not dissimilar to some of the bomb trials in the 1970s. In 1893 a German named Brall and his wife came to England and settled in London. During their first year here Mr Brall found work as a skilled cabinet-maker and both he and his wife became members of the Autonomy Club, which was at the time the best-known anarchist meeting place with much talk, discussions and dancing. Brall himself was involved in revolutionary politics and was visited frequently by known anarchist activists. About a year after they had come to England, the Brall's home was raided by six members of the Branch under Inspector Sweeney, and enough evidence was gathered from his house for Brall to be charged under the 1883 Explosive Substances Act for having in his possession explosive materials. As is usual at such a trial the evidence was of two kinds – firstly, that demonstrating the

---

[17] Sweeney, *op. cit.*, p. 186.

revolutionary and violent connections and tendencies of the accused and secondly, the hard evidence of materials for manufacturing bombs. In addition Brall was charged with coining (counterfeiting).

The evidence presented by the prosecution included a large quantity of leaflets and papers from anarchist and socialist groups, some in Dutch and French, including a pamphlet entitled *Scientific Revolutionary Warfare* which contained details of how to make bombs, and Sweeney commented: 'This pamphlet was a very remarkable work, and the mere possession of it unexplained should be made as serious an offence as the possession of explosive materials.'[18] An explosives expert, called by the state, described his examination of the nitric acid, sulphuric acid, methylated spirits, and a small quantity of fulminate of mercury together with several blank cartridges found at Brall's home. Three other pieces of evidence against Brall were also presented – an electric battery (an ignition mechanism), a large hole dug in his back garden (the police suggested for concealing bombs), and a reported explosion in the Bralls' flat (while conducting an experiment). For the defence it was submitted that the literature found by the Branch was nothing extraordinary for a politically active person to have – moreover some of the newspapers were in a language the defendant could not read. Several anarchist witnesses appeared to testify that Brall did not belong to those sections of the movement who believed in bombing. As to the hard 'evidence' the defence said there was a reasonable explanation for every item – most of the chemical substances had been left by a fellow workman studying medicine who asked Brall to look after them for him (an explosives expert called by the defence said that there was insufficient material to make a bomb anyway). The hole in the garden was simply for keeping rabbits in. And the reported 'explosion' was merely an attempt by Brall to clear his blocked chimney flue with a small quantity of gunpowder – a working-class practice attested to by several respectable witnesses. Finally, Brall's boss testified that several of the 'suspicious materials' were commonly used by skilled cabinet-makers – methylated spirits, sulphuric acid, and electric batteries were used for cleaning brass.

By the end of the defence case even the judge was in some difficulty and the jury took just fifteen minutes to acquit Brall of the charge. Brall had attracted the attention of the Branch because he was a foreigner and was active in anarchist politics, and when the speculative raid on his home produced 'explosive substances' its case seemed

[18] *Ibid.*, p. 272.

complete. After the trial Sweeney commented: 'We had fully expected that he would be found guilty and sentenced to a long term of imprisonment.'[19] On this occasion Sweeney and his fellow officers did not get the extra cash reward from the state that they had received so many times before.

At the turn of the century the Branch, although now permanent, was still very small, with only some fifteen to twenty officers based at the Yard. In most areas of London and the provinces the political surveillance of the socialist movements rested with the local police and the CID. One important by-product of the Branch's surveillance of immigrant political groups was the weight its reports gave to the lobby to restrict immigration to this country. Although a Royal Commission reported in 1903 that the number of immigrants in Britain had doubled between 1881 and 1901 no action was taken until a Home Office committee report came out in 1905 based largely on police and Branch information. This report stated that these immigrants, particularly from Poland and Russia, had bad habits which demoralised those living in already crowded conditions. Moreover most of them were settling in the working-class areas of London. In the same year the Aliens Immigration Act was passed which gave the Home Secretary powers to issue deportation orders on the advice of the police, magistrates and the Special Branch. This was the first Act to restrict immigration to Britain.

By 1905 the Branch had been called in to help the police with the suffragettes, but like the police it had a problem in trying to get information on their activities – for neither had any women officers. The Branch's activities were limited to guarding Ministers and trying – vainly – to keep an eye on the assumed leaders of the movement. Much has been written of this great struggle but the perplexities caused to the authorities are worth recalling:

'There was an uncanny ingenuity about their methods of annoyance ... Many of them were perfectly rational ladies in private life, but they drew into their ranks a number of mentally unbalanced women ... They were amply supplied with money and they had a host of sympathisers all over the country. A high-powered car met them at the prison gate and spirited them out of London to an unknown destination.'[20]

[19] *Ibid.*, p. 277.
[20] Thompson, *The Story of Scotland Yard* (1935), p. 190.

In addition to the disruptions caused by the suffragettes, the police throughout the country had to contend with a series of major industrial strikes between 1911 and 1914 – a period that became known as the 'Great Unrest'. It is not only the number of strikes which were worrying to the state (872 in 1911, 834 in 1912, and 1,459 in 1913), but the increasingly radical ideology of the socialist movements. The importation into Britain, as it was viewed, of communist and anarcho-syndicalist ideas from Europe and America brought a militancy which countered, temporarily at least, the developing parliamentarianism of the left. Moreover the syndicalists, the shop stewards movement and the communists organised themselves in non-hierarchical groups that were not amenable to co-option and infiltration. The outbreak of the First World War had several effects. It divided the socialist movement in Britain and, more importantly, divided the common interests of the working classes of Europe through the dominance of nationalism.

Before the war the Branch numbered around fifty men and its actions had been largely in response to specific areas of political activity – the Irish, the anarchists, the suffragettes, Indian students or aliens. There was as yet very little record-keeping and no systematic surveillance. Its responsibilities, as they had evolved since its formation thirty years before, were the guarding of Ministers and royalty, 'watching out' for violent political plots (bombings and assassination), and the irregular watching at ports for 'undesirables'. Its field of activity was limited to London – the day-to-day work of keeping watch on political and industrial groups in London and the country still remained with the local police as a by-product of their public-order role.

The First World War and the October Revolution

In June 1913 Sir Basil Thomson became head of the Criminal Investigation Department in succession to Sir Melville Macnagthen. Thomson was the son of the Archbishop of York and after completing his education at Eton and Oxford he joined the Colonial Service. In Fiji, Tonga and New Guinea he 'put down' native wars and then was assigned to educate the sons of the King of Siam. Later he became Deputy Governor of the Prison Service at the Home Office and then Governor of Dartmoor prison where there had been several riots:

'his qualities as a gatherer of intelligence in the Colonial Service had not gone unnoticed in Whitehall. . . . (his appointment) was mainly on account of his handling of the problem of foreign immigrants and his detailed knowledge of the habits and methods of habitual criminals.'[21]

Thomson was to remain in command until 1921 and he became increasingly involved in the work of the Special Branch of whose later practices he was in many ways the fashioner. The reasons for this however had more to do with the demands of war than with Thomson personally. During war the dividing lines between 'crime', 'political opposition', and 'aiding the enemy' are hard to draw for agencies of state, and throughout the war the CID and the Branch operated as one unit. At the start of the war the CID numbered seven hundred men of whom over one hundred were members of the Branch. The work of the Branch continued to include its pre-war duties but these were now extended to cover national security (the detection of spies and saboteurs) and, for the first time, the surveillance of the socialist movement as a whole. As an aspect of its national-security role it was to play an important part in the watch for spies, a function it shared with the newly-formed MI5.

The war generated paranoia, and patriotic Englishmen 'saw' spies in every imaginable situation. Letters and messages flooded in to the police and the Branch, and the Branch had to take on a large number of pensioners to cope with all the letters. The work of the Branch was limited to forwarding likely leads to the local police; it became directly involved only if something extraordinary transpired. The opposition of the socialist movement to the war posed more than a few problems for the police and the Branch. In 1914 the TUC and the Labour Party Executive endorsed the war and the left wing resigned in protest. The rejection of the war from a pacifist position embraced both conscientious objectors and socialists opposed to fighting an imperialist war. Prominent among the groups in opposition were the Independent Labour Party, the Union for Democratic Control, The Non-Conscription Fellowship, the Fellowship of Reconciliation, the syndicalists and the Rank and File Movement. Resistance to the war gained momentum with the introduction, for the first time in Britain, of conscription in 1916. In this war three out of ten conscientious objectors were sent to prison (compared with three out of one hundred in the Second World War).

The restrictions on the press during the war worked more by self-censorship than by direct state intervention, but there was one occa-

---

[21] Deacon, *A History of the Secret Service* (1969) p. 169.

sion which called for exceptional measures. One afternoon in 1915 there assembled in the Home Secretary's room at the House of Commons a formidable gathering of Ministers and civil servants. At the meeting were the Lord Chancellor, the Attorney-General, the Director of Public Prosecutions, and the Permanent Under-Secretary for the Home Office. The subject under discussion was the daily insistence by *The Globe* newspaper that Lord Kitchener had resigned – it appears he was on a secret mission in Serbia but his long absence lent credence to the story. The government had issued a denial but *The Globe* took no notice.

'*The Globe*', said the Attorney-General, 'must be taught a sharp lesson. We must suppress it for a time.'[22] As legal proceedings would be a long and public process, Thomson, the head of the Branch, was sent for and briefed on the situation. Charged with teaching *The Globe* a lesson Thomson was in something of a quandary as to how he should effect his brief. After entering *The Globe* offices Thomson, without seeing the editor, went straight to the print-shop and saw the foreman:

> 'Supposing you wanted to take away some part of this machinery which would make it impossible to run the machines again until it was restored and yet do no damage to the plant, what would you take?' 'Oh, that's easy,' said the foreman, and he led me to a certain engine from which he took a portion which I could carry away in my hand, I thanked him and carried it away. That was how the Globe was suppressed until such time as the directors of the newspaper had come to an arrangement with the Government.'[23]

Towards the end of 1916 the work of the Branch took on a new significance at the instigation of the Prime Minister, Lloyd George. While he was Minister of Munitions he had set up a directorate of intelligence to watch and report on industrial unrest and subversion in the massive arms-production industry. When he became Prime Minister Lloyd George lost this facility, so he asked Thomson to provide him with regular reports from the Branch. Thomson commented on his new role: 'Pacifism, anti-conscription and Revolution are now inseparably mixed. The same individuals took part in all three movements. The real object of most of these people, though it may have been subconscious, appeared to be the ruin of their own coun-

[22] R. Jackson, *Case for the Prosecution* (1962) p. 147.
[23] Thomson, *My Experiences at Scotland Yard* (1922) p. 124–125.

try.'[24] As a result of this initiative the Special Branch became an important influence on Lloyd George and his Cabinet. Thomson made detailed reports in person to the Cabinet, at first fortnightly and then weekly, on the reported activities of revolutionary movements in Britain. The information for these reports came from several sources such as the literature of the socialist movement, transcribed reports of public meetings by uniformed police and Branch officers, informers in the movements, and from a small number of officers infiltrated into organisations.

What is clear from the work of the Branch during the war is that surveillance was not limited to revolutionary groups; it extended to many of liberal inclinations, including members of the Labour Party who became involved in anti-war activity or industrial action. In short, everyone who was ideologically to the left of the Tory Party became a potential subversive. Despite Thomson's reports, Cabinet understanding was – to say the least – somewhat warped. Thomson's diary entry for 22 October 1917 reads as follows:

'I handed in my report on the activities of the pacifist revolutionary societies for the War Cabinet, who were not disposed to take doses of soothing syrup in these matters. Being persuaded that German money is supporting these societies, they want to be assured that the police are doing something, I feel certain there is no German money, their expenditure being covered by the subscriptions they receive from cranks.'[25]

Within months it was being suggested that Russian money was financing the movements in Britain.

In May 1917 a series of strikes started in different areas of the country and Thomson was instructed by the War Cabinet to draw up a list of the ringleaders to be arrested under the Defence of the Realm Act. However, Thomson stayed his hand when he learnt that 'the Cabinet had sent the King and Queen to the strike areas' and it was agreed to wait and see the effect of the visit. On 16 May Thomson wrote: 'The effect of the King's visit North has been excellent.'[26] But although Rochdale and Manchester went back to work Liverpool and Sheffield workers came out on strike and Lloyd George instructed the police to 'Proceed against the intimidators.' Seven of the ten militants on the

[24] Thomson, *Queer People* (1922) p. 269.
[25] Thomson, *The Scene Changes* (1939) p. 359.
[26] *Ibid.*, p. 338.

Branch's list who could be found were arrested but this only increased the strikers' determination and a reluctant TUC was asked to intercede by the Cabinet to bring the strike to an end.

The success of the October 1917 Revolution in Russia encouraged socialist movements all over Europe, and Britain was no exception. In the months that followed many Councils of Action were set up by socialists modelled on the Soviets, and the Bolshevik cause gained a large measure of support. The police and the Branch were stretched all ways, desperately trying to keep up both with the new groups sympathetic to communist ideas and with strikes in industry. In August 1918 the police went on strike and the Branch was given the job of infiltrating the ranks of the militant police unionists and reporting on their activities to the Cabinet.[27]

Early in 1917 a plot to assassinate Lloyd George and other Cabinet Ministers was uncovered by a 'tip-off' to the Branch. The reported plan was to assassinate the Prime Minister while he was playing golf at Walton Heath by the use of a blow-pipe which would emit a small dart tipped with curare – a deadly South American poison. After the mail of the conspirators was opened and proof obtained of the plot four people were arrested and put on trial. The trial at the Old Bailey took five days and the jury found three of the four guilty of conspiracy to murder – the arch-conspirator Mrs Wheeldon was given ten years' penal servitude, George Mason, her son-in-law and a chemist, got seven years, and Winnie Mason (her daughter) got five years. (A second daughter, Harriet Wheeldon, was acquitted). This story has been told many times in histories of the police but the truth of the case may well be very different. Let us reconstruct the events of December 1916 and January 1917.

Mrs Wheeldon and her two daughters had been militant suffragettes for many years and, also being socialists, they opposed the war, particularly after the introduction of conscription. Mrs Wheeldon's son was a conscientious objector who was on the run from the authorities, and she often extended the hospitality of her home in Derby to other conscientious objectors passing through the city. Like many other socialists at this time she was inclined to employ the use of very strong words in reference to members of the Cabinet, the Prime Minister, and the King, in her daily conversation. The other group of 'plotters' involved in this scenario were based in the intelligence department of the

[27] See pp. 68–69.

Ministry of Munitions (created by Lloyd George in 1915). The three men involved were Major Lee, head of one of the sections of the intelligence department; Herbert Booth, who started work with the department in September 1916 and who acted as middle-man; and Alexander Gordon, who was employed by Booth and Lee as an agent-provocateur.[28]

On 26 December 1916 Gordon was sent to Derby by Booth to present himself to Mrs Wheeldon as a conscientious objector on the run, and as on many such previous occasions he was afforded the generous hospitality of the Wheeldon household. Three days later Gordon introduced Booth to Mrs Wheeldon as 'Comrade Bert', a fugitive from the army. Within four days Major Lee himself went to Derby to meet the conspirators and arranged for all the Wheeldon mail to be opened. The crux of this case revolves around the four phials of poison Mrs Wheeldon received in the post from her chemist son-in-law in Southampton. The Crown case rested on the alleged plot to kill Lloyd George and Arthur Henderson, a Labour MP who joined the War Cabinet (a 'class traitor' in Mrs Wheeldon's terms). Much was made of Mrs Wheeldon's remarks about the Prime Minister, the Cabinet and the King, the inference being that this was the kind of person – suffragette, pacifist and socialist – who would perpetrate this deed.[29]

Mrs Wheeldon's version is very different. She told the court it was true she had voiced strong opinions about the Prime Minister and others but this was not the same as acting on them. Gordon had come to her posing as a conscientious objector and had said he had helped men escape from concentration camps.[30] As a result of the escapes guard dogs were now being used and Gordon suggested poison was needed to overcome this obstacle. In exchange for getting the poison for Gordon he promised to help her fugitive son escape to America. She admitted sending for the poison and receiving it, but this was then handed over to Booth (Comrade Bert). Therefore at the time of her arrest the poison was in the hands of Booth and Gordon. Mrs Wheeldon categorically denied the alleged 'plot' of assassination. At

[28] Thomson notes in his *Story of Scotland Yard* (p. 240) that Gordon had a thick criminal-record file.

[29] The use of the beliefs and life-styles of defendants in political trials – although theoretically inadmissible – is a consistent feature of state prosecutions.

[30] When the prisons could hold no more conscientious objectors, camps were opened in various parts of the country where the men were employed as forced labour.

the trial only Major Lee and Herbert Booth appeared as prosecution witnesses – the key witness, Gordon, was not presented by the state. The case against Mrs Wheeldon and the three others thus rested on a couple of letters, the poison phials (the purpose of whose acquisition was in dispute) and the sole evidence of Booth as to the nature of the 'plot'. Mrs Wheeldon was eventually released before the end of her prison sentence because of ill-health and died shortly afterwards.[31]

The two years immediately after the end of the First World War saw the exacerbation of the political and industrial struggles which had emerged in 1917 and 1918. In 1918 there were 1,252 strikes with the loss of 6 million working days, and in 1919 more than 1,400 strikes and the loss of 34 million working days (involving two-and-a-half million workers). Indeed things were so bad that Thomson recalls the occasion Lloyd George summoned him to No. 10 to reassure a group of Tory and Labour MPs that the politically subversive elements in the country were under control. Thomson told them: 'The routine of the "Home" section of my staff was to attend subversive meetings all over the country and to obtain evidence of money passing from Russia to the extremist section of Labour.'[32] In the period immediately after the armistice the various intelligence departments set up by the different Ministries continued to gather information independently. The inefficiency of this arrangement became apparent to Lloyd George and his Cabinet who, having been impressed by Thomson's performance during the war, decided to hive off the Special Branch at Scotland Yard from the CID and give it the co-ordinating role. George Dilnot, in his book *Scotland Yard*, succinctly describes Thomson's job as being to 'save England from "Red" machinations'.[33] Thomson, while retaining the position of Assistant Commissioner, was also given the grand title of 'Director of Intelligence'. This arrangement came into force in May 1919 and lasted until 1922 when the Special Branch was again placed within the auspices of the CID – albeit still with a large measure of independence.

The cause of Thomson's dismissal in 1921 and the end of this special arrangement have often been interpreted as resulting from a disagreement between Thomson and the new Commissioner of the Metropolitan Police. The reasons offered by Thomson himself are

[31] See *Political Spies and Provocative Agents*, written and published by F. W. Chandler (1933).

[32] Thomson, *The Scene Changes* (1939) p. 387.

[33] Dilnot (1929) p. 264.

two-fold. Firstly, it appears that a few days before his dismissal four young Irishmen got in to the grounds of Chequers (the Prime Minister's official out-of-town residence) and painted 'Up the Sinn Fein' on the summerhouse. The police guarding the grounds – Lloyd George was not there – arrested the four and sent them to Thomson at Scotland Yard. He satisfied himself that it was only a prank and with a warning let them go. However when Lloyd George heard of the event he took a different view; he was very shaken that such a thing could happen. Thomson was summoned to the Commons and found himself confronted by Lloyd George, General Horwood (the Commissioner), Mr Shortt (Home Secretary) and others. Lloyd George launched into a damning attack backed by General Horwood. The meeting broke up and Thomson was informed by the Home Secretary he was to retire five years before his time, and this was immediately followed by a visit by Sir Warren Fisher, the Permanent Under-Secretary at the Treasury, who on Lloyd George's orders offered Thomson a generous pension providing he left immediately and without a fuss. Thomson had, at sixty, few options.

Clearly the anger of the Prime Minister marked the end of a long-standing relationship, for Lloyd George and Thomson had worked closely together since 1916. Thomson himself believed that some of the subjects of his reports – the Labour leaders – had brought strong pressure to bear. The truth of the matter probably lies less in the antagonisms between the individuals than in the struggle between the various agencies. The police (including the CID) resented the independence of the Branch, particularly as much of the Branch's reputation depended on reports from police officers up and down the country. More importantly, the War Office was adamant that the newly-formed MI5 should continue in the post-war period. In this unequal struggle Thomson lost out, and MI5 staked its claim to extend its anti-espionage activities to anti-subversion as well. Because MI5 was more secretive and less accountable this change had many attractions. The Branch retained a marginal interest in espionage by thereafter acting as the arresting officers for MI5, although their work of keeping political subversives under surveillance continued in a more limited fashion. But let us return to 1919 and the formation of Thomson's independent squad.

Although the war ended in 1918 many of the British troops were not disbanded for about two years. In January 1919 military riots broke out in Folkestone, and a little later troops seized Calais. Other troops had to be sent to surround them. In London some soldiers drove their trucks to the War Office and blocked the entrance, and later, three thousand troops, en route through London, marched on Whitehall. They were disarmed by the Guards. During this period, in which occurred the police strike of 1919, strikes on the 'Red' Clyde, and opposition to Britain's help for the counter-revolutionary White Russians, the Branch concentrated its attention on the Bolsheviks and those sympathetic to their cause. Today it is difficult to imagine that a body such as The Soldiers', Sailors' and Airmen's Union could be regarded as revolutionary, but in 1919 this was so. The Union 'had wholeheartedly accepted the Soviet idea and was in touch with the more revolutionary members of the London Trades Council . . .'[34] One of the responses of the Branch in 1920 was to help a group of White Russian emigrés produce forged copies of the Bolshevik daily paper, *Pravda*. The paper, an exact likeness of the real thing, carried a series of boastful tales of Bolshevik executions, terror squads, and murders. The London printer insisted on including the firm's imprint on the paper, and the emigrés were grateful to the Branch for providing a Yard guillotine to chop this off the bottom of the page. In 1921 the *Daily Herald* exposed the affair and the Home Secretary admitted in the Commons the role of state employees.[35]

In 1922, the year of independence for the twenty-six counties, the Irish problem was again brought home to the English when the Chief of the Imperial General Staff, Field Marshal Sir Henry Wilson, was assassinated in London on 23 June. The two Sinn Fein members who shot him were caught and hanged. The Branch came in for particular criticism as their special responsibility for Ireland was meant to preempt such events. As if to restore its jaded name the Branch got to work up-dating its intelligence on Irish groups in England and on 11 March 1923 – acting on the instructions of the Home Secretary – it deported one hundred members of Irish political groups in England. The chosen one hundred were arrested, and taken by destroyer to Ireland where they were immediately interned. The legality of the acts by the Home Secretary and the Branch was challenged in the House of Lords, which held the deportation to be illegal and the state had to pay out £50,000 in compensation to the men.

On the home front the formation of the Communist Party in 1920 meant that another group had to be watched. One of the many sources

[34] Thomson, *Queer People* (1922) p. 296.
[35] *Daily Herald*, 28 February 1921.

of information on their activities was the well-tried practice of Branch
officers attending political meetings. However, it was not always easy
for them to gain entry to those held indoors. So it was that in April
1924 two Special Branch officers were discovered under the platform
of the Rehearsal Theatre where the Communist Party was holding a
conference. Once discovered they were so keen to get away that their
notebooks were left behind. The Labour government Home Secretary,
Mr Henderson, was questioned by MPs and Lieutenant-Commander
Kenworthy (Liberal member for Hull City) refused to withdraw the use
of the term 'spies': 'I addressed my question to the Home Secretary. I
was not attacking the minions of the law at all. I was attacking the
policy of the Department.'[36]

During the 1926 General Strike all the forces of law and order were
pitted against the unions, but the part played by the Branch was
marginal to that played by the police, the Special Constabulary, the
army and the emergency apparatus of the state.

The hunger marches and the IRA

One movement which had occupied the attention of the Branch for
many years was the National Unemployed Workers' Movement
(NUWM). The first self-organised groups of unemployed were the
ex-servicemen who came home from the war to find not a new world
but widespread poverty – by 1920 unemployment was over two
million. In 1921 the NUWM was formed and Wal Hannington was appointed as organiser.[37] Much play was made by the authorities during
the 1920s over communist influence within the NUWM, but although
they were a strong influence on national decision-making it is
ludicrous to suggest they were 'in control' of the mass movement at
local levels. In the community the NUWM branches organised
marches and petitions, as well as helping their comrades tackle the
social security officers to gain their full entitlements. The first hunger
marches organised on a national basis were in 1922 and 1925, and
these were followed by five more between 1929 and 1936 – in 1929,
1930, 1932, 1934, and 1936. Throughout this period there were dozens
of pitched battles between the unemployed and the police, who often
used systematic baton charges. In Belfast two men were killed when the
police opened fire in 1932 and during this period hundreds of workers
were arrested.

[36] *The Times*, 15 April 1924.
[37] See W. Hannington's, *Never on Our Knees* (1967).

An examination of the police records for this period has revealed extensive infiltration between 1929 and 1935.[38] Throughout this period there was a Branch informer on the national decision-making council of the NUWM – and there is no evidence from the books later written by the movement's leaders that they were aware of this. Secondly, prior to each of the national marches detailed reports prepared by the local police were sent into Scotland Yard from each of the starting points. For example just before the 1932 march the following 'very urgent and confidential' memo was sent out by Scotland Yard:

'24.10.1932: To assist the Commissioner in taking any action he may consider necessary in connection with the Unemployed Demonstrations, will you please report as early as possible the names and addresses of any local or other leaders of the Communists or Unemployed against whom you possess evidence of incitement to create disturbance, or of participation in disturbance that have occurred.'[39]

Within forty-eight hours various provincial police forces reponded with information on 'militants' – names, addresses, police records and notes, and sometimes photographs as well. In addition to all this the Branch placed all the national leaders under surveillance and its *Daily Bulletin* for 17 October 1932 recorded the movements of Wal Hannington, Emrhys Llewellyn and Harry Pollitt. Some of those actively sympathetic to the poverty of the unemployed were also watched. They included the Secretary of the National Council for Civil Liberties, Ronald Kidd, whose movements were noted in a report sent by the Commissioner to the Home Secretary in March 1936. The summary of this report stated that Kidd was 'well-known for his antipathy against the police and their methods'.[40] Detailed transcripts of speeches made at meetings of the unemployed were also in the police files, and these included speeches by Clement Attlee (leader of the Labour Party), Aneurin Bevan MP, and Arthur Horner, an official of the miners' union.

The information from the 'informer' in the NUWM national council, headed 'The following information has been received', was both

[38] See 'The Police and the Hunger Marchers', by Ralph Hayburn, in the *International Review of Social History*, Vol. 17, no. 3, pp. 625–644 (1972).

[39] *Ibid.*

[40] See Kidd, *British Liberty in Danger* (1940) for his account of police activity at this time.

regular and detailed. It included notes on the discussions in meetings, circulars and maps of planned marches. What was the effect of all this information? Clearly it did not stop the movement's activities, but it did allow the police to be well-prepared for 'any eventuality'. Moreover, the near-paranoia in some of the filed reports and the over-reaction of the politicians produced in turn a violent response from the police on almost every occasion.[41] The activities of the unemployed were completely legitimate political actions within the liberal-democratic system – marching, petitioning and making speeches – yet the Branch and the police infiltrated the movement, followed its leaders, attacked peaceful marches, and prepared lists of 'militants' to be arrested if the chance arose.

The size of the Branch varied only slightly during the 1920s and 1930s. At the end of the First World War there were one-hundred-and-fifty officers but this dropped to one-hundred-and-twenty by 1920 – a level that remained constant until the mid-1930s. In 1934 it was announced that sixty-four additional officers had been assigned to Branch work, bringing the total to two hundred. The reason given for the increase was subversive activity, which as usual was attributed to external rather than internal causes: 'The large increase in personnel will enable Lord Trenchard to deal more effectively with certain political elements in this country which have within recent months shown a pronounced tendency to work in closer alliance with foreign factions of a similar nature.'[42] In the latter part of the 1930s Branch surveillance extended to the supporters of the revolutionary struggle in Spain, and particularly to the volunteers who went to join the International Brigades.

As war with Hitler loomed on the horizon in 1939 the attention of the Branch had yet again to be devoted to Ireland. In January 1939 the IRA launched a massive bombing campaign which lasted until February 1940. Between January and June 1939 there were 127 bombings in which one person was killed and fifty-five injured. In August a bomb in Coventry Street in London killed five and injured eighty. Immediately the bombings started parliament passed the Prevention of Violence (Temporary Provisions) Act, 1939.[43] The Act gave wider

[41] In 1934 the Home Secretary, in a widely reported speech, called on the people of London to keep their children off the streets and to batten down their windows as the 1934 march approached London.

[42] *Daily Mail*, 6 December, 1934.

[43] The Act was intended to last for two years, but it was reviewed yearly until 1954.

powers of search to the police, the power of detention for five days (which meant suspension of habeas corpus), and the power of immediate deportation by the Home Secretary. In addition, suspected IRA sympathisers could be required to register with the local police. To exercise the power of deportation and registration the Home Secretary had to be 'reasonably satisfied' that a person was connected with the IRA. Ronald Kidd, the Secretary of the NCCL, observed that sufficient powers already existed without the introduction of a measure which did not afford protection to the individual against arbitrary power. Hundreds of Irishmen and women were deported and interned when they arrived in Ireland; many were jailed in England; and two, Peter Barnes and Frank McCormick, were hanged for the Coventry Street bombing.

The Cold War and the Campaign for Nuclear Disarmament

The practices of the Branch after 1945 are largely indicative of their methods today, comprising both long-standing responsibilities and new ones arising out of more recent political activities. The same contradiction remained – between the liberal-democratic right to pursue political ideas and actions contrary to those of the prevailing order, and, on the other hand, the consistent surveillance and harassment of those engaged in activities perceived to be a danger by the agencies of the state. Two police histories written in the early 1950s recognise the supremacy of the latter position. Writing in 1950 Hart stated that the Branch is 'the political police for the whole country. It aims at collecting information about "undesirable" political persons and movements wherever their headquarters are situated.'[44] Sir Harold Scott, Commissioner of the Metropolitan Police (1945–1953) wrote in 1954:

'The Special Branch is a part of the CID, and is primarily an intelligence department. Its business is to keep a watch on any body of people, of whatever political complexion, *whose activities seem likely to result sooner or later* in open acts of sedition or disorder.'[45]

Scott's description of the scope of the Branch's surveillance is adequate to justify the inclusion of every politically active person. The history of the Branch's work shows this to be exactly the situation. Although there has been a dominant interest in extra-parliamentary groups,

[44] J. Hart, *The British Police* (1951) p. 117.
[45] Sir H. Scott, *Scotland Yard* (1957) p. 219. My emphasis.

liberals and socialists (of all complexions) have also come under their eye.

In March 1946 Albert Canning, who had been head of the Branch since 1936, retired and was replaced by Commander Leonard Burt. Although Burt had started as a policeman in the CID he was seconded for the duration of the war to MI5 and there headed the section devoted to foiling German espionage. One of the problems faced by Burt in his new job was an unusual one for the Branch – the curtailment of their powers. Some time after the end of the war protests were made to the new Labour Party Home Secretary by local Communist Party groups that the Branch had planted agents in their organisations. The Minister thought such activities un-British and ordered the infiltration to stop, which most of it duly did. However, just over a year later thousands of people from the East End proceeded to occupy empty houses and flats around the centre of London. The homeless squatters took everyone by surprise in a highly-organised coup, and the Home Office quickly reversed its previous ruling.

The Cold War and the beginnings of Britain's MacCarthyite era – when a purge of Communists from the Civil Service was undertaken – also led to a closer working relationship between the Branch and MI5 on the question of espionage. Not all Branch officers were engaged on this liaison work with MI5. It has been the practice for a senior officer of the Branch to be permanently seconded to this duty, and all other officers liable to be called on are specially vetted by MI5. The Branch also extended its surveillance at ports and airports beyond the rather *ad hoc* practice of the 1920s and early 1930s. This work included watching for the following: aliens who had previously been deported, individuals whose criminal activities abroad made them undesirable entrants, 'known' foreign agents, and known British and foreign political activists. In respect of the latter, movements in and out of the country are noted and filed. For this purpose the Branch officer (or often the Passport Officer if he is on duty alone) has a little black book with the names and addresses of those in whom the Branch and police are interested.

In the late 1940s there was a series of dock strikes in London and Merseyside; the government were convinced that Communists and political extremists were behind the strikes. The Branch set up a special squad to find the ringleaders. Part of their ploy was to discredit one of the organisers of the unofficial Port Workers' Committee for London with his union. Branch officers hid in the vicinity of a meeting room in Canning Town and recorded a speech by the organiser in question, and their records of the meeting were used by Arthur Deakin, then General Secretary of the Transport and General Workers Union, to expel the man from his union. In April 1951 seven dockers, including the already victimised man, were arrested and brought to trial. The primary charge was inciting the dockers to strike contrary to a 1940 wartime Act still in force, and the bulk of the evidence against them was speeches recorded by Branch officers. At the trial Branch officers admitted they had often not transcribed the whole of a speech, but only that part they considered might be used in evidence, and one officer admitted he had been following one of the defendants for two years.

The role of the uniformed police in the gathering of political intelligence has already been mentioned in relation to public order, but there is one practice which is little realised. One of the consequences of the anti-communism (that is, anti-leftwing) purges in the Civil Service and government-contract firms, which started in 1948, was that Chief Constables throughout the country were given instructions to compile lists of people believed to be members of the Communist Party and its front organisations. Copies of these lists are collated nationally by the Special Branch (who also forward copies to MI5). This practice continues today and it is well-known that one of the sources of local information is the corner newsagent who is regularly asked for the names and addresses of those people ordering the *Morning Star*. Another of the lists held and up-dated by the local police is of registered aliens. One of the reasons for holding these lists is the restriction on political and trade union activities placed on aliens – under the 1908 Act they may not be active in a trade union unless they have been employed with a particular firm for at least two years. Such activities can lead to a recommendation for deportation, or to a refusal when application is made for naturalisation. And as has already been noted it is the Branch who vet all applications and put in a report to the Home Secretary.

It was the organised opposition to the government's H-bomb policy and the farce of the state's civil defence programme which presented the Branch and the police with an almost insurmountable problem from the mid-1950s. CND, and later Direct Action and the Committee of 100, embraced not just a few hundred hard-core activists but many thousands of people from every kind of background. There were teachers, students, middle-class mothers, vicars, social workers, civil servants, academics and many more. This was in addition to support from the left of the Labour Party, most trade unions, and the Communist Party. Demonstrations at local and national level did present a problem of public order for the police and Special Branch, but there were other considerations which necessitated an attempt (and this was all it could be) to place on file all those taking part. One reason was that many of those concerned with intelligence and surveillance saw people's participation as being tantamount to having communist 'sympathies'. Another more direct reason was that some of these people might seek to gain employment as civil servants in a research establishment, try to join the Army or police, or a firm doing sensitive work for the Ministry of Defence. Particularly after the events which led to the setting up of the Radcliffe Commission in 1962 this latter factor became crucial to the Branch and the police (and to the other agencies). Yet again the line between 'legal' democratic action and 'illegal' action lost its meaning as files were opened on all and sundry.

A foretaste of police interest came in 1957 when a group of mothers in Mill Hill organised a meeting at a local Congregational Church hall. After the meeting a uniformed police officer approached the organiser of the meeting and asked for the names and addresses of the speakers and organisers. 'Never fear', said the policeman, 'this is just a normal sort of thing. We always check on this sort of meeting.' The organiser was also asked who arranged meetings and marches and for the names of those taking part. Sydney Silverman, a Labour MP, commented: 'The wickedness is hidden in its insidious courtesy.'[46] Some of the methods used by local police to gather information were to attend meetings like the one above; to note letters to the local paper for names and addresses of CND sympathisers; to note the registration numbers of cars parked outside meetings and add the owners' names from the records; to take photographs of those on marches in the cities; and in other areas to ask for prints from the local papers (which usually obliged). At national level the Branch received lists from the local police forces to which were added the names of those signing petitions to parliament, those writing to the national press, pictures from the files of national newspapers, information sent in by the patriotic public; these were in addition to information from their usual means of surveillance.

One of the many examples of their methods which came to light in this period was in 1962. Mrs X who worked in a small village in the south of England was visited at work by a policeman who proceeded to ask if her son was a communist; he went on to say that he might be a security risk. The only basis for this questioning was the fact that the eighteen-year-old son was the local secretary of CND and active in the

---

[46] *Reynolds News*, 30 June 1957.

Anti-Apartheid Movement. The NCCL wrote to the Chief Constable about the case and asked whether this was connected with the compilation of lists of political activists. They received the stock answer to such enquiries: 'With regard to the statement alleged to have been made by the Constable, this is not true, and no such list is in the process of being prepared.'[47]

If the police and the Branch were hard put to keep track of all those sympathetic to the disarmers then something close to panic ensued in April 1963 when the 'Spies for Peace' pamphlet was published giving full details of the state's underground network of Regional Seats of Government. While the national media largely observed the restrictions of the D-Notices no such inhibitions could stop the duplication of the information in the pamphlet by hundreds of groups up and down the country. Each leaflet had to be followed up by the local police in the vain hope it would lead back to the originators. The possibilities of the source of the leak abounded – had it been planted by the Russians, had it been leaked by a member of the government or worse still by a member of one of the intelligence agencies? The Home Secretary declared: 'This is the work of a traitor.'[48] Despite all the efforts of the police, the Special Branch and the intelligence agencies, no-one was found.[49]

The year of 1961 was a critical one for the Branch, because both the CND campaign was in full swing and the Radcliffe inquiry into the efficiency of the security services was under way. In part this inquiry reflected on the efficiency of the Branch, but even before the report came out the Branch began its own internal reorganisation. In the period immediately before the reorganisation, 1955 to 1961, the strength of the Branch had increased from 150 to about 220 officers. All of these were based at Scotland Yard. Outside London, apart from at the major ports and airports, the role of the Branch was undertaken by officers of the CID from the uniformed branch seconded temporarily to these duties when the need arose. The secondment was unofficial in that there was no authorised establishment allowed for the duties (i.e. no money and resources); moreover there was no chance

[47] Letter to the General Secretary of the NCCL from Sup. Gunning of the Surrey Constabulary, dated 19 October 1962.
[48] *Daily Mail*, 15 April 1963.
[49] The impact of the 'Spies for Peace' pamphlet and the reaction to its publication is documented in *Resistance Shall Grow* (1963); the story of how the information got out is in 'Inside Story', No. 8, March/April 1973.

for promotion and it was generally considered as a dead-end job. The net effect was that centrally the Branch was relatively well-organised but everywhere else it had to rely on an *ad hoc* system.

After 1961 several changes were made. The first change was the decision to extend the Branch to cover the whole country and not just London. Secondly, it was decided that each regional squad, although nominally answerable to the Chief Constable, would in fact report directly to the Branch at Scotland Yard. Thus both the Branch at the Yard and the Home Office could request information of the regional squads without going through the usual channels.[50] Thirdly, it was decided that each of the regional Branch squads should collate and assess the intelligence gathered on subversive groups by the local police forces; carry out surveillance of firms engaged on state contract work; and handle applications for naturalisation. Finally each of the regional Branch squads were to comprise not less than six officers permanently seconded from the CID departments and each was to be headed an an inspector. When these changes became effective over one hundred officers had been assigned to Branch duties outside of London, bringing the total number of officers in the country to about 450. Hence, although MI5 had been operating on a country-wide basis in relation to internal surveillance since the 1920s, the Branch, however, did not follow suit until the 1960s.

The Radcliffe report, published in 1962, extended the work of the Branch into the vetting of civil servants – a process which happens on appointment and when promotions are made to sensitive or high-grade posts. Prior to this date it appears that only irregular checks were made with the Criminal Records Office and the Branch's Registry files. The administrative staffs at the Yard were increased to cope with this new check. In 1964 it was the turn of the Branch men themselves to be screened for security risks – that is, for subversive histories (of them or close relatives), deviant characters, or financial indebtedness. Each of the officers was screened by two Branch superintendents, and these two officers were in turn themselves given the once-over by MI5. The screening included an interview at home with the officer and his family, the questioning of neighbours, of the children's school head and teachers, the visiting of known friends and a personal interview with the two referees provided by the officer in question. Every stage of an officer's life was examined, from school through all the subsequent

---

[50] MI5 inquiries are directed through Branch Headquarters at the Yard, and only rarely is there direct contact with provincial offices.

stages of his career in the uniformed police and the Branch. It is not known whether any bad apples were thrown up.

During the period after the Second World War there were three heads of the Branch. The first, already mentioned, was Commander Burt who retired in 1958 to be succeeded by Deputy Commander E. W. Jones. Jones retired in December 1966 and Detective Chief Superintendent Ferguson G. D. Smith took over as head of the Branch. Like Burt before him Ferguson Smith had for many years been the liaison officer with MI5 in espionage cases. Apart from the Commissioner of the Metropolitan Police, the head of the Special Branch is the only other officer at the Yard able to communicate directly with the Home Office without going through the usual channels. He is also on occasion asked to report on a case directly by the Cabinet Office on behalf of the Prime Minister.

This brief history of the Branch has shown how and when the different responsibilities emerged, and how, since its formation, it has acted against political groups and individual activists. What must now be outlined is the way in which the Branch operates today and what methods are available to it.

PART II *THE SPECIAL BRANCH TODAY* 1964–75

The headquarters of the Branch is on the top floor of Scotland Yard in Victoria Street, though some of the specialist squads operate from offices dotted around London (for example, the Irish Squad). The current head of the Special Branch is Deputy Assistant Commissioner Victor Gilbert, who took over when Ferguson Smith retired in October 1972. Under Gilbert are the three Commanders in charge of the main sections of the Branch – Administration, Ports and Operations (currently Commander Matthew Rodger).[51]

The day-to-day working of the Branch involves it with two other national agencies – the Home Office and MI5. In addition to checking espionage the other area of joint interest to the Branch and MI5 is in-

---

[51] In 1970 all London police ranks were brought into line with those of the regions and the head of the Branch became Deputy Assistant Commissioner instead of a Commander.

ternal subversion. All the information held by the Branch compiled from country-wide reports is made available to MI5. The reverse however is not the case; MI5 may or may not respond to a request for information by Branch officers. This practice stems from their respective historical roles: the Branch operates only partially undercover while MI5's work is totally undercover. Moreover MI5 has nearly ten times as many people working on internal subversion as the Branch. The tacit superiority of the Branch over the CID at the Yard is reversed in their relations with MI5. It would be easy, therefore, to underestimate the importance of the Branch's work in deference to the larger and more secretive body. But to do so would be to misunderstand the nature of the state's intelligence-gathering. Put quite simply the rationale is that two sources of information are better than one and in practice at least five independent sources are available. A secondary rationale is that the Branch is able to approach people openly and ask for information, and what is given freely does not necessitate the subterfuge and expense of secrecy and infiltration. It is also a mistake to underestimate the role of the uniformed police in intelligence-gathering for both of the above reasons.

The Special Branch has a much closer relationship than MI5 with the Home Office. This is primarily because the Branch is the main source of information for the Home Office in an area for which the Home Office is primarily responsible – the centuries-old one of maintaining internal order.[52] The intelligence about political movements which is presented by the Branch in their regular reports to the Home Office is a compilation of both their own efforts and those of the uniformed police throughout the country. Branch reports represent their assessment of new groups and new developments, or relate to a known event (like a future strike, or a recent demonstration). Regular reports of this kind are submitted to F4 Department in the Home Office – the one responsible for public order, security liaison and subversive activities. This department in turn will reach its own assessment of the subject area of a report and, if necessary, pass on its own report to the Deputy Under Secretary in charge of the Police Department, and so on up the line to the Home Secretary. At another level will be the Branch investigation of a particular event (a bombing, inflammatory speech or allegation of Branch interference). To this extent much of the traffic between the Branch and the Home Office is often in response to an outside demand from parliament or the press.

[52] See chapter 4 for the relationship of the Home Office to MI5.

The formal chain of accountability for the Branch is through the Commissioner of the Metropolitan Police, but in practice the head of the Branch reports directly to the Permanent Under-Secretary and/or the Home Secretary on matters of general policy. However it would be incorrect to think the policy of the Branch is determined by the Home Office. Constitutionally the Branch is part of the police force and answerable to the law and not to parliament, therefore while the Home Office lays down (in reality, agrees) guidelines for action, operations are firmly in the hands of the Branch.

When a Labour MP attempted to find out the cost of the Branch in early 1970 he was informed that 'there is no separate Estimate for the Special Branch and no detailed financial information concerning this branch is published.'[53] Similarly when Eric Moonman MP asked the Home Secretary to make a statement on the extent and nature of the Branch's political records he was told by Mr Callaghan, in a written reply: 'The security of the state necessarily requires that I should be in possession of certain information about political affiliations, which it would not be in the public interest to disclose.'[54]

Responsibilities and staff

The historical account of the Branch showed the development of its areas of responsibility from the 1880s. Today its duties include:

1. The guarding of royalty, ministers and visiting public dignitaries. This traditional role is somewhat changed today. The guarding of the Royal Family and of senior Cabinet ministers is undertaken by officers from the CID trained specially in protection duties and seconded from Scotland Yard. (They are also armed.) The Branch provides personal guards for visiting dignitaries particularly as an important part of its work centres on the surveillance of emigré groups, e.g. of the Portuguese community prior to the visit of Caetano in 1973.

2. The watching of ports and airports. This continues to be undertaken by the Branch though during 1973 the demands placed on it as a whole necessitated the recruitment of officers direct from the CID to take on some of this work, which released trained Branch officers for investigations and surveillance. With the aid of the little black book these officers watch for terrorists, undesirable political and criminal

[53] Letter from House of Commons Library to Peter Jackson, MP, 12 January 1970.

[54] *The Times*, 18 March 1970.

entrants, and log the movements of known political activists in and out of the country.

3. The watching and guarding of embassy buildings, and of individual diplomats at certain times, and work related to this. Warnings are given of possible threats against the embassy and its personnel; lists of potential 'assassins' are compared when a figurehead is due to visit; surveillance of the embassy of an 'unfriendly' country may be carried out (although this is mainly carried out by MI5); and embassy officials may be 'warned-off' certain activities via a Foreign Office man.

4. The Branch's relationship with MI5 over espionage has already been noted: it includes forwarding to MI5 intelligence in this field; assisting in the last stages of surveillance; making arrests, preparing evidence for court, and appearing at trials.

5. The surveillance of subversive organisations is dealt with in detail on pp. 135 ff. The continuing responsibility for Irish affairs has meant that one section of the Branch has always been engaged in this field, moreover its brief includes the whole of Ireland (north and South). Not surprisingly the strength of the Irish squad has been supplemented several times in recent years.

6. The monitoring of aliens entering the country and the vetting of applications for naturalisation for the Home Office continues to be one of its duties. (This work is related to 7 below.)

7. The Branch contributes to the preparation of lists of foreigners, and those of foreign parentage, in anticipation of a state of war existing between Britain and another country. The precedents for this operation were clearly set in 1914 and in 1939 when hundreds of Germans were interned within hours of the outbreak of war, and the movements of many others were restricted to their immediate locality. The preparations of the state for any eventuality require a continual assessment of exactly who should be interned in certain circumstances, so that the national and local leaderships of political groups must be determined.

8. The Branch also has a special responsibility for offences against the Official Secrets Acts.[55]

9. Finally, in 1973 it was assigned the duty of investigating offences in relation to the conduct of elections. This was previously carried out by the CID at the Yard.

The work of the Branch outside of London (while it excludes certain national functions) embraces the surveillance of subversive groups in

[55] See p. 207 for example of their role in the *Railway Gazette* case.

the community and in industry, aliens, and ports and airports. Each of the forty-one provincial forces now has a small squad of officers permanently assigned to Branch duties. The size of these groups varies but is generally between eight and twelve officers. The chain of communication is similar to that of the Branch nationally, but the responsibility to the local Chief Constable is mainly theoretical, and communications are usually carried out directly between the regional Branch squad and the headquarters in London. Much of the initiative and information comes from London, for example details of local political activists will often be supplied by Scotland Yard to supplement that gathered regionally. It should be noted here that the lack of democratic accountability evident in the relationship of the police to the local authorities is even greater where the Branch is concerned.

As has been the practice for many years today's Branch recruits directly from the constables of the uniformed police after they have served the statutory two-year probationary term. The volunteer recruits must in addition to passing a security screening be able either to write shorthand or speak a foreign language. The former skill is useful for recording political speeches and the latter for the monitoring of immigrant communities. Today the Branch represents an alternative career structure to that in the CID or the uniformed police, and to this extent there is a certain amount of rivalry between the personnel of the three groups.

One of the more confusing aspects of the Branch is the reported number of officers permanently engaged in its work. Since the 1920s no official figures have been given to parliament and estimates have rested on the 'informed' opinions presented in the press – which themselves vary widely. (In the wake of the Lennon murder in 1974 the press estimates varied from 300 to 1,000.) In broad terms from the beginning of the century to the late 1940s the size of the Branch fluctuated between 100 and 150 officers (except for wartime when the numbers rose to 800). From the late 1940s to the early 1960s the numbers increased slowly to the 200–225 mark. After the 1968 demonstrations and increased militancy on the Left, the strength of the Branch increased to 300. After 1970 the numbers rose, and by 1975 there were 550 officers working from Scotland Yard. Prior to 1968 the Branch was often supplemented by the temporary secondment of CID officers in relation to a specific event, like the 1939 IRA bombing campaign. However, the permanent increase in the size of the Branch is of recent origin and is a reflection of the state's response to increased militancy by political movements.

These figures refer only to the number of officers at national level. After the establishment in 1961 of small permanent squads outside London, the numbers of provincial Branch officers increased first from 50 to 120, and today are close to 450. The total strength of the Branch which was under 200 in the 1950s, was just over 1,000 full-time officers in 1975.[56] The low-level intelligence-gathering by the uniformed branch and CID has also correspondingly increased, and there are signs that part of the training of new constables will in future include a course in 'intelligence work'.

The Special Branch and the Left

Any consideration of who is placed under surveillance rests on criteria laid down by the Branch as to which groups constitute a threat to the security of the state and its personnel. During the 1950s references were commonly made to the monitoring of 'Communists' and all radical political activity was subsumed under this term. By the late 1960s the more colloquial terms were 'subversive' and 'terrorist'. The state's characterisation of a wide range of political activities as either 'Communist' or 'subversive' represents a handy means of portraying alien or violent interests at work. The Branch's current pre-occupation is with 'subversive' activity, against which it argues stronger measures are justified. Of course these terms have never in reality correctly described the positions of those placed under surveillance by the Branch and other state agencies. The liberal and the socialist (of the Labour Party variety) have been of as great an interest as the avowedly revolutionary. An historical study of the Branch (and the other agencies) shows only one consistent criterion – for 'subversive' read 'all those actively opposed to the prevailing order'.

The reassertion of extra-parliamentary action since the late 1960s has caused major problems for the Branch. In addition to the traditional political parties and reformist pressure groups, the left in the 1940s and 1950s largely comprised the Communist Party (and those pressure groups in which it played a major role), the left of the Labour Party, and trade union activists. Most of the organisations in which they were active were stable and centrally-organised. After 1968 the extra-parliamentary left took on a qualitatively new dimension. Its central characteristics (particularly as it has affected Branch work) were

[56] From a Commons reply given by Mr Jenkins in 1974 it can be estimated that the annual cost of the Special Branch is £5–6 million. *Hansard*, 20 June 1974, p. 46.

that its modes of action were not directed through the traditional channels (i.e. the parliamentary road to socialism) and that its 'organisation' was largely non-hierarchical and decentralised. The reassertion of militant (and often unofficial) industrial action by workers, the emergence of several socialist organisations in addition to the Communist Party (the International Socialists, the Workers' Revolutionary Party and the International Marxists), and the libertarian left (particularly in the local community), combined to present the Branch with many headaches. The life-style of many younger political activists constitutes a major obstacle for surveillance, as they tend to be the kind of people who move frequently, do not have telephones, change jobs, and do not necessarily leave forwarding addresses: more than once policemen or Branch officers have been known to say: 'Take me to your leader'. All these problems became apparent during the Bomb Squad investigation of the Angry Brigade when it was later admitted that the list of 'suspects' still numbered 137 people after many months of investigation.[57]

The Left is often said to have a misplaced conspiracy theory about the actions of the state and the ruling class in Britain; however, such theories are not the prerogative of the Left alone. The intelligence agencies of the state, including the Branch, have their own theory of the 'international communist (or anarchist) conspiracy' which seeks the overthrow of civilised societies and the democratic way of life. Such a simplistic notion leads some on the Left to dismiss the activities of the Branch on the basis of their supposed general lack of understanding of ideological questions. Again this is to misunderstand their function. In a society where they seek to uphold the prevailing order (of which they are part) the level of understanding required is that necessary for them to do their job, which is in effect to pre-empt over the long-term any revolutionary movement that threatens to gain mass support.

Sources of information

What then are the methods of information-gathering used by the Branch? Although it is impossible to enumerate all the methods, the following are some of those in most common use. (What may however come as a surprise is that about 75 per cent of all the information monitored by the Branch is either publicly available or freely given.)

1. All the names of political activists appearing in the press – national and local – are noted and indexed (especially if they appear in the *Mor-*

[57] See p. 48.

ning Star, *Socialist Worker* or *Workers Press*). Extra prints of demonstration pictures in newspapers can be requested of the paper's photographic department and the cuttings library will be used for background research; journalists are also asked for additional information on the subjects of their stories. This information is usually forthcoming in return for earlier (or potential) 'tip-offs' from the officer concerned. This source also extends to local newspapers. A Branch officer will pay occasional visits to the paper and strike up a friendly relationship with the leading reporters – the information requested varies from the address of people writing left-wing letters to the details of people attending the local trades councils.

2. All those signing petitions to parliament are indexed, even in the most innocuous causes.

3. Letters come in from members of the public, describing some activities of their neighbours, or with pictures of demonstrations naming someone they know.

4. The papers, magazines and leaflets of political groups contain much information of interest to the Branch. Where possible they subscribe to publications through a box number; in other cases Branch officers can on occasion be seen visiting left-wing book shops and information centres in search of new items.

5. Following raids by the Branch and the police the contents of address books, letters, cheque-stubs etc. are assiduously noted (and cross-indexed) to try and determine 'friendship networks' in cases of current surveillance.

6. In cases of high-level surveillance there will be information from telephone-tapping and mail-opening.

7. Trials of members of certain groups are watched for those who attend or help the defence (for example, in 'anarchist', Irish, trade union, and cases involving black people). Branch officers man the two entrances to the court – the public gallery, and the one into the main body of the court for the defence, press, friends of the defendants. And sometimes a room is rented opposite the court to photograph those going in and out.

8. Approaches for information are made to employers and state officials of all kinds, like social security officers, doctors, and teachers. For example, during the 1972 school students strikes in London several headmasters are known to have been approached for lists of those absent from school.

9. Meetings and demonstrations. A report on all demonstrations and any public meetings of significance is prepared either by the Branch

officer, or by a CID/uniformed policeman in attendance. The contents of speeches are noted and if made by a 'ring-leader' will be transcribed and held for future use. In addition at most demonstrations there is a Branch photographer, and at major ones video-cameras are used to film the whole length of a march. Observation of private meetings usually entails secretly observing those who attend and watching for any new faces. When the International Marxist Group moved into new premises in Caledonian Road in July 1974 they received an unexpected visit. A man called asking for a Mr Ross. Thinking he meant Comrade Ross the IMG worker said he was not in to which the caller replied: 'Well, there shouldn't be any problem. Its about the surveillance on Saturday. Mr Ross always lets us use the front room to watch the pub over the road.'[58] The pub in question is a traditional meeting place for left-wing groups.

10. There are individuals who give information to Branch officers. The need to get information was well-expressed by a security man after the Aldwych shooting who said: 'We have to get knowledge of who is saying what, and who is planning what. And we have to try and find out who is likely to be planning something and why.'[59] The level of Branch intelligence is not as sophisticated as this – though that of MI5 is – but it is the job of Branch officers to contribute to this understanding. There are five main types of informants, each with his own motives for passing information. There is the 'innocent' informer, active in an organisation or at his place of work, who tells the Branch officer only what he considers to be common knowledge ('everybody knows'). In the same category is the reactionary who is motivated by malice to give information on those he considers to be a danger to society or to threaten his own interests within the context of his work. Both of these categories are unpaid and are generally motivated either by a misguided sense of duty or by a sense of self-importance, though it is not unknown for those asked for information to refuse and then to tell the subject of the inquiry. Then there is the 'innocent' revolutionary who also communicates what 'everybody knows' – this kind of 'informer' is more common than generally realised. The paid informer is usually recruited by the Branch officer who recognises the need for help and pays small, irregular sums across (£5 to £10 a time), though this is comparatively rare. More commonplace is the 'paid-in kind' informer who is effectively blackmailed into giving information because the officer has some hold over him or her – embarrassing personal infor-

---

[58] *Guardian*, 12 July 1974.
[59] *Guardian*, 12 February 1973.

mation or the threat of bringing criminal charges on some minor offence. Finally, there are the undercover Branch men and women. Undercover work is mainly undertaken by the other intelligence agencies, although the Branch does employ a certain number of officers in this way. The numbers involved at any moment are quite small – usually not more than twenty or thirty officers. One area they seem to specialise in is the infiltration of *ad hoc* campaigns where few of the people know each other.

Having considered the methods by which the intelligence is gathered, let us look at how it is stored. There are three levels of classification in the Branch's Registry – the cards, the files, and those under 'active' files in current surveillance. In 1965 it was estimated that the Branch held records on more than two million people in this country.[60] The number is now nearer three million people though most of these warrant only an index card kept in the rows of steel filing-cabinets. A card will be opened on an individual whose name crops up through one of the means suggested above – letter to a paper, signing of a petition, secretary of a local group. For all practical purposes this is low-level surveillance which seeks to determine the size, affiliation and location of the politically active community in Britain. The next stage is when a file is opened on an individual and while several million may warrant index cards relatively fewer individuals are assigned a personal file. A file will be opened where an individual is considered to be an activist (militant) or occupies a position of importance in a left-wing group. The shop steward, black activist, and the persistent squatter will be placed alongside the left-wing lecturer, solicitor, journalist, and the full-time official of a radical group. The progression from the card index to the file-system is by no means automatic; it depends on whether a case investigation or a piece of 'inside' information brings a name and activities to its attention. This, in turn, is partly determined by the third category – that of surveillance.

Most surveillance is undertaken because of the investigation of a 'case' (leaking of an official secret, a strike, or a bombing). Firstly, the

---

[60] *The Observer*, 31 January 1965. There are three main Registries of intelligence information held by the state's repressive agencies: the Special Branch (who also have access to the criminal records held by the uniformed branch); MI5 whose files while covering much the same areas as the Branch are more numerous and more extensive; and thirdly, those of military intelligence which are handled by the Defence Intelligence Staff (DIS).

people who crop up in the course of an investigation are likely to be put on a file. Secondly, there is the on-going surveillance of certain groups. In this area would fall *ad hoc* committees (like the Stop the Seventy Tour Committee or the Vietnam Solidarity Campaign); permanent groups considered revolutionary (like the International Socialists, black groups, trade union branch committees, or claimants' unions); and more liberal organisations (the National Council for Civil Liberties or community groups) who have access to cases and information of interest to the Branch. Except in a specific investigation direct surveillance (like tailing) is rare and periodic, and is usually undertaken to check on new friends and activities in order to update the file record. The number of people under permanent surveillance is very limited and is usually in response to a specific event such as a strike or a planned demonstration.

Special Branch operations

The description given here of the Branch's means of intelligence-gathering and its methods of classification may have left the impression, despite the reservations expressed, of an all-embracing agency prying in depth into the lives of millions. This impression is not entirely justified. Of the five hundred officers based at Scotland Yard a substantial number are employed in two of the three main sections – Ports and Administration. Each of those involved in the third section, Operations, is assigned to one or more specialist areas, for example, to cover the Portuguese community in London, the black organisations, or Arab groups. Two or more officers are assigned to each interest area and their work is supervised by an Inspector who is in turn responsible for several groups in which the Branch has an interest. Within their speciality officers are expected to remain conversant with new faces, groups and publications. An important part of this is to establish friendly relations with key people in the field. Typically the officer seeks to appear sympathetic to the cause he is monitoring, and in order to gain the trust of his contacts will appear to be understanding about their problems (political or personal). In short, his skill is to establish a friendly and sympathetic relationship with people whose political activity is of interest to the Branch. Although this practice works very effectively, there have been numerous occasions when the officer has been taken for a ride. However, it would be a mistake to think Branch officers spend all their time working within their specialist area. Over a year much of their time will be spent on other duties like checking on naturalisation, doing a stint at the ports, joining a squad investigating a crime, or helping in the preparations for the visit of a foreign dignitary. In fact it is doubtful whether much more than half their working hours are directly concerned with their specialist political intelligence-gathering. On the other hand it would be wrong to underestimate how much information a few Branch officers are able to gather from a couple of days' work a week, for though this information by no means represents a complete picture, the effectiveness of their operations has been amply demonstrated over the years.

When a specific investigation is undertaken a squad is formed for the purpose (for example, the Yard Bomb Squad and its regional counterparts). These squads jointly comprise Branch and CID officers (usually from Criminal Intelligence). The reason for the union of these two branches lies in the particular skills of each group. While the Branch officers are interested in, and trained to look for, items of political significance, the CID officers are skilled at looking for evidence. The CID provides the ordinary detection work and the Branch the political understanding, and this distinction relates back to the recruitment of officers from the beat and the different training given to them. Squads of this kind are placed under the command of senior CID officers, while the Branch appoints a liaison officer (of Inspector rank or above) who is not a permanent member of the group. The work of such squads is mainly concerned with applying the usual methods of detection in criminal cases; surveillance; and carrying out raids on members of the 'suspect' group.

The information held by the Branch on the active political community in Britain is in itself a major intrusion into people's political freedom, but it is the actions of the Branch against individuals and groups that highlights the danger of a political police force. One of its common modes of action is to carry out raids on the homes of activists and on the offices of organisations. Raids in the context of political activity can be divided into three kinds. Firstly, there are those designed to catch a specific person (which is rare); secondly, those that can only be defined as 'fishing expeditions' (by far the most common form of raid); and finally, there is the 'face-saving' raid intended to create the impression that 'something is being done'. A classic example of the latter category occurred in 1966 when Mr Heath, as leader of the Opposition, received (together with fourteen other MPs) a fake invitation to attend a reception for the Deputy Premier of South Vietnam. Mr Heath (and the others) were duly turned away when they arrived at the Dorchester Hotel. Some days later it was reported that Branch officers 'made a series of lightning raids . . .'[61] In the event it appears they raided four or five offices and homes of members of the Committee of 100 and CND, and nothing was found although 'samples were taken away'. No-one was subsequently reported to have been arrested. Even in the first category, where the raid is intended to arrest a specific person, the procedure is open to abuse. When Wal Hannington was arrested in 1932 for alleged sedition the Branch raiding party took away 5 cwt of material from the headquarters of the National Unemployed Workers' Movement. Later the NUWM sued the police for this action and were awarded damages. At the hearing their counsel D. N. Pritt made a timeless comment on this practice:

'What disturbs my clients, and what they really desire to have stopped is that police officers can walk into the offices of a perfectly legal organisation, and, under the guise of arresting an individual, proceed to make a clean sweep of all documents, including accounts, collection cards, and to remove them all to Scotland Yard.'[62]

The blanket surveillance of demonstrations, political meetings, and industrial struggles by the Branch needs to be made quite clear. In September 1974 *Time Out* published extracts from the 'general orders' for London police, which related to 'Public and other events'. These extracts confirmed that the Branch is informed in advance of *all* political meetings known to the local police, and that – should Branch officers not attend – a report on all meetings is forwarded to them. The only political activities excluded from these orders would appear to be those concerning parliament and local councils. The most revealing aspect of these instructions relates to the part played by the Branch after an arrest:

'Whenever persons are arrested for offences connected with political activities including minor breaches of the peace and cases of slogan-daubing, etc., enquiry is always to be made of Special Branch to ascertain whether anything is known about the accused before the case is dealt with at Court. This enquiry will be in addition to any other searches made. Results of all cases are to be submitted to Special Branch.'[63]

Two comments on this statement will suffice. Firstly, it appears that in

[61] *Sun*, 25 August 1966.
[62] Wal Hannington, *Never on Our Knees* (1967) p. 279.
[63] *Time Out*, 20 September 1974.

addition to the usual check through the Criminal Records Office to see if there are any previous convictions, the Branch records are also checked. These records include information on people previously unconvicted of any offences as well as much personal data. All this of course begs a question. Are the records of the Branch supplied to the prosecution solicitors at the trial? And, if they are, is this not likely to increase the prosecution's chance of getting a conviction, particularly when used by the prosecution in examining defence witnesses.[64] Secondly, it appears that *every* incident however minor resulting from political activity is recorded.

Finally, the 'fishing expedition', although in regular use, is particularly prevalent when an investigation lasts for several months or more. The investigations into the Angry Brigade, and the Irish bombings which started in 1972, led to several hundred 'fishing expeditions'. Raids intended to make an arrest were very rare compared to those where large quantities of documents were taken away and recorded. Banking on the presumption that little attention would be paid to the complaints of those raided when bombs are going off around the country, the Branch exploits the opportunity to up-date their information on a whole range of political groups. A classic example was recorded by the *Sunday Times* in 1972.[65] Armed with a two-year-old list of supporters of the Irish Solidarity Campaign (which mainly comprised English supporters of the Irish cause) the Branch carried out a series of raids on activists in the International Socialists, the International Marxists and the libertarian left. The particular raid reported on this occasion started at 6.15 am at a Bloomsbury flat occupied by four young people and lasted for eight hours. Among the four hundred items carted off 'for examination' were: six chopsticks, two clothespegs, one empty coughdrop tin, a sheet of paper with the words 'shish-kebab' written on it, one pair of children's wellington boots and one lavatory roll. All these highly explosive items (for the raid had been carried out under a warrant related to the possession of explosive material) may seem ludicrous but as one of the occupants commented: 'after a while the most normal, silly things cease to be normal'. Of course there were other items taken of more direct 'intelligence' use, like research papers for a thesis on Cuba, address

[64] In the Stoke Newington Eight trial the prosecution had detailed files on the character and activities of several defence witnesses within minutes of their going into the witness box.

[65] In an article by Nicholas Tomalin and Diane Fisher, 19 March, 1972.

books, letters, pamphlets and leaflets. The upshot of this raid was that while no charges relating to explosives were ever brought against the people, a mass of very useful personal and general political information had been added to the files. A similar series of raids was carried out again in April 1973.[66] Throughout this whole period no evidence emerged to link members of any of those political groups raided with the IRA bombing campaign.

Some examples of Branch operations

One key area in which the Branch contributes to the state's monitoring is industry. Its interest starts at the top with the union leaders and extends to trade-union activity in the factory. Its attention is partly directed at firms undertaking contract work for the state, but this area is more the responsibility of other agencies. Most of the Branch's activity is in private industry, especially in strike situations. What is to the trade unionist legitimate activity in furtherance of a pay claim or against an arbitrary management decision becomes, in the eyes of the Branch, industrial unrest led by politically motivated militants. Shop stewards, branch secretaries and political activists are key targets. The Branch officer will first establish contact with a senior member of a firm and then create a working relationship with the personnel manager. Peter Laurie puts the Branch's view well:

> 'He (the Branch officer) sets about getting information in the usual way: he starts with the security officer, or one of the directors, or a trade-union official, and works down from one well-disposed person to another until he establishes a network of contacts on the shop floor, among the people who are likely to cause damage either by sabotage or revolution.'[67]

The Branch's activities in industry are both direct and indirect. When a question of public order arises, such as a strike, march or picket, the local police are briefed by the Branch on the 'ring-leaders' and these are the people who tend to get arrested. At any resulting trial of workers the Branch provides pictures of the event, and sometimes, transcribed notes of speeches made, to support the police case. It is their indirect intrusion into industrial affairs which is the more pernicious. Collusion between management and the Branch can lead to dismissal, blacklisting, or the continual failure to get promotion. Once

---

[66] See *Time Out*, 27 April 1973.
[67] Laurie, *Scotland Yard* (1972) p. 200.

sacked, militant workers can find themselves blacklisted throughout the industry in which they are skilled. For many years such a 'blacklist' has existed in car-making, building, engineering and aircraft-manufacturing. At other times it may be the firm which approaches the Branch for information on a prospective employee, which is usually readily given. This practice is quite normal for foreign firms based in this country especially the American and European ones.[68]

One area of industrial struggle in which the Branch has taken increasing interest is factory occupations. The economic recession has caused a rapidly increasing list of bankruptcies. As companies cut-back by closing 'loss-making' plants in order to preserve their profits, workers in these plants are forced to act to keep them open and thus protect their jobs and livelihoods. Between March 1971 and July 1974 there were more than 100 factory occupations.[69]

One such factory was Strachan's in Eastleigh, Hampshire, which made van bodies for Fords. On 1 March 1974 Strachan's parent company, Giltspur Investments, announced the closure of the Strachan's factory (together with another at Hamble in Hampshire). When this decision was announced the workers decided on an occupation and elected a works' committee. A statement by the committee made their intentions clear: 'Since the closure of Strachan's, we have said and meant that the occupation of the factory is purely an attempt to get this factory reopened, and to give back to our members the right to work. We have permitted all potential customers the freedom of the factory.'[70] Unknown to the workers the management of the factory had been in touch with the local Special Branch office in Southampton for nearly eight months, since August 1973. During a seven-week strike at the factory in August and September 1973 the chief accountant of Strachan's, Mr Norman Grist, was visited by an officer from the Branch officer at Southampton, who showed interest in the political activities of one of the workers.

'... a Special Branch detective pretending to be a commercial traveller went round the plant and confirmed that the worker was known to him.

As a result of this Grist has paid a number of visits to police at Southampton. They told him they were from the Special Branch ... Grist claims that detectives told him that the dispute was

[68] See p. 82 for the Air France example.
[69] *New Statesman*, 13 September 1974.
[70] *Socialist Worker*, 20 April 1974.

political, and controlled by "outside forces".'[71]

The Branch officers told Grist the names of the ringleaders and of three others described as 'sleepers' who were in sympathy with them. The 'outside forces' was said to be the local branch of the International Socialists (IS) at Portsmouth. In fact the IS branch, understandably acting in support of brothers in the struggle, had collected money to help support the workers and had distributed leaflets informing the workers how to claim social security benefits (that is, telling them their legal rights).[72]

When the Home Secretary, Mr Jenkins, was asked in the Commons to justify the intervention of the Branch in this industrial dispute he said the Chief Constable of Hampshire 'had reason to believe that public disorder might have resulted from the incident . . .'. Jenkins went on to say that the Branch

'has no interest in trade unions as such. It is interested only in subversion and possible subversion. Subversion can come from a variety of quarters. I think that it is most important that the Special Branch should be neutral in its attitude to differences between trade unions and employers . . .'[73]

Clearly, the workers in the Strachan's occupation could be forgiven for thinking otherwise.

Another area of Special Branch surveillance is universities and colleges. Several examples in this field have come to light but the three cases below each illustrate a different aspect of Branch work.

In 1968 a Persian student at the School of Oriental and African Studies was approached via another student to come to an informal meeting with someone from Scotland Yard. At the meeting the student in question sensibly had in attendance his father (a solicitor) and another solicitor, much to the discomfiture of the two officers who were ostensibly from the Aliens Department of the Home Office. During the two-hour conversation they said they wanted information on radical students and advance notice of demonstrations. In the end the student simply asked if they wanted an informer, and when they said 'Yes', he said 'No'.[74]

In 1968 a student at Sussex University who had monitored a local

[71] *Sunday Times*, 14 April 1974.
[72] *Socialist Worker*, 20 April 1974.
[73] *Hansard*, 20 June 1974.
[74] *Guardian*, 20 June 1969.

police broadcast and then turned up at a suspected burglary was unfortunately discovered to have done so by the police at the scene. To listen to police broadcasts is technically an offence, and later the student alleged he was approached by two men from the local Branch who asked him to supply them with information about political activities on the campus. This he refused to do. Not surprisingly the Chief Constable of Sussex denied that any approach had been made.[75]

Then there was the case of the politics student at Nottingham University who was similarly asked for information and also refused. It later was asserted by David Winnick, Labour MP for Croydon South, that the student had been approached by an official of the West Nottingham Constituency Labour Party to meet a man from the MOD.[76]

The Branch has had several problems in its surveillance of the black community, not the least of which is that there are very few black policemen in the Metropolitan Police and the Branch. The black community has proved very difficult for the Branch to gain 'informers' in and it has had to resort to other tactics in order to gain information (like offering inducements for information, doing deals over possible charges, 'arranging' arrests). The difficulty the Branch has in getting information on the black community was shown in 1969. On 16 December 1969 the race relations correspondent of *The Times*, Peter Evans, rang Tony Smythe, then General Secretary of NCCL and asked if he knew anything about a meeting on police and immigrants the following day. Smythe said he did not and that he had not been invited. The next day, 17 December, Chief Superintendent Merrick of A7 (the Yard's Community Relations section) rang Smythe and asked what he knew of the meeting – and got the same reply Evans had received the day before:

> 'Mr Merrick then said that a Special Branch officer had suggested that I was organising the meeting and that I would be going to it. I repeated that this was not true, and Mr Merrick went on to say that the Special Branch officer had reported that I had "denied" any connection with the meeting.'[77]

Peter Evans was the only person through whom the details of the original conversation could have leaked to the Branch, and it

[75] *Daily Telegraph*, 20 December 1968.
[76] *The Times*, 11 December 1968.
[77] Extract of a letter from Smythe to the Home Secretary, Mr Callaghan, 18 December 1969.

transpired that he had mentioned the conversation to some six people. Smythe observed that 'it seems likely that one of his contacts, without his knowledge, was a Special Branch informant.'[78] When the Home Office eventually replied to Smythe's letter on 25 March 1970 it stated that 'there had been a misunderstanding'. The police knew a press conference was being planned at which 'allegations would be made that many Metropolitan police officers were racialists and antagonistic towards coloured people. The Metropolitan police were understandably concerned . . .'.[79] The letter side-stepped the central question by suggesting that 'it was thought possible you [Smythe] might be present', and then went on to deny that Chief Superintendent Merrick ever mentioned the special Branch in his conversation. Smythe contested this suggestion but there is no recorded reply.

After 1970 the Branch and the police started to harass the political activists in the black community in a systematic way. In August 1970, after the Mangrove demonstration, the Home Secretary Mr Maudling called for a report on the black community. The *Guardian* reported: 'He will have a complete dossier within 48 hours. The Special Branch has had the movement under observation for more than a year (and) Police now regard Black Power as, at least, worthy of extremely tight surveillance . . .'[80] Derek Humphry observed this period as a *Sunday Times* reporter and later wrote:

'there were a disturbing number of arrests of Black militants in 1970, and their trials dragged on through 1971, causing hardship to the men and women concerned and wasting thousands of pounds of public money. Quite a few were acquitted or received nominal sentences; some received suspended sentences.'[81]

This is an understatement of the effect of the actions of the Branch and police against both groups and individuals in the black community. The diversionary effect of becoming engaged in trials is not lost on the Branch, nor are the months spent in custody (although the eventual trial more than likely does not lead to a prison sentence).

Whenever a foreign head of state visits this country it is customary for the emigré community to come under surveillance. For example,

[78] *Op. cit.*
[79] Letter from Elystan Morgan MP on behalf of Mr Callaghan, 25 March 1970.
[80] *Guardian*, 12 August 1970.
[81] Humphry, *Police Power and Black People* (1972) p. 98.

prior to Bulganin's visit in the 1950s the Russians passed over a comprehensive list of those living in Britain who might take some kind of action: this list closely matched that prepared by Britain's security forces. Similarly, when the now-deposed President Caetano paid a goodwill visit to Britain – as an old NATO ally – in the summer of 1973, the Portuguese community and those opposed to Portugal's African policy had pressure put on them not to do anything (and presumably a list was also exchanged). Reams of newsprint was devoted to such stories as: 'Using Cannon Row as their headquarters the detectives will infiltrate demonstrators, keep watch on violent extremists and bring back intelligence reports about any plans for breaches of law and order.'[82] The pressures brought to bear on aliens living in this country can be considerable, for permits to remain here may not be renewed, applications for naturalisation turned down, or deportation orders issued. During the Caetano visit the British-based Committee for Freedom in Mozambique, Angola and Guinea was 'advised' by visiting Branch officers 'not to do anything'. The near-paranoia of the security agencies was directed at pre-empting any kind of demonstration during the pomp and ceremony of this official state visit.

In September 1971 when Ewald Katjevena, a representative of the South-West African People's Organisation arrived from Brussels at Dover he was stopped and his briefcase searched. After the customs man discovered who he was another man appeared and

'Proceeded to look through all the papers in Katjevena's briefcase and addresses in his diary. When (Mr X) came across a letter from someone in this country referring to a proposed conference to be held by SWAPO in Brussels, he photocopied the list of addresses in Katjevena's diary, a document on the objectives of the conference and its supporters, and the telephone number of the SWAPO President.'[83]

When the Home Office were asked to comment on the powers of immigration officials the reply was that officials have a legal right to read and copy all papers and documents brought into this country.[84]

The impending investiture of Prince Charles as Prince of Wales in July 1969 heralded a high-level campaign by the Branch and the police

---

[82] *Sunday Telegraph*, 15 July 1973.
[83] *Inside Story*, June 1972.
[84] *Guardian*, 21 December 1971.

against the Welsh nationalist movement in which the police sought to gather information on the members of the movement. The Superintendent at Holyhead sent the following 'Confidential' instruction to all stations in Anglesey:

> 'In connection with the proposed investiture of the Prince of Wales at Caernarvon in 1969, the activities of the members of the above mentioned societies are being watched (the Welsh Language Society and the Welsh Nationalist Party). Please submit to this office full details of all persons presently known to be connected with any of these societies or being sympathisers therewith. Details should include, if possible, full name and address, date and place of birth and particulars of any vehicles they own or use ... Details of movements or activities in connection with these societies should also be reported ... It is emphasised that this subject must be treated VERY CONFIDENTIAL.'[85]

The Branch on the other hand supplemented the small Welsh squad from London and proceeded to plant a number of agent-provocateurs in the nationalist movement. The Chairman of Plaid Cymru, Phil Williams, wrote of their activities: 'What we have seen in Wales is a positive sales campaign to promote violence among a body of young people.'[86] Several agents-provocateur were exposed – one left a gun in a student's flat (the student sensibly threw it away); another was heard ringing 'Inspector Carlisle' from a pub; and the car of a third was traced through the licensing authority who gave the scarcely-guarded reply: 'When the police register a car privately, we aren't allowed to reveal the owners.' Again in 1973 the Plaid issued a press statement warning their members that Branch agents-provocateur were again touring Wales in search of outlets for guns and explosives.

Finally there is the case of David Ruddell, a 29 year-old teacher. Ruddell spent most of his early working life abroad teaching English to foreigners – working at one time for Voluntary Service Overseas. In the spring of 1972 he returned to England and taught for the summer term at a school in Bournemouth. At the end of term he got a job as a liaison officer at a camp for Ugandan Asians near Lingfield, and this work ended in December 1972. All this is quite straight-forward, for David Ruddell could be described as a 'do-gooder' helping those less fortunate. However, in January 1973 the Bournemouth school

---

[85] *Planet*, June/July 1972.
[86] *Ibid.*

received a call from the police asking for Ruddell's address, and when a reason for giving the information was asked for vague references were made to 'political' matters. Meanwhile Ruddell applied for a job with Leicester education authority to teach English to Ugandan Asians for which he was well-qualified. His application was rejected without interview although weeks later advertisements for the job were still appearing. Two applications by him for degree courses were also turned down. Meanwhile in March, the director of studies at the Bournemouth school, being a friend of Ruddell's told him of the police telephone call. When more information was requested of the police over the telephone (in Ruddell's presence) the reply was 'It's political. Hammer and Sickle business.' ('Hammer and Sickle' is one of the Branch's short-hand expressions for 'politically undesirable'.) When Ruddell sought another job, a friend and prospective employer at an organisation called Christians Abroad rang the local Sergeant who had originally contacted the school, and he also referred to politics and its being a 'Hammer and Sickle' business. The conversation was then cut off – at the police end – as the enquirer was clearly not conversant with the usual methods of checking on people. However, when the director of studies approached the policeman he began denying any knowledge of all the previous conversations, or that there was any interest in Ruddell, and this conversation itself was cut-off in mid-sentence. Ruddell's only past political activity was support for CND in the early 1960s, his work for the anti-apartheid society at his teaching college, and his membership of the Labour Party. Corinna Adams, who wrote up the story, commented: 'At best, they have subtly slandered him. At worst, they have ruined a career. Who's next?'[87]

Conclusion

It should be clear by now that the Special Branch has been actively engaged in the surveillance of political activists since its inception in the 1880s. For many years the pretence was put forward that there are no 'political police' in Britain. The mythology of the mass media and the literature on the Branch prior to the late 1960s attributed to it much of the glamour stemming from its (marginal) spy-catching activities. Alternatively it was presented as an agency dealing with those who resorted to violent methods in furtherance of their political aims.

[87] *New Statesman*, 7 October 1973.

A 1955 article in the *Daily Mail* characterised this attitude:

> 'Fundamentally the job of the Special Branch is to see that the people of Great Britain can sleep safely in their beds and not wake up to learn of an outrage that occurred in the night at the hands of some foreign agent, some political fanatic, or some home-grown lunatic.'[88]

Only rarely is there recognition of activities such as mail-opening and telephone-tapping. It was this conspiracy of silence which had caused Claud Cockburn to comment in 1933: 'What I do mind is the hypocritical pretence that the high-minded British government wouldn't dream of doing anything so terribly un-British.'[89]

Since the beginning of the 1970s the work of the Branch (and the other intelligence agencies) has come to be more openly admitted, which is not to say that the public is any better informed of their activities. In 1971 David Wood, one of *The Times* political correspondents wrote in an article on the Branch:

> 'I for one share Michael Foot's liberal horror of a society in which ideas have to be policed as lawless acts. Yet this is hypocrisy, the liberal fallacy. The idea precedes the act, and the best hope of counteraction lies in catching the criminal idea on the wing. We are hypocrites to pretend otherwise.'[90]

The contention that we live in a society where, increasingly, it is ideas which are policed is still one many people are not prepared to recognise. Yet this is precisely the premise of the Special Branch.

[88] *Daily Mail*, 18 August 1955.
[89] Patricia Cockburn, *The Years of The Week* (1971) p. 82.
[90] *The Times*, 18 January 1971.

4 MI5

The work of two agencies has been considered so far, the police and the Special Branch. While the work of the Special Branch is relatively shrouded from public view the work of MI5 and the other military intelligence agencies is rarely even raised as a topic for discussion. Many volumes have been written about the war-time exploits of Britain's military forces and their intelligence wings. Some of these have also covered counter-espionage activities against the Germans, and then later against the Russians. However, the concern here is not with these aspects of their work, but rather with the activities of these agencies in maintaining the interests of the state internally.

Two aspects of their work necessitate widespread surveillance of the population: firstly, in respect of what they term 'subversive' activities, and secondly, where anti-espionage security amongst state employees extends to those who are investigated because they (or their friends) are considered potential security risks. The line between these two areas is, as will become apparent, all too often non-existent. This chapter is therefore concerned with internal surveillance and not with espionage by foreign powers. One point of clarification may be helpful at this stage: various titles have been used over the years for MI5, which is also called DI5 or the Security Service. Moreover some writers use the general term 'Secret Service' in reference to the work of MI5. Here the term MI5 will be used throughout.[1]

The material in this chapter falls into three parts. Firstly, there is a short historical account from the creation of MI5 through to 1945. This is followed by a description of MI5's operations in recent times and its structure. Finally, there is a section on the military intelligence agencies which take an interest in internal affairs.

The formation of MI5

Prior to the formation of MI5 in 1909 there were a number of bodies concerned with the internal security of the state. The historic role of

---

[1] MI6 is concerned with intelligence gathering from and activities outside the U.K., while MI5's sphere is limited to the U.K. and Britain's remaining colonies. MI6 is sometimes referred to as the 'Secret Intelligence Service' (SIS).

the Home Office has always been to ensure the safety of the state and this necessitated the maintenance of an *ad hoc* network of spies and informers from the onset of industrial capitalism in the eighteenth century.[2] This *ad hoc* system became institutionalised with the formation of police forces from the 1830s, and the establishment of the Special Branch from the 1880s. The home-based army also played an intelligence role but this was – in the nineteenth century – geared to its involvement in specific struggles (for example, Luddism and Chartism). Military intelligence developed significantly only from the 1850s when the advance of British imperialism demanded more sophisticated methods.

The other Ministry to have an interest in internal politics was the Foreign Office, which had a well-tried undercover intelligence service abroad, and in the latter part of the nineteenth century became deeply involved in subversive movements throughout Europe and Russia. Foreign Office interest in internal politics stemmed from the communities of political exiles who came to Britain in the latter part of the last century.[3] To the Foreign Office these exiles were a source of information and a recruiting ground for potentially valuable agents; it therefore adopted a tolerant attitude towards the refugees. On the other hand, the Home Office, the police and the Special Branch viewed these groups as potentially subversive and a threat to the state. As a result of this a working hostility developed between the Foreign Office on the one hand and the police and Special Branch on the other, with the former holding much information which it did not pass on to the latter.[4]

One well-known event in which the interests of the Foreign Office and the Home Office conflicted was the Siege of Sydney Street in 1910. This is usually portrayed as the hunting down of a group of anarchists led by 'Peter the Painter'.[5] The anarchists involved in the siege were from a small colony of Letts who had originally lived on the Russian Baltic coast. 'Peter the Painter', who escaped from the Sydney Street shoot-out, was almost certainly an agent-provocateur sent over by the Ochrana (the Russian secret service) to instigate criminal acts in the anarchist community here. Deacon, in his *History of the Secret Service*,

[2] See pp. 102–103 for the activities of the Home Office during the time of the Chartists.
[3] See pp. 105 ff.
[4] The Foreign Office intelligence agency also maintained a strong branch in Ireland.
[5] See chapter 3 for details on the anarchists and the Czarist secret service.

suggests that 'Peter the Painter' escaped with the tacit help of the police from the house in Sydney Street before the shooting began. He goes on to say that this was in the nature of the 'quid pro quo arrangements in the field of Secret Service in which governments undoubtedly engage'.[6] The folk-story of Winston Churchill's visit to the siege to boost the morale of the besiegers is probably only part of the truth. 'It is far more likely that he knew all about the ramifications of counter-espionage which this siege involved.'[7] Given the nature of the Czarist secret service, and its known policy of seeking to cause the deportation or imprisonment of anarchists in Britain, this version seems closer to the reality of those times.

MI5 came into being on 28 August 1909. The Committee for Imperial Defence had a sub-committee concerned with internal security, censorship and the protection of British ports and harbours. What particularly concerned the sub-committee were the spying expeditions openly undertaken by German officers ostensibly on holiday in Britain. The possibility that spy-rings were being created worried them even more. One of the junior officers on the sub-committee was a Captain Vernon Kell, and he was asked to head a small unit to watch German activities in Britain.[8] Initially Kell was assigned a small office and a clerk and up to the outbreak of the First World War his staff remained quite small – in 1914 there were three in-vestigators, three senior officers, and seven clerks. One of the officers was Inspector Melville, who had been moved over from the Special Branch. The lack of a large staff meant that Kell had to establish good working relations with the other agencies already concerned with aliens and naturalisation, active political groups, and observation of movements at the ports.

Kell's opposite number in the Special Branch was Inspector Quinn, its operational head. From 1913 Kell also worked with Thompson, the head of the Special Branch, although over the war years a certain amount of professional rivalry arose between them. Kell reported to the Director of Military Operations, while Thompson reported to the Home Secretary or directly to the Cabinet. Both MI5 and the Special Branch were concerned with espionage and sabotage by German agents. (However, although the Special Branch was active in

[6] Deacon, *The History of the Secret Service* (1969) p. 173. Deacon bases this inter-pretation in part on a book about the event by Gerald Bullett, *Statement*.

[7] Deacon, *op. cit.*, p. 173.

[8] Kell's cover was as 'The Commandment of the War Department Constabulary.'

monitoring political groups and industrial militants, MI5 did not
come to take an interest in these areas until after the end of the war.)

Between its formation in 1909 and the end of the war in 1918 MI5
began to evolve some of the working principles under which it
operates today. For instance, in order to take command of MI5 Kell
had to take on civilian status. Recruits to MI5 were largely from
military or police backgrounds and had to be British-born; aliens and
naturalised people were not considered – though ironically Kell's own
mother was half-Polish.

Despite its comparatively small strength MI5 was the instigator of
the 1911 Official Secrets Act and during the war was to pioneer the art
of mass mail-opening.[9] When war broke out spy-scares swept the land
and German agents were 'seen' everywhere. In October 1914 the
Home Office issued a statement to reassure the nation of the state's
efforts in tracking down the spy-rings. The statement said that 120,000
inquiries had been made and 6,000 house searches conducted.
However, 'Although it was fairly confidently believed that all German
agents in Britain had been rounded up, the Government quite
deliberately fostered fear of spies. *In this way every citizen became an
auxiliary of the counter-espionage.*'[10]

The October Revolution of 1917 evoked two major responses from
the British state. The first, and lesser known, was its effort inside Russia
against the Bolsheviks. In August 1918 an expeditionary army of
British and French troops landed at Archangel and fought against the
revolutionary armies until the former withdrew in September 1919.
The army also gave massive supplies to the White Russians. Meanwhile
MI6 poured in agents and several million pounds in a vain effort to
subvert the revolution.[11] This attempt at direct intervention in the
revolution was motivated partly by the general fears of the ruling class
that communism would sweep through Europe (there were attempted

[9] For details on the 1911 Official Secrets Act see Ch. 1; for details on mail-
opening see Ch. 5.

[10] Bulloch, *MI*5 (1963) p. 97. My emphasis. It is interesting to note in passing
that the claims of success in foiling German espionage efforts during the First
World War usually fail to mention the loss of four warships (three with full
crews) through sabotage: *HMS Bulwark* (1914), *Princess Irene* (1915), *HMS Natal*
(1916) and the battleship *Vanguard* (1917) – the saboteurs were never caught.
(Bulloch, p. 92–93.)

[11] Several books were later written by these agents telling of their work. One
such book, *The Story of ST25* by Sir Paul Dukes is subtitled *Adventure and Romance
in the Secret Intelligence Service in Russia* (1938).

revolutions in Holland and Switzerland in 1918) and partly in defence of British 'interests' – £50 million of British capital was invested in Russia.

The second response was inside Britain itself. The intelligence agencies and the government rarely sought to distinguish between the various strands of the socialist movement in the post-war period; to them all socialist action aided the Bolshevik cause and threatened the security of the British state.[12] The separation of the Special Branch from the CID at Scotland Yard after 1919, the assignation of the title of 'Director of Intelligence' to Thomson, and the continuing Branch reports direct to the Cabinet were only some of the measures taken to counter the threat of internal subversion.

From spying to subversion

The rising militancy of the socialist movement after the war together with the success of the October Revolution and the spread of communist ideas to Britain convinced the military minds of the need to link counter-espionage and counter-subversion. What is characteristic of this period (and still exists today) is the notion that but for the importation of ideas from 'across the Channel' English men and women would have been forever happy with the prevailing conditions. The belief in 'foreign elements' at work was a convenient excuse for political surveillance: 'It's (MI5's) primary duty then as now was to prevent and detect espionage and sabotage, but to do so, agents of the department had to know what was going on in all the organisations and societies in which Britain's potential enemies within her shores might be found.'[13]

At the end of the war a new department was formed in the War Office – the Directorate of Military Intelligence (DMI). It was from this time that MI5, which had been known as M.O.5 during the war, gained the appellation MI, for Military Intelligence. The DMI was itself an attempt to create a co-ordinating body for all the intelligence agencies, encompassing those working both externally and internally.

While MI5 under Kell, and the Special Branch under Thomson, closely co-operated during the war there remained an implicit sense of rivalry – particularly on Thomson's part. He had visions of extending

[12] See chapter 3 for an account of some of the struggles at this time and of the Special Branch's activities.

[13] Bulloch, *op. cit.*, p. 155.

his empire by recruiting a team of spies to act abroad. The upstart organisation, MI5, limited his ambitions. This implicit rivalry during the war came to a head in the period immediately after the cessation of fighting. Between 1919 and 1921 Thomson, the 'Director of Intelligence', operated the Special Branch not just as an agency for gathering political intelligence but also as a counter-espionage organisation, while Kell, with MI5 attached to the newly-formed DMI, was also operating in the latter field. A clash was inevitable, and the out-come was never really in doubt. Whatever specific reason was offered for Thomson's sacking by Lloyd George in 1921, the competition between MI5 and the Special Branch underlay this decision. Within months of Thomson's departure the Special Branch lost its indepen-dent status and was back under the wing of the CID at the Yard. A clear field was thus left for MI5 whose secretive and wholly undercover methods of operation had many advantages for the state. From then on MI5 was the key agency concerned with counter-espionage; the Special Branch's role was limited to helping in the final stages of an investiga-tion, making the arrest, and appearing in court. In the field of internal subversion the two organisations shared the responsibility, with MI5 operating completely undercover and the Special Branch only marginally so. With the passage of time MI5 came to be a much larger organisation than the Special Branch with greater funds and fewer restraints.

The 1920 Official Secrets Act, the 1920 Emergency Powers Act and the formation of the British Communist Party were all the concern of Kell's agency.[14] After the immediate post-war struggles between the state and socialist movements, the ruling class began preparing itself for the 1920s, and MI5 played its part. The state was

> 'not averse to using MI5 as a long-term weapon to prepare for the General Strike which they were convinced would come sooner or later . . . the counter-espionage organisation played a leading role in foiling some of the plots centring around the events leading up to that strike, as well as a somewhat dubious role in manufacturing propaganda in the form of various "Red Scares" '.[15]

A part of these preparations was the announcement in the *London Gazette* in 1924 that Kell and his deputy had retired. In fact this state-ment was intended to deceive the people and parliament as to the new

---

[14] See chapter 2 for MI5's part in formulating the 1920 Official Secrets Act.
[15] Deacon, *op. cit.*, p. 256.

and more sensitive role now being undertaken by MI5 in industry and socialist movements. Its work now 'called for new techniques and, above all, for a new type of agent who could infiltrate among the workers without arousing suspicion.'[16]

On several occasions prior to this the Special Branch and MI5 had come under attack in parliament. This usually occurred when the annual Secret Service Vote for 'the foreign and other secret services' came up for consideration. In 1913 the sum agreed to was £46,840; in 1918–19 it was £1,150,000 and in 1919–20 some £400,000. In December 1919 a supplementary sum of £200,000 was agreed by parliament, and one MP took the opportunity to ask a question.

> *Mr A. Short:* Apart from the use of that service as a diplomatic weapon, there was a growing volume of opinion, particularly among the organised working class, that the fund was being used for purposes alien to its usual purposes.
> *Mr Baldwin* replied: He had no knowledge of the way in which the money was spent.[17]

And again in May 1920 the Chancellor, Mr Chamberlain, declined to give details of the Secret Service Vote.

> *Captain Benn:* asked if the Secret Service had not in recent years altered from being a purely military service to being a political service.
> *Mr Chamberlain:* said he was not aware of any such change; but if he were to answer even harmless questions, the service would cease to be secret . . .[18]

On 8 October 1924 the Labour government was defeated in the House of Commons because of its withdrawal of the prosecution against John Campbell, the acting editor of the Communist Party journal, *Workers Weekly*. In the ensuing General Election the Labour Party was defeated and the Tories returned to power. Labour's defeat was sealed by the publication of the notorious Zinoviev Letter. The 1,200-word letter, produced on the official notepaper of the Third Communist International, purported to be a communication between Gregory Zinoviev, the President of the International, and Mr A. McManus, a member of the Communist Party and the British representative on the International's executive committee. The letter suggested

[16] Deacon, *op. cit.*, p. 255.
[17] *The Times*, 10 December 1919.
[18] *The Times*, 12 May 1920.

that the British comrades should be working to create a revolutionary
insurrection and included the directive that 'Armed warfare must be
preceded by a struggle among the majority of British workmen, against
the ideas of evolution and peaceful extermination of capitalism. Only
then will it be possible to count on the complete success of an armed insurrection.'[19] At this time ruling-class paranoia over the revolution in
Russia and the militancy of socialist movements in Britain was at a high-
point. Many in the Tory Party, the press, the Ministries and the intelligence agencies considered the Labour Party and the MacDonald
government as being only one step removed from the Russian
Bolsheviks – the reality of MacDonald's reformism and clear hostility to
the working class notwithstanding. What tended to confirm this belief
was the strong lobby within the Labour ranks for a trade agreement
with Russia. When the election was called this put an end to the ratifica-
tion of the Anglo–Russian trade treaties then before parliament.
However, the proposed treaty together with the Zinoviev letter 'enabled
the Conservative Party to paint MacDonald as the dupe and abettor of
Bolshevism's subversive aims'.[20]

The Zinoviev plot involved two groups of conspirators. Firstly, there
were the two White Russians who forged the letter and Zinoviev's
signature. Secondly, a group in Britain who sought to exploit the
letter's implications and who provided 'proof' of its authenticity –
these were a middle-man named Thurn, members of MI6 and MI5,
the top personnel at the Foreign Office, and the Tory Party. The two
forgers in Berlin were Alexis Bellegarde and Alexander Gumansky,
who were both members of an exiled White Russian organisation, the
Brotherhood of St George. The precise route of the letter to Britain is
still uncertain but what is clear is that a copy was in the hands of the
Foreign Office by 10 October. Thurn also had a copy and touted it
around trying to ensure that its contents were made public. At the
Foreign Office, the head of MI6, Sinclair, got together with Admiral
'Blinker' Hall (the ex-chief of the Naval Intelligence Department) and
several others. The upshot was that Thurn appeared to have been paid
£7,500 by Tory Party Headquarters and they in turn arranged for the
letter's publication in the *Daily Mail*. Throughout Sinclair master-
minded the operation. The publication of the letter was essential to the
plotters to bring it to public attention, but it was even more important
for the Foreign Office to authenticate the letter's origin.

[19] Quoted by Deacon, *op. cit.*, p. 256.
[20] Chester, Fay and Young, *The Zinoviev Letter* (1967) p. 33.

Before looking at the motivation of the Foreign Office it must be asked what the Prime Minister, MacDonald, was doing about the letter?[21] MacDonald, who was away from London campaigning in the country and his own constituency, had been sent a copy of the letter by the Foreign Office – who, as already mentioned had a copy on 10 October. MacDonald instructed the Foreign Office to establish the authenticity of the letter and, pending the outcome of this, to draft a protest to the Russian government. On 23 October MacDonald got a copy of the draft protest which he returned uninitialled – that is, no authority to act was being given until proof of the letter's origin had been established. On 24 October, without the permission of the Prime Minister or any other member of the government, the Foreign Office sent the protest to the Russian embassy and without waiting for a reply the whole story was given to the press – four days before the election. The publication of the protest to the Russians itself served as authentication of the letter's contents and origin.

This unauthorised action by the Foreign Office was no accident. The top administrator at the Foreign Office, Sir Eyre Crowe, the Permanent Under-Secretary, and Sinclair, head of MI6, were convinced that a new Labour government would seek to limit the work of the secret service. 'And once a small, but powerful group of threatened men had convinced themselves that the letter was genuine, their incipient institutional paranoia made it almost inevitable that they should become equally convinced that Ramsay MacDonald was secretly plotting to prevent the letter's publication.'[22] It is clear MacDonald had no such intention, but the informal network of conspirators within the Foreign Office and outside expressly set out to do the maximum damage to the Labour Party. The steps taken by the Foreign Office to authenticate a letter they wanted to believe was genuine were laughable. Trevor-Roper describes the report from Sinclair to Sir Eyre Crowe as follows:

> 'It amounts to simply this: our man in Riga (which was not then in the Soviet Union) says that he knows of a conversation between Chicherin and Zinoviev which proves the letter to be genuine. That so contemptible a snippet of unverifiable gossip from an un-identified and distant source – and Riga was notoriously the factory of anti-Soviet propaganda and fiction – should have been sent, as authoritative proof of fact, by the Head of the Secret Service to the Permanent Under-Secretary of the Foreign Office, shows

[21] MacDonald combined the posts of Prime Minister and Foreign Secretary.
[22] Chester, Fay and Young, *op. cit.*, p. 108.

that MI6 under Admiral Sinclair, had lost all contact with rational methods . . .'[23]

What must remain a strong suspicion in this whole affair is that one of the SIS's notorious anti-Russian spies, Sydney Reilly (who was conversant with all means of forgery), set the whole operation up in Berlin. Moreover, the unidentified source in Riga used by Sinclair may well also have been Sydney Reilly. Although the Labour Party had its suspicions about the document it was not until 1966 that most of the story came out when the widow of Alexis Bellegarde, one of the two White Russians, spoke to the *Sunday Times*.

Immediately after losing the election the Labour Party, not knowing the whole story but at least being aware of how the Foreign Office's release of the protest without MacDonald's agreement influenced the result, launched into an attack on the intelligence agencies in general. *The Daily Herald* declared that 'the cleaning up of Scotland Yard and of its allied and associated departments will be one of the first jobs of the next Labour government.'[24]

At the Labour Party Conference the next year the call to expose the spies on the working class was repeated. No Labour government has however instituted a full-scale investigation into internal surveillance and curtailed the spying activities of these agencies on working-class movements. For all their huff-and-puff when in opposition the Labour Parliamentary Party when in office has not wanted to appear less patriotic than the Tories.

The recruitment of new agents and personnel to MI5 continued throughout the 1930s and the source of recruits extended from the tried and trusted ex-Army and colonial officers to include people from all parts of the country and from many different occupations.[25] A teacher recruited in 1936, Dick Goldsmith White, later went on to head both MI6 and MI5.[26] On the one hand intellectuals were recruited for assessment and decision-making jobs at Headquarters, and on the other people were engaged who could pursue their normal occupations while reporting back either on an organisation they had joined or the industry they worked in. Many of the new recruits

[23] Trevor Roper, *The Philby Affair* (1968) pp. 70–71.
[24] 6 November 1924.
[25] Of this period H. Trevor Roper commented that 'no one was more fanatically anti-communist, at this time, than the regular members of the two security services, MI6 and MI5.' *The Philby Affair* (1968) p. 28.
[26] See p. 189.

became field operatives who joined subversive organisations, and their role was to participate in the activities of the group and attempt to rise to positions of influence. These agents of MI5 were to remain under-cover at all costs in order to gather 'long-term' intelligence. In the 1930s

> 'MI5 planted its agents in every organisation which could possibly be used by an enemy or which could cause trouble for Britain by its aims and methods.'[27]

Only on rare occasions have the undercover activities of long-term MI5 agents come to light. One such case occurred in 1938 when a member of the Communist Party, Percy Glading, was charged with the possession of documents taken from Woolwich Arsenal. Glading was a former worker at the munitions plant and three men actually working at the factory were charged with him (one was acquitted). Glading was given a six-year sentence and the others three and four years respectively. Glading's undoing was to enlist the aid – in photographing plans and documents – of a trusted fellow-member of the Communist Party. This was Miss X, who had joined the Party in 1931 on the in-structions of MI5. For seven years Miss X was a 'sleeper'. First she had become a member of the Friends of the Soviet Union and then she got a typist's job with the Anti-War Movement. Having established her credentials she joined the Communist Party and in 1934 was sent on a mission abroad for the Comintern. At the trial Miss X gave a full and damning account of Glading's activities.

In 1936 five workers at the Royal Dockyards were summarily dis-missed by the Admiralty. There had been some acts of sabotage at the dockyard but whether all the five men, who were work-mates, were responsible was never established. However, the Admiralty acting on 'information received' from MI5 decided they were and got rid of them. The men protested vocally against their dismissal and on 26 January 1937 the Labour opposition put down a censure motion, which was lost by 145 votes to 330. The government position was put by the First Lord of the Admiralty, who said that 'we were confronted with the difficulty that the information at our disposal was necessarily secret and confidential and was obtained from sources which, while legitimate and reliable could not in the interests of the security of the State, be disclosed.'[28] The Labour MPs attacked the idea of a secret

[27] Bulloch, *op. cit.*, p. 156.
[28] *Hansard*, 26 January 1937.

'trial' without the recourse to law; they pointed out that even in Official Secrets' cases such evidence is usually presented *in camera* and that the sources are not usually revealed. Mr Baldwin, the Prime Minister, was intransigent and this case was a precursor of the post-war purges which allowed only marginal rights of appeal against dismissal.[29]

The outbreak of civil war in Spain in 1936 led to the formation of many groups in Britain in support of the Republican cause and, later, Britons joined the ranks of the International Brigade fighting against Franco. MI agents joined these groups in order to gain information on the British left's involvement. To this end they even 'helped the representatives of Republican Spain in England to buy arms or recruit men for the war there.'[30] One or two men had also been infiltrated into the ranks of Sir Oswald Mosley's fascist movement. But it was not until the late 1930s that equal attention was being paid to the fascist as opposed to the socialist movements in Britain.

Three major disasters at the start of the Second World War led to an immediate enquiry into the efficiency of MI5 and the removal of Kell. The first two disasters concerned MI5's responsibility for counter-espionage: three explosions at the Royal Gunpowder factory at Waltham Abbey in Essex and the sinking of the Royal Oak with the loss of 633 men in Scapa Flow. The third concerned MI5 itself. At the outbreak of hostilities MI5 had been moved lock, stock and barrel to Wormwood Scrubs prison. A few months later the prison was hit by a bomb which, with great accuracy, landed on the MI5 Registry of files. Churchill immediately constituted a high-level inquiry by Lord Swinton, William Armstrong (later Sir William, who recently retired as head of the Civil Service) and Kenneth Diplock (now Lord Diplock). Sir Vernon Kell was retired and replaced by Sir Charles Petrie, who had previously worked for the Indian police in gathering political intelligence. It was also at this time that MI5 was formally separated from Military Intelligence, although it retained the designation 'MI'. In fact this was only a recognition of the independence of MI5 which had been the practice over the previous twenty years.

A year after the war ended Sir Charles Petrie was replaced by Sir Percy Sillitoe. This appointment caused much resentment within MI5, as the talented number two, Guy Liddell, had been expected to take over; instead Attlee appointed Sillitoe who has been described as 'the

[29] See p. 165 ff.
[30] Bulloch, *op. cit.*, p. 156.

self-advertising policeman'.[31] Sillitoe started his police career with the British South African Police Force and returned to England to become the Chief Constable of Glasgow and then of Sheffield.[32] This appointment also ended the tradition of making a military man the organisation's head and thereafter the Director-Generals of MI5 have been civilians appointed from within MI5 (with one exception).

In the period between 1909 and 1945 the respective roles of the police, the Special Branch and MI5 were evolved and refined. Whereas the police and the Special Branch tended to act immediately on the information they received MI5 adopted a different policy. Sillitoe brings out this distinction in his book: MI5 was to collect 'information about people who intend to subvert British institutions and also devise ways and means of countering their activities. The Department's job is to identify the enemy, to find out what he is doing and by what methods he is working; then *to pursue and neutralise him*.'[33] The policy of making public disclosures only as a last resort applied as much to internal political surveillance as to counter-espionage by foreign powers, for an arrest or a scandal brought unwelcome publicity. It should also be noted that in this period MI5 was responsible for the internal security of Commonwealth countries and this took on a new dimension after the Second World War. This was not only in response to the start of the Cold War and Russian designs on Third World countries, but because demands for liberation from direct political rule by imperialist countries were gaining force within these countries themselves.

MI5 1945–1975

This historical account, from 1909 to 1945, has shown the development towards MI5's two central roles – counter-espionage from 1909, and counter-subversion from the 1920s. The following sections cover aspects of MI5 that are relevant today: the introduction of Positive Vetting, Ministerial responsibility, the organisation of MI5, and finally, two specific areas of their surveillance are considered – MPs and industry.

[31] Trevor Roper, *op. cit.*, p. 65.
[32] When Sillitoe in turn retired in 1953 he agreed to go to South Africa at the request of Sir Ernest Oppenheimer, the Chairman of De Beers Consolidated Mines and of the Diamond Corporation, to investigate diamond trafficking which was causing the companies considerable losses.
[33] Sillitoe, *Cloak Without Dagger* (1955) p. xiv. My emphasis.

The 'purges' and positive vetting

In 1948 MI5, the Special Branch and the police, who had been compiling and revising their list of members of the Communist Party, gathered in the process evidence of Party members employed in sensitive Ministries, key private firms, and trade unions. It was this evidence, together with pressure from the USA, which convinced the Labour Home Secretary and the Prime Minister of the need for a formal purge procedure. Moreover, prior to the official announcement about the purge it was reported that MI5 had vetoed the appointment of several people engaged to work in firms employed by the Air Force and the Navy.[34]

In March 1948 Mr Attlee announced in the Commons that no person 'known to be a member of the Communist Party or to be associated with it' would in future be employed on secret state work.

In 1952 it was decided that a much greater in-depth investigation into an individual's life and background was necessary. This was called Positive Vetting. What was not known then is the fact that the 1952 introduction of Positive Vetting and its practical application was the result of an agreement between Britain, America and France. Sir David Maxwell-Fyfe, the Tory Home Secretary, gave an interview in October 1954 to the *US News and World Report* in which he spelt out the arrangement:

> *Sir David:* We have this three country agreement. The French adopted it too.
> *Q:* What is this three country agreement?
> *Sir David:* It was an agreement as to Positive Vetting.
> *Q:* Was this during the war or since?
> *Sir David:* No, since about two and a half years ago.[35]

In 1956 the Report of the Conference of Privy Councillors into the defection of Burgess and Maclean agreed that in addition to suspected communist sympathies, character 'defects' should also be grounds for exclusion for many state posts – 'failings such as drunkenness, addiction to drugs, homosexuality, or any loose living'. The Report found that 'It is right to continue the practice of tilting the balance in favour of offering greater protection to the security of the State rather than in the direction of safeguarding the rights of the individual.'[36]

[34] *Daily Express*, 16 March 1948.
[35] *U.S. News and World Report*, October 1954.
[36] *Report of the Conference of Privy Councillors,* Cmnd 9715 (1956) para. 16.

The Report explicitly stated that

'One of the chief problems of security today is thus to identify the members of the British Communist Party, to be informed of its activities and to identify that wider body of those who are . . . sympathetic to Communism . . .'[37]

Yet what is clear from this and other official statements is not only that the Communist Party was watched and infiltrated, but that the net spread to those individuals who were thought of as being 'sympathetic to Communism'. And even in cases where Communist Party members were dismissed or moved it was not being alleged that they were actually undertaking espionage activities, but that by engaging in political action they had become 'potential risks'.[38]

Between 1948 and 1955 some 135 civil servants were said to have been affected by these procedures. Of these some resigned (24), some were dismissed outright (25), and some were transferred to 'non-sensitive' work (86). No figures have ever been made public for those whose applications for a transfer were turned down, whose promotion was vetoed, or of those whose application to join the Civil Service was rejected on grounds of their alleged communist or left-wing activities supplied by the intelligence agencies.

In response to the purges the Campaign for the Limitation of Secret Police Powers was set up in 1956 and it produced two reports on the activities of MI5 and other investigating agencies.[39] Many eminent people became sponsors of the CLSPP including G. D. H. Cole, Ritchie Calder, Henry Moore, Terence Rattigan, A. J. P. Taylor, Sybil Thorndike, and Peter Ustinov. The sponsors also included a number of Liberal and Labour MPs. The Campaign brought to light many cases of discrimination against communists and left-wing activists outside the Civil Service.

For example, there was John Clother, who was destined to have a bright future in the army when a sympathetic commanding officer showed him a letter from the War Office: 'Sapper J. Clother, R.E. 23182346, is on no account to be commissioned.' Clother's problem appears to have been his father, who was a JP and an active member of the Labour Party and the Peace Pledge Union. In another case a qualified teacher was refused employment by Renfrewshire County

---

[37] Cmnd 9715, *op. cit.*, para. 7.
[38] This Report only contained those details of its workings considered suitable for publication, *op. cit.*, para 3.
[39] *The Secret Police and You* (1956); *A Year with the Secret Police* (1957).

Council because her husband was a communist, and a woman cashier was dismissed from a club for civil servants in Cheltenham because her husband belonged to the Young Communist League. Then there was the case of Ronald Frankenberg, a young anthropologist, who went to the West Indies to carry out research on a Nuffield Foundation grant. He was refused permission to land and had to return to Britain. When the matter was raised in parliament the Colonial Secretary said Mr Frankenberg was considered 'a bad security risk', and no further grounds were given.[40] His past political activity was solely as an active member of the Socialist Society at Cambridge and Manchester universities.

In 1957 the Association of University Teachers held a long and heated debate on the question of whether lecturers should supply information to MI5 and other agencies. Members of the Association were divided as to their position. Professor Montrose of Belfast University said:

> 'I cannot see it is in any way consistent with the work of the university teacher to be asked to give information. We ought to make it clear that this Association is quite convinced that no person can with honour remain a university teacher and at the same time agree to be a secret agent for the government in this work.'[41]

Professor Briscoe, of Imperial College, said he saw no difference between these inquiries and those made by potential employers. The difference is that while employers make inquiries from references provided by the undergraduate, MI5's investigations are made without the knowledge of the student. The President of the AUT, Lord Chorley, said in a House of Lords debate that there were many recent cases in London where lecturers had 'been asked to report not only on students, but on their own colleagues – teachers with whom they are working.' And later, at the AUT Conference Lord Chorley elaborated on the point of his objection: 'If teachers are being asked to report on the general loyalty of colleagues it means, in effect, that they are being encouraged to act as spies – to find their way into their colleagues' studies, even to pry into the drawers of their desks.'[42]

The concern of the state over Communists in public service had, in the purge, centred particularly on those who held positions within the

[40] *The Secret Police and You* (1956) p. 9.
[41] Meeting of AUT at Cardiff, May 1957.
[42] *Ibid.*

Civil Service trade unions. In 1963 Mr Cyril Cooper, the General Secretary of the Society of Technical Civil Servants, was barred from acting on behalf of his members in negotiations. Mr Cooper appealed against this decision, under the procedure agreed, and was given an interview by the Three Advisers.[43] He stated that he had left the Communist Party many years ago. The questions asked at his interview with the Three Advisers give some insight into the mentality behind the purge programme. Mr Cooper was interested in ballet and opera and while in Moscow for a few days he had attended the Bolshoi Ballet: 'I was asked, if I was interested in opera, why I had not gone to Vienna.'[44] Mr Cooper continued: 'I was then asked if we had any artistic friends. I confessed to that; to meet the question, "Aren't all of these long-haired people of one political persuasion?" I begged leave to doubt this, whereupon the questioner expressed his thought that they were.' Mr Cooper's appeal was unsuccessful and despite a campaign by the NCCL the ban was never withdrawn.

Two general comments can be made about the security programme. Firstly, the standards of Positive Vetting are today applied not just to civil servants but as a matter of course to all military personnel, their families and relations.[45] Secondly, the emphasis today is on seeking to exclude from *entry* into state service those with 'subversive connections'. And this necessitates the investigation of *all* applicants, most of whom never get appointed.

MI5 and Ministerial responsibility

The Denning Report (which resulted from the Profumo affair in 1963) sought to define the status of MI5 in the following terms:

'The Security Service in this country is not established by Statute nor is it recognised by Common Law. Even the Official Secrets Acts do not acknowledge its existence. The members of the Service are, in the eye of the law, ordinary citizens with no powers

[43] The 'Three Advisers' was an appeals mechanism appointed by the government.

[44] *The Times*, 10 June 1963.

[45] In 1964 MI5 compiled a booklet called *Their Trade is Treachery*, which was distributed to a wide range of civil service personnel. The booklet, which is a classic piece of institutional paranoia, opens with the following words: 'Spies are with us all the time . . . This booklet tells you about the great hostile spy machine that tries to suborn our citizens and turn them into traitors . . . (and) how to avoid pitfalls, which could lead to a national catastrophe or a personal disaster – or both.' (HMSO, 1964.)

greater than anyone else. They have no special powers of arrest such as the police have.'[46]

Taken at face value this statement is undoubtedly true, but what are its implications? The reality of course is that not having created MI5 parliament is impotent to question its policies and actions, and Ministers – of both parties – have always refused to divulge any information to the House of Commons. Despite this some notion of parliamentary accountability is necessary if monies are to be annually allocated to its work and its failures are to be explained away. Yet even this aspect has been shrouded in secrecy for it was not until the publication of the Denning Report in 1963 that MPs and public were told that the Home Secretary had had a responsibility for MI5 since 1952.

During the Second World War the Prime Minister, Winston Churchill, and his advisers had a considerable degree of influence on the agency. Prime Ministerial responsibility for MI5 was confirmed in 1945 by the report of Sir Findlater Stewart which said that the Director-General of the Security Service should be given the maximum freedom of operation: 'having got the right man there is no alternative to giving him the widest discretion in the means he uses and the direction in which he applies them – always provided he does not step outside the law.'[47] The implication here, which was to be confirmed later, was that the Prime Minister would have a general responsibility for MI5 but would in no sense be in a position to control or indeed even know about the day-to-day operations of the agency. In March 1950, after the Fuchs case, the Prime Minister, Mr Attlee, said in a statement to the Commons that he personally accepted responsibility for MI5. And Sir Anthony Eden revealed in 1955 that a secret inquiry into the efficiency of MI5 was carried out on Attlee's instructions immediately after this statement: its findings were to produce few changes and the agency was found to be well-equipped for the job in hand.

The question of responsibility was doubly confounded because it was the Treasury who issued all the directives related to the purge programme and its Minister who answered questions in the Commons. However in March 1951 the Secretary to the Cabinet, Sir Norman Brook, recommended in a report to the Prime Minister that responsibility should be transferred to the Home Secretary. Sir Nor-

[46] The Denning Report, p. 91.
[47] *Op. cit.*, p. 79.

man suggested that Sir Findlater had put too much stress on the defence aspect in the work of MI5: 'In practice the functions of the Security Service are much more closely allied to those of the Home Office, which has the ultimate responsibility for "defending the realm" against subversive activities and preserving law and order.'[48] The nature of the suggested relationship was that the Director-General should be able to consult with a Minister 'for advice and assistance on policy aspects of his work', while leaving open the power to 'arrange a personal interview with the Prime Minister', without going through the Home Secretary.

This confidential report was to be formalised when the Tories came back into government and on 25 September 1952 the Tory Home Secretary, Sir David Maxwell-Fyfe, issued a directive to the Director-General of the Security Service which set out this relationship. As this directive is the only public statement defining the accountability of MI5 to parliament and government it is worth quoting in full.

1. In your appointment as Director-General of the Security Service you will be responsible to the Home Secretary personally. The Security Service is not, however, a part of the Home Office. On appropriate occasion you will have right of direct access to the Prime Minister.

2. The Security Service is part of the Defence Forces of the country. Its task is the Defence of the Realm as a whole, from external and internal dangers arising from attempts at espionage and sabotage, or from actions of persons and organisations whether directed from within or without the country, which may be judged to be subversive of the State.

3. You will take special care to see that the work of the Security Service is strictly limited to what is necessary for the purposes of their task.

4. It is essential that the Security Service should be kept absolutely free from any political bias or influence and nothing should be done that might lend colour to any suggestion that it is concerned with the interests of any particular section of the community, or with any other matter than the Defence of the Realm as a whole.

5. No enquiry is to be carried out on behalf of any Government Department unless you are satisfied that an important public interest bearing on the Defence of the Realm, as defined in para. 2, is at stake.

[48] *Ibid.*

6. You and your staff will maintain the well-established convention whereby Ministers do not concern themselves with the
detailed information which may be obtained by the Security Service in particular cases, but are furnished with such information
only as may be necessary for the determination of any issue on
which guidance is sought.[49]

In effect, the directive begs more questions than it answers. Does it
mean MI5 is 'responsible to the Home Secretary' in the same sense as
civil servants in the Home Office are to the Minister? Clearly not, for it
is not 'part of the Home Office'. So what does it mean? Who decides
which 'internal dangers' arising 'from actions of persons and
organisations' are 'judged to be subversive of the State'? How can MI5
fail to show 'political bias' when its responsibility is to defend the
status quo against all those seeking radical change? Future Home
Secretaries were clearly being told that only the most general matters
could be discussed between them and the Director-General – information would only be given 'as may be necessary' when MI5 itself sought
guidance.

Of course back in 1952 parliament knew nothing of this directive –
which only became public knowledge with the publication of the Denning Report in 1963. Questions on security continued to be directed
to, and answered by, the Prime Minister. Mr Macmillan did tell MPs in
1961 of the Home Secretary's responsibility on matters of discipline,
pay and organisation, but no-one took this to mean that he had
anything more than a nominal role. Indeed in 1963 the then Tory
Home Secretary, Henry Brooke, answered MPs' questions as follows:
'The Security Service is, after all, a secret service . . . this is part of its es-
sence. Its cost is borne on the Secret Vote and one must bear in mind
therefore that the number of parliamentary questions which could be
put to me with any hope of an answer being properly given is very
limited.'[50]

A number of changes followed the 1963 Denning Report. In
January 1964 a permanent body, the Security Commission, was
created. A judge, Mr Justice Winn, was appointed its first chairman.
And when Labour won the 1964 election Mr Wilson appointed George
Wigg as the Paymaster General, with the job of trying to ensure that no
scandals arose to embarrass his term of office. In the end parliament
and public were no less confused than they had been before as to the

[49] *Op. cit.*, p. 80.
[50] Quoted by Thompson in *Big Brother* (1970) p. 77.

respective functions of the Prime Minister and the Home Secretary.
Though, as a correspondent noted at the time, to an MP it does not
'make much difference whether the Home Secretary or the Prime
Minister fobs him off'.[51]

The question however still remains: what if anything do Ministers
know of the operation of intelligence agencies for which they are
theoretically responsible? When the Commander Crabbe fiasco was
debated in 1956 the Labour MP, Mr Bellinger, who had been a
Minister of War in the Attlee government, said:

> 'Having been in charge of a service department myself, I should
> like to know whether he [the Prime Minister] is quite sure that
> Ministers, and Service Ministers in particular, have complete con-
> trol over their secret service . . . I should not be at all surprised if
> Service Ministers, in particular, do not know what their
> Intelligence does. Yet they are asked to take complete respon-
> sibility for the expenditure of these secret service sections of their
> Departments without knowing one iota of what is happening.'[52]

And later in 1968 a former naval intelligence officer, Donald
McLachlan, wrote in an article for the *Daily Telegraph*:

> 'I was not amused, but somewhat surprised to learn lately from a
> former Foreign Secretary and from a former head of the Foreign
> Office, that they know next to nothing of the organisation and
> assessment of secret intelligence for which some years ago they
> had been responsible.'[53]

In reality it is probably the Prime Minister (via the Secretary to the
Cabinet) who has the most contact with the Director-General of the
Security Service, for as Williams concludes in *Not in the Public Interest*:
'The Maxwell-Fyfe Directive of 1952 has, in the end, done little to alter
the pre-1952 position.'[54] It is the occasional and publicly-exposed
failures of MI5 which have called it to give some account of its activities: but what of its 'successes' about which we know nothing?

The organisation of MI5

The historically evolved roles of MI5 are to foil the spying efforts of the
Communist and other 'unfriendly' countries (counter-espionage), to

[51] *Daily Worker*, 15 October 1963.
[52] *Hansard*, 9 May 1956.
[53] *Daily Telegraph*, 26 September 1968.
[54] D. Williams, *Not in the Public Interest* (1965) p. 169.

track down or stop perpetrators of sabotage (counter-sabotage) and to pre-empt any revolutionary potential which may arise in the land (counter-subversion). To suggest that these three roles can be easily distinguished in practice would be misleading. What unites them is the prime function of MI5 – the maintenance of the prevailing order, against external and internal challenge. Effective counter-espionage demands that in order to catch the few who indulge in spying, many thousands of people are subject to surveillance and investigation by the intelligence agencies, particularly since spying these days extends beyond the purely military, into matters of economic and political interest to foreign powers. These powers are not limited to the 'Communist bloc' but are world-wide. Equally the definitions of 'sabotage' can range from a deliberate act to destroy a machine or engine through to the paralysing of an essential industry by prolonged strike action. A complete picture of MI5's operations obviously cannot be presented; however, some aspects of its overall organisation can be constructed.

The shroud of secrecy about MI5's activities also extends to the name of its top man, the Director-General, of the Security Service. His identity is always known by foreign intelligence agencies, both friendly and unfriendly, and it is known by many in government, in the Civil Service, and the media: the only ones who do not know are the British people. The publication of his name in the press (like that of the head of MI6) is governed by the convention that silence will be maintained unless his name is revealed in the foreign press – then it can be made public here too. (This is what happened in the case of Sir John Rennie, the last head of MI6, after his name appeared in a German magazine.) Ironically it is the good old tradition of giving medals and titles to top ranks which is one of the best guides as to who is currently head of MI5. In 1966 the Queen's New Year Honours List (published each year on January 1st) carried the information that MI5's chief Sir Roger Hollis was 'lately attached to the MOD' (he got the KBE) thus signalling his retirement.[55] Similarly his successor was later honoured as 'E. M. Jones, attached to War Office'. The latter, now Sir Martin Furnival-Jones, retired in April 1972 but his successor remained incognito until the beginning of 1974. Yet again the give-away was the honouring of the MI5 chief. The *Sunday Express* pointed out the revelation but it did not name him; all it said was that the Director-General

---

[55] Hollis had joined MI5 from the British-American Tobacco Company which he had represented in China.

who works from a 'West London headquarters' had been given a 'fairly high honour' by the Prime Minister. When asked for a comment the Ministry of Defence said: 'We understand this gentleman does not want any publicity and we have no information about him.'[56]

A careful examination of the Queen's Honours List for 1974 produced the following: 'KCB – Michael Bowen HANLEY, Ministry of Defence'. Unlike all the other recipients no specific job was assigned to him. Another check with *Who's Who* and *The British Imperial Calendar* (an annual listing of all executive officers in the Civil Service) showed Mr Hanley's name to be absent, which is another indicator as to the identity of the MI5 chief – he is excluded from both these publications while in office.[57]

The money voted by parliament in the annual Secret Vote goes towards the activities of MI5 and MI6 (the military intelligence agencies are funded separately). Every MP knows this money is only a fraction of the money needed to run these two agencies – the rest is hidden in other estimates, particularly those on defence.[58] Their total cost is not known but the public figure should be multiplied by five to reach the real level of expenditure. In the immediate post-war period, 1945–1951, the Secret Vote went up from £2·5 million to £4 million a year. By 1963 the figure was £7 million and two years later in 1965 it was £10 million. Between 1966 and 1969 the Labour government held back any increases, however by 1972 the figure had risen to £13 million, and by 1973–74 to £15 million. What is clear is that the total sum has more than doubled in the last ten years. The Secret Vote is the one exception to the rule that the Public Accounts Committee of the Commons may inspect the accounts of all departments without reservation. Moreover, the accounting for the Secret Vote which had been undertaken by the Treasury was transferred in 1969 to the Cabinet Office.[59]

Few commentators and writers make any reference to the staffing of MI5 but it has certainly more than doubled since the 1950s. Its strength then was estimated to be around fifteen hundred and is now between four and five thousand.

Perhaps one of the most significant factors affecting the kind of staff

[56] *Sunday Express*, 6 January 1974.

[57] Sir Michael Hanley, like Sir Maurice Oldfield, head of MI6 is a career security-officer who rose through the ranks. (*Private Eye*, 30 May 1975).

[58] The passing of the Secret Vote is usually a mere formality for only rarely have MPs used this as an opportunity to try and get more information.

[59] *Daily Telegraph*, 21 March 1969.

required by the agency has been the loss of the Empire in the post-war period, for MI5's overseas role is now very limited. A number of ex-colonial police and intelligence officers still occupy high positions in the agency, but they are a dying breed. The recruitment of personnel is now more usually from the police and Special Branch, the military (particularly their security and intelligence agencies), and the Civil Service (mainly for administration). In addition there are also lawyers, journalists, psychologists, sociologists, chemists and technicians. However, there is still a tendency in recruiting headquarters staff to opt for those from trusty military or public service backgrounds who are thought more likely to be loyal.

MI5 interest in universities and students serves a double function – to keep under surveillance potential troublemakers and to gain recruits. This involves contacts on the staff and in the administration of most of Britain's universities and colleges: 'The young men who work for the department were thoroughly vetted, and all-but-selected before they had any notion that the secret service had any interest in them . . .'[60] After their names have been suggested and a security check made on their backgrounds, some potential recruits are initially invited to an interview and asked to provide information about their campus, while others are recruited only after they have completed courses.

The recruitment of students today usually starts with an informal approach by someone known to the student. It appears that the methods used to be more direct, for example in one case letters were sent to more than twenty students at Cambridge University.[61] One inquisitive student who attended the interview following the letter at the War Office was told: '(we need) a report from time to time on the political actions and attitudes of some undergraduates, and occasionally a full report in reply to a specific inquiry . . .'[62] And in 1973 it was reported that among the files discovered during a sit-in at Edinburgh University were those concerning two students recruited by MI5.[63]

*MI*5 *'s internal structure*

The internal organisation of MI5 has three components: 1) headquarters staff responsible for the collation, recording and assess-

[60] *Sunday Times*, 23 March 1961.
[61] *Black Dwarf*, May 1969.
[62] *Ibid.*
[63] *Daily Mirror*, 17 May 1973.

ment of intelligence; 2) the field force of undercover agents and those engaged on surveillance duties; 3) the scientific and technical branch. Under the Director-General are at least six departmental heads – the Directors of the Counter-espionage Branch, the Protective Security Branch, the Counter-Sabotage Branch, the Counter-Subversion Branch, the Scientific and Support Services Branch, and a Director for the Registry and Administration. The Branches under the first four Directors are then divided into Sections, then Sub-Sections (or 'desks' as they are commonly referred to). For example, one Section, 'K.9' is reportedly concerned with investigating defectors (including resignations) from MI5.[64]

A central part of the organisation is the Registry, where files from all the Branches are co-ordinated and indexed. In addition to the files there are 'source books' which contain an up-to-date appraisal of specific fields. In 1961 Chapman Pincher suggested that the Registry held details of over two million people on file and the figure is probably more than double this today. In the same article Pincher said the staff of the Registry are 'mainly young daughters of Society and Service families recruited largely on the recommendation of girls who have worked there previously. The MI5 chiefs believe this is the best way of keeping out pro-Communist girls who might destroy valuable records.'[65] Apart from satisfying continuous internal demands for information the Registry also searches through its files when another agency asks that a check (known as a 'trace') be made on any known subversive or pro-communist activities by the named individual. These requests can originate from a large number of sources – the army, the Special Branch, the Foreign Office, and other state departments. Usually checks of this kind also involve the Registries of the Special Branch, MI5 and Defence Intelligence Staff (DIS).[66]

The field force of MI5 comprises two groups, those engaged in general surveillance duties (who work in teams of four to eight, keeping an eye on diplomats and trade union leaders, for example) and those operatives working largely undercover.

Also, like the Special Branch, MI5 recruits informants in all areas of political activity. One unsuccessful attempt to recruit an informer came during the Angry Brigade trials when a girl who had been asked to put up bail money for one of the defendants was approached. The

---

[64] *Workers Press*, 27 December 1973.
[65] *Daily Express*, 10 January 1961.
[66] For DIS see p. 191.

initial approach was made through a family friend who in turn
brought along his MI5 boss.

> 'He knew that I'd put up bail for this girl and told me that I could
> get to know "certain things". That I could get to know certain
> people – people I didn't know then, but whom I've met since. He
> told me that he could understand my scruples – that I felt I would
> be spying on my friends. But that I wouldn't really – we all
> believed in the same thing etc. and that I needed a "job and direc-
> tion in life".'[67]

Many of those working at Section level at MI5 headquarters come
from the professions and include psychologists, economists, journalists, and sociologists. Their job, together with other members of the
Section, is to assess the data assembled from field operatives and from
routine monitoring by the administrative staff.[68] These assessments,
together with recommendations for action, may be for internal use
within MI5; or for consideration by another intelligence body like the
DIS; or for the information of the Prime Minister via the Cabinet
Office.

While MI5 holds an overall responsibility for protecting the secrets
of the state it is not answerable for the actions of all civil servants. Each
Ministry has its own security force and the Secretary of State for a
department is held to be responsible for the security of personnel and
documents under him. MI5 does advise these security units and carries
out periodic inspections of security procedures. The Investigating
Officers of each Ministry's security division are responsible for both
personnel and physical security. These Officers are frequently retired
police officers (some from the Special Branch) or ex-servicemen. MI5
checks out the records in its Registry in response to enquiries from
Ministries, who themselves hold comparatively few records.

Essentially MI5 attempts to work unobtrusively, gathering information and, if necessary, communicating it to selected people, often via a
third party. This could include an adverse report on an applicant for a
'sensitive' job, a report to a private contractor about one of his men, an
indirect tip via the Special Branch regarding the 'leadership' of a strike
or of subversive actions or speeches by militants, or tipping-off a journalist that a particular person or incident is worth investigating.

---

[67] *Socialist Worker*, 5 March 1975.
[68] See the chapter on the Special Branch for examples of this.

MI5 and MPs

It is often assumed that only those active outside the corridors of power are of interest to agencies like MI5. But industrialists, journalists, and academics are also frequently placed under surveillance. In practice every new MP immediately acquires a dossier in the Registry files, and this is usually fatter if he comes from a Labour Party background. The verbal evidence given by Sir Martin Furnival-Jones, the Director-General of MI5, to the Franks Committee in 1971 confirmed that MI5 has evidence that the Russians are interested in public figures as potential sources of all sorts of information, from state secrets to the personal foibles of important people: '(the Russian Intelligence Service) are very active in the press world, in Fleet Street, and they are very active among the political parties, around the Palace of Westminster.'[69] On the delicate subject of MPs and the possibility that some of their immediate friends might be in touch with spies Sir Martin said in reply to a question:

'I do not think I can answer that question. It would involve my having indulged in an activity in which I certainly do not indulge, and that is informing myself of the total circle of acquaintances of every MP . . . I can certainly say that very many MPs are in contact with very many intelligence officers.'[70]

A little later Sir Martin expanded on the Russian interest in MPs: 'No doubt many MPs, many people enter the House of Commons in the hope of becoming Ministers. If the Russian Intelligence Service can recruit a backbench MP, and he continues to hold his seat for a number of years and climbs the ladder to a Ministerial position, it is obvious the spy is home and dry.'[71] It is also obvious that MPs and Ministers are, in the eyes of MI5, as much of a threat to security as civil servants – perhaps more so because the state has less control over them.

Two reported cases of MI5 surveillance of MPs concerned Labour MPs: the first at the time of the 1945 Attlee Government and the second in 1961. In the first case a Labour MP had visited Greece on behalf of the National Union of Students, and while travelling round the country had been captured by the guerrillas. He was taken to see their leader, General Markos, and given a letter for the United Nations

[69] Franks Committee, Vol. 2, p. 246.
[70] *Ibid.*, Vol. 2, p. 250.
[71] *Ibid.*, Vol. 2, p. 253.

which explained their political position. On his return to Britain the MP told the Minister at the Foreign office of his experience and of the letter, but much to his surprise the Minister seemed to know all about his movements in Greece and even quoted parts of conversations he had with a number of Greek officials. His surprise was compounded when an ex-MI5 employee (who had resigned in protest at their methods) told him he had been shadowed both in Greece and on his return: 'Now you are back in England again, an MI5 man has been sent to your home town to keep an eye on you.'[72] The Labour MP finally decided to go and see the Prime Minister, Mr Attlee, who did not believe his story but promised to check. A few days later Attlee apologised to the MP.

> 'He explained that he had looked in the suspects book and had found the MP's name was there. He said that what had happened had been done by the Secret Service people and had not been authorised by him. He told the MP that he himself had torn the page out of the book and that he hoped he would forget about about it.'[73]

The 'suspects book' referred to was one compiled by MI5 with the names of 'important figures' whose allegiance was in doubt.

In the period after the 1959 General Election the Labour Party underwent nearly four years of internal dissension between the reformist leadership of Hugh Gaitskell and the Labour left. The issues dividing them ranged from Gaitskell's leadership, and his desire to remove Clause Four (the commitment to nationalisation) from the party's programme, to the Labour Party Conference decisions in favour of nuclear disarmament. The Labour Party parliamentary leadership at this time was convinced that the only way to regain power after ten years in opposition was to excise the radical elements within the party in order to become more appealing to middle-class voters. Part of this face-lift was an approach by the Labour leaders to MI5 to investigate, on their behalf, MPs considered to be 'crypto-communists'.[74]

A committee of three MPs was set up by the Labour leaders to investigate those left-wing Labour MPs thought to be 'fellow-travellers' – the three were Gaitskell, George Brown and Patrick Gordon Walker.

[72] *Reynolds News*, 11 August 1957.
[73] *Ibid*.
[74] These events were partially revealed by Chapman Pincher in November 1966 and more fully in June 1968.

The committee understandably could not approach the Tory Home Secretary in order to make contact with MI5, so an approach was made to Chapman Pincher, who said: '. . . Mr George Brown, then deputy leader, asked me to provide him with the names, addresses and telephone numbers of the heads of MI5 and the Secret Service, which I did.'[75] A meeting took place between the committee and MI5, and the names of fifteen Labour MPs were handed over to MI5 for investigation. These investigations were conducted by MI5 between August 1961 and January 1962, and involved 'telephone-tapping, shadowing, the opening of mail, examination of bank accounts, and other methods used by Intelligence services.'[76] When the six-month investigation ended MI5 informed Brown that there was no evidence of 'fellow-travelling' MPs in the Labour Party. However, in reality, it appears the Tory Home Secretary learned of the investigation and ordered it to cease and forbade MI5 to present any evidence against a member of parliament.[77] But MI5 did provide evidence that a member of Transport House (the Labour Party national headquarters) was taking money from Czech intelligence officers in return for information. According to Pincher the man in question admitted the truth of the allegation and was quietly dismissed from his job.

It later became clear that not only the Labour leaders were worried about Labour MPs; the Tories up to October 1964 had authorised tapping the telephones and opening the mail of an unspecified number of MPs. When questioned in the Commons, Harold Wilson, the Prime Minister, said: 'When we came into office naturally I found out what was going on. I felt that the system of the previous government in which MPs' telephones were being tapped should be changed.'[78] For the Tories Mr Heath responded by saying that he saw no reason why MPs should be exempted from security procedures.

MI5 and industry

From the point of view of the state, one of MI5's functions is to watch for 'the instigation of strikes . . . in order to serve the purposes of some foreign power.'[79] What a trade unionist may regard as a strike for an

[75] *Daily Express*, 28 June 1968.
[76] *Ibid.*
[77] Sir Tufton Beamish, Tory MP for Lewes, claimed that six of the fifteen MPs investigated were still in the Commons in 1967. *Daily Mail*, 15 February 1967.
[78] *Daily Telegraph*, 12 April 1967.
[79] Williams, *Not in the Public Interest* (1965) p. 137.

increase in pay, can be construed quite differently by those dedicated to preserving the status quo: it may be seen either as an act which furthers communist interests in the long-term Cold War struggle or, as is becoming more fashionable, it may be seen as a direct assault on the very fabric of capitalist society. The monopolisation and nationalisation of key industries together with the long-term economic recession serve to make the productive system more vulnerable to trade union action and to make these actions themselves of critical importance to MI5 in maintaining the security of the state and the prevailing order.

Surveillance of industrial struggles is carried out both by full-time undercover agents of MI5 and by people already working in industry who are recruited by agents to pass out information on a long-term basis. This surveillance covers both private industry and those concerned with state-contract work.

A case that arose in 1962 was one of the rare occasions when MI5 officers appeared in court. Kodak Ltd. brought a charge under the Prevention of Corruption Act against two of their employees for allegedly giving industrial secrets to East German Intelligence via a contact man. The contact man was Dr Soupert, a Belgian chemical engineer, who was confronted by Belgian Intelligence with evidence of his passing industrial secrets, and for a time he became a double-agent. Part of the deal was that he should name his sources and these he alleged included two Kodak employees in England who were subsequently arrested. The men pleaded not guilty and after an eight-day trial were acquitted by the jury on all counts. The key prosecution witness was Dr Soupert, who was provided with a secret address by MI5 for the duration of the trial. In the witness stand Soupert admitted that he had signed a contract with Kodak worth £5,000 if he came and gave evidence at the trial. At the end of the trial the defence counsel summed up in the following terms: 'This Court is not an instrument of MI5, it is not an instrument of Kodak Ltd., nor is it a rubber stamp for the authorities, the police or what may be called the "powers that be".'[80] One of the two acquitted men was a member of the Communist Party, active in union affairs, and a past Vice-Chairman of the Association of Cinematograph and Television Technicians (ACTT). The events leading up to the trial had involved Belgian Intelligence 'tipping-off' MI5, and MI5 presenting their 'evidence' to Kodak who brought the charges. MI5 officers then took care of Soupert while he was here for the trial. Yet the court was told from the start 'that no state security was

[80] Payne, *Private Spies* (1967) p. 189.

involved', so why did MI5 intervene so directly in aid of a private firm?[81]

Another case, of a man working at a Vickers Armstrong aircraft factory, was recounted in *The People* in 1966 – with a headline which read 'For 14 years Fred fooled the Commie bosses'.[82] Being a patriot, Fred, who operated under the code-name George, became a member of the Communist Party and within the factory was for a time elected to the shop stewards' committee. In return for these services Fred got several hundred pounds from his security contacts.

At national level there is evidence that MI5 gathers information on wage-claims. In 1972 it was reported that the eight members of the executive committee of the Associated Society of Locomotive Engineers and Firemen had their telephones tapped during a dispute

3.   An unidentified cameraman taking pictures outside a courtroom where workers were demonstrating in support of the Shrewsbury 24 who were on trial.

[81] *Ibid.*, p. 187.
[82] *The People*, 16 January 1966.

with British Rail. And during the miners' strike in the same year an ex-MI5 agent said that a meeting between NUM chiefs and a leading member of the Communist Party was bugged. The meeting was held in a cafe and an agent planted a briefcase containing a tape recorder within range of their conversation.[83] In 1975 it was revealed that during redecorations of the Communist Party HQ in King Street in London a powerful bug was found built into the wall of a conference room.[84]

The interest of MI5 in private companies who undertake contract work for the state needs spelling out in detail. Production work for Ministries is partially fulfilled by state-owned factories, where the Ministry concerned is responsible for security. Most work however is done under contract by private industry and it is MI5 who have the responsibility for security and surveillance within the 4,500 firms concerned. These firms are not allowed to employ aliens on classified contract work, nor anybody that MI5 finds politically unacceptable. Each firm is sent a 'secret aspects letter' with the contract for work; a manual of security procedures; and the firm's security officers are encouraged to participate in special courses organised for them by MI5. What is less well-known, however, are the two other aspects of this programme. The first is that the contractor's employees are subject to Positive Vetting:

> 'In principle the application of the purge procedure and Positive Vetting to contractor's employees is on the same basis as in the public service. In practice these personnel security procedures, though sometimes calling for delicate handling, do not appear to present contractors with major difficulties or embarrassment.'[85]

Positive Vetting involves the preparation of an in-depth report on the personal lives and political activities of those investigated. The extension of this procedure to those outside state employment in industry represents a substantial intrusion into areas of industrial struggle and individual job opportunities. It serves the function not merely of ensuring security for state secrets but also of seeking to eliminate the possibilities of strikes and other industrial action in these industries – a factor not entirely unwelcomed by the employers: 'Contractors such as Costains are reported to have in the past sacked unskilled labourers

---

[83] *Workers Press*, 27 December 1973.
[84] *The Times*, 8 February 1975.
[85] The Radcliffe Report (1962) p. 29.

whom the Security Service found politically unacceptable for work on certain construction projects.'[86]

In addition, MI5 employs a specially recruited and trained team of agents known as Security Advisers who act on behalf of the contracting state department and work in close liaison with the security officers and managements of the firms concerned. Most of these Security Advisers are recruited from the police or from the police constabularies of the armed forces.

The Military Intelligence Agencies

Until the end of the nineteenth century internal intelligence was gathered by the Home Office (discussed in chapter 3) and external intelligence by the Foreign Office. The Foreign Office co-ordinated the expansion of the British Empire and the protection of British markets in these countries. Deacon observed of this period that 'It was sometime during the middle of the nineteenth century that the tendency grew in Britain for the Secret Service to be regarded as something which was not mentioned in polite society.'[87]

In the latter part of the century the War Office (Army) and the Admiralty created small intelligence departments independent of the Foreign Office. A year after the start of the Crimean War in 1855 the War Office set up a small unit behind the facade of the Topographical and Statistical Department. This was formally recognised as the Intelligence Branch of the War Office in 1871, and its central functions – as defined in 1896 – were 'the preparation of information relating to the military defence of the empire . . . (and that) relating to the military geography, resources and armed forces of foreign countries and the British colonies and possessions . . .'[88] In 1887 the Admiralty set up a Foreign Intelligence Committee under Captain W. H. Hall (whose son was later chief of the Naval Intelligence Department, NID). However the Foreign Office and the military were not the only ones gathering intelligence; the Colonial Office (created 1801) and the India Office (created as the Board of Control in 1784) also ran a spying system in their areas of interest. Additionally, information came to them from

'indirect means by various societies which provided funds for exploration in remote parts of the world. Much that was contributed towards the cost of obtaining intelligence came,

[86] Thompson, *Big Brother* (1970) p. 67.
[87] Deacon, *op. cit.*, p. 122.
[88] *Op. cit.*, p. 124.

sometimes unrequested, from the pockets of private individuals whose motives were either purely patriotic, or those of unbridled curiosity.'[89]

An attempt at co-ordinating the various interests and agencies was the Colonial Defence Committee set up in 1878 and in 1895 the Cabinet Defence Committee was created. In the wake of Britain's defeat in the Boer War this latter committee became more high-powered with a new title – The Committee for Imperial Defence (1902); its chairman was the Prime Minister. The Committee's main task was to co-ordinate plans by military and civil branches of government in preparation for war. During the First World War the main intelligence agencies were MI5 (created in 1909 by the Committee for Imperial Defence), MI6 (the Foreign Office agency with a growing independence, also known as the Secret Service and SIS), Military Intelligence (based at the War Office), and the Naval Intelligence Department (at the Admiralty). The Air Force Intelligence department was created during the 1920s after the formation of the Air Ministry in 1918.

In the inter-war years the Committee for Imperial Defence was serviced by a sub-committee called the Joint Intelligence Committee (JIC):

'The Joint Intelligence subcommittee's mission was to provide accurate information from every point of view upon a problem under consideration. Its membership comprised a Foreign Office representative, as chairman, the three Deputy Directors of (service) Intelligence, a member of the Department for Overseas Trade, and other departments as necessary.'[90]

During the Second World War JIC serviced the Chiefs of Staff Committee (COS) and after the war it was transferred to the newly-formed Ministry of Defence.[91]

Structural changes 1945–1975

After the war the introduction of the purge procedure and Positive

[89] *Op. cit.*, p. 134.
[90] F. A. Johnson, *Defence by Committee* (1960) p. 244.
[91] The Ministry of Defence was formed in 1946, and replaced the Committee for Imperial Defence. The Admiralty, War Office and Air Ministry continued as independent departments until the reorganization of 1964 when they were unified under the MOD.

Vetting placed a greater emphasis than in the past on the security as distinct from intelligence aspects of these agencies. Each of the three services – Army, Navy and Air Force – operated both an intelligence agency and a security agency, and MI5 and MI6 each had a section devoted to its own internal security.[92] Since the First World War all of the service Ministries had had an internal security force, and the principle was well-established that a Minister (now the Secretary of State) was responsible for the 'safety' of his or her departments, personnel, buildings and documents. The start of the Cold War saw all these internal Ministry security-units re-vamped and increased in personnel.

In 1946 a small co-ordinating unit was created, known as the Joint Intelligence Bureau (JIB). The first Director of JIB was Kenneth Strong (later Major-General Sir K. Strong), who spent a year prior to this as head of the Political Intelligence Department at the Foreign Office. JIB was the first professional attempt to co-ordinate intelligence from all Ministries, and it remained a small though influential unit despite hostility from the long-standing service intelligence agencies. The scope of JIB was not merely to provide analyses based on military considerations: it covered the political, economic, and psychological aspects of subjects connected with the national interest – in other words, the security of the British state. Its staff included 'economists, engineers, geographers, scientists and doctors as well as Service officers.'[93]

JIB was in fact to be a prototype for the reorganisation of defence intelligence in 1964 and Strong commented on its relevance to the traditional agencies:

> 'The speed and complexity with which military, political economic, scientific and social factors can interact, and the rapidity of social and political change, makes completely anachronistic the type of Intelligence-estimating machinery that leans heavily on elaborately insulated departments . . .'[94]

When the reorganisation occurred JIB was absorbed into the new Defence Intelligence Staff (DIS), and Strong became its first chief – as Director-General of Intelligence at the Ministry of Defence.

[92] These agencies are: Air Security and Air Intelligence; Navy Security and Navy Intelligence; Army Security and Army Intelligence (the latter is more usually referred to as the Army Intelligence Corps).
[93] Strong, *Intelligence at the Top* (1968) p. 223.
[94] *Op. cit.*, p. 224.

In 1964 the structure of Britain's defence organisation underwent a major reorganisation with the old Admiralty, War Office and Air Ministry being absorbed into the Ministry of Defence. Each service was still to be responsible for intelligence-gathering and security within its own field:

> 'Senior officers of each service will still be responsible for their professional views on subjects which primarily concern their own Service. But the staff as a whole will be integrated . . . (and will also produce) a Defence intelligence viewpoint on matters which are of interest to the MOD.'[95]

The latter part of this statement is a reference to the continuation of the role played by the now-integrated JIB. The 'Defence intelligence viewpoint' therefore must be understood not just as a consideration of purely military matters, but in the terms of Strong's statement on the wide-ranging interests of JIB. Strong's number two in the new DIS as Deputy Chief of Staff Intelligence was Vice-Admiral Sir Norman Denning – previously Director of Naval Intelligence and later the Secretary to the D-Notice Committee.

What should not be confused at this point is JIB and JIC. JIC, the Joint Intelligence Committee, continued and collated reports from the DIS, MI6 and MI5. The Chairman of JIC is always a senior Foreign Office civil servant of Deputy Under-Secretary rank who is responsible for intelligence and strategic affairs – Sir Bernard Burrows and Sir Denis Greenhill have both been its chairman. JIC has recently become known as the Defence Intelligence Committee (DIC), and its present-day job extends far beyond the purely military and diplomatic:

> '(Their duty) is to supply responsible Ministers and officials with up-to-the-minute intelligence on critical matters, forecasts of trouble or other significant developments, and long-term round-ups. Their sphere of action extends far beyond that of defence in the narrowest sense, to include political and economic matters and so on: in fact all matters of potential interest to the government, and particularly to the FCO (Foreign and Commonwealth Office) and the Department of Defence.'[96]

The respective importance of DIC and the DIS must be made clear – DIC is a co-ordinating committee, while DIS is a massive organisation

---

[95] White Paper, *Central Organisation for Defence* Cmnd. 2097, p. 7.
[96] MacDermott, *The New Diplomacy* (1973) p. 137.

DEFENCE, PRESS AND BROADCASTING COMMITTEE

'D' NOTICE NO 10

BRITISH INTELLIGENCE SERVICES

This Notice should be read in conjunction with 'D' Notice No 1.

2. The broad functions of the Security Service and the Secret Service (often referred to as MI5 and MI6) are of course widely known. The Security Service is responsible for countering threats to the Realm arising from espionage, subversion and sabotage and the Secret Service exists to provide HM Government with secret intelligence concerning foreign powers. Both Services must operate as far as possible in conditions of secrecy.

3. Attempts are made by foreign powers to plant stories in the British Press. A variation of this technique, which must be taken into account where the activities of foreign intelligence services are concerned, is the planting in an overseas newspaper or other publication of a piece of information about British Intelligence matters with an eye to stimulating the British Press not only to republish the story but also to expand on it.

4. You are requested not to publish anything about:

a. secret activities of the British intelligence or counter-intelligence services undertaken inside or outside the UK for the purposes of national security;

b. identities, whereabouts and tasks of persons of whatever status or rank who are or have been employed by either Service;

c. addresses and telephone numbers used by either Service;

d. organizational structures, communications networks, numerical strengths, secret methods and training techniques of either Service;

e. details of assistance given by the police forces in Security Service operations;

f. details of the manner in which well-known intelligence methods (eg telephone-tapping) are actually applied or of their targets and purposes where these concern national security. Reference in general terms to well-known intelligence methods is not precluded by this sub-paragraph;

g. technical advances by the British Services in relation to their intelligence and counter-intelligence methods whether the basic methods are well-known or not.

5. You are also requested to use extreme discretion in reporting any apparent disclosures of information published abroad purporting to come from members or former employees of either Service. If you are in any doubt please consult the Secretary.

6. You are also requested not to elaborate on any information which may be published abroad about British intelligence.

7. On all these limitations some relaxation may be possible: please consult the Secretary.

Date of issue 16 August 1971

4. The D-Notice reproduced above is one of a series issued to all national, regional and local media – newspapers, television and radio.

with more than ninety departments.

The last major change to the intelligence structure in recent times has been the appointment of a Co-ordinator of Intelligence and Security in the Cabinet Office. The current holder of this office is a career diplomat, Sir Peter Wilkinson, who was appointed in January 1972. It is popularly believed that he was the first to undertake this job but in fact Sir Dick Goldsmith White, previously head of MI5 and then of MI6, was the first, when he retired from MI6. He held this position for about two years before finally retiring at the end of 1972.

The role of the Co-ordinator in the Cabinet Office is to present assessments and reports to the Prime Minister. It is this function, rather than the notion of the Co-ordinator directing or controlling the intelligence establishment, which is the reality, although it is probably true that the attitudes of the Prime Minister are brought to the attention of the agencies more frequently than in the past.

A typical example of the work of the Co-ordinator occurred in the summer of 1973. The visit of the now-deposed President Caetano of Portugal was preceded by evidence of massacres by Portuguese troops in Mozambique and in this country his arrival was expected to spark off vocal demonstrations by opponents of the Portuguese regime. It was reported that Sir Peter prepared for Mr Heath 'forecasts and recommendations from Scotland Yard and the Security Service' on the expected demonstrations, and 'interim summaries of Secret Service findings following an investigation into reports of the Mozambique massacres.'[97]

MI6

The head of MI6 from 1951 was General Sir John Sinclair who resigned in the wake of the Commander Crabbe incident in 1956. The new chief was Sir Dick Goldsmith White, who had been head of MI5, and he remained in the post until 1969. The long tradition of independence of MI6 from direct Foreign Office control much annoyed the Ministry and their views found the sympathetic ear of the Prime Minister, Harold Wilson, who appointed a Foreign Office man, Sir John Rennie, over the head of the internal candidate of MI6 (the number two). While head of MI6 Sir John was listed as Deputy Under-Secretary at the Foreign Office, and Superintending Under-Secretary

[97] *Sunday Express*, 15 July 1973.

of the Library and Records Department, the Research Department, and the Planning Staff.[98]

Sir John's departure, due anyway in 1973, was preceded by two events. The first was the arrest and conviction of his son on a drugs charge; the second was the publication of his name in the German magazine *Stern*. By tradition – one through which the public is kept in the dark – the heads of MI6 and MI5 are not named until their retirement unless their names should appear in the foreign press. On this occasion however Sir John's successor was named in the press within weeks of his appointment. This time it was the American magazine *Newsweek* which published the name of Maurice Oldfield, the current head of MI6. Ironically, his name did not appear in the European edition which is sold in London, but several British papers reported its publication in America and hence evaded any likelihood of giving offence to the authorities.[99] By appointing Oldfield Mr Heath reasserted the principle of favouring an internal candidate.

MI6 is responsible for gathering intelligence and espionage activities outside of the United Kingdom and its few remaining colonies. The areas in which MI6 is especially proficient are the old colonies, where as MI5's responsibility ended MI6 took over, and in Western Europe. A rare example of MI6's work in Western Europe came to light in 1972. While British intelligence agencies were concerned with the activities of the Angry Brigade and the IRA the West German agencies were trying to track down the Red Army Faction (the 'Baader–Meinhof' gang). In June the West German police entered an apartment flat in Stuttgart with guns blazing and shot dead a British 'businessman', Ian MacLeod. Initially it was represented as an 'accident'; however two weeks later a German paper, *Bild am Sonntag*, said that MacLeod was a British agent who had infiltrated and was working with the Red Army Faction. The object of the operation had been to find out if the guerrilla group had any connections with similar groups in Britain.[100] And in August 1973 the West German government admitted that it acted on requests from the American, French and British intelligence agencies to tap the phones of private citizens. A German law of 1968 recognised the right of the old occupying powers to make such requests. A spokesman said:

[98] *British Imperial Calendar*, HMSO, 1973.
[99] See *Time Out*, 10 August 1973, for Oldfield's biography and his reported base.
[100] *Time Out*, 7 July 1972.

'The three powers have repeatedly made use of the above-mentioned possibility to request a surveillance measure.'[101]

The gathering of intelligence in foreign countries is not the prerogative of MI6 alone, and the Foreign Office (to which MI6 is 'related') itself mounts a large intelligence-gathering operation on questions of political, diplomatic, and economic importance: 'The truth is that diplomats are, in the nicest sense of course, licensed spies.'[102] Like the intelligence agencies the Foreign Office receives daily information reports from the Government Communications Headquarters (GCHQ) in Cheltenham, whose Director is Sir Leonard Hooper. GCHQ monitors and decodes all radio, telex and telegram communications in and out of Britain, including the messages of all foreign embassies based in Britain, finance and industrial companies, and individuals of interest to the state agencies. In addition to decoding, GCHQ also codes messages from Britain's agencies to overseas outposts. The relationship of MI6 to the Foreign Office is formally through the Permanent Under-Secretary who is the top man in the Ministry. A Deputy Under-Secretary of State is chairman of JIC, and several senior executives liaise with MI6. But MI6, like MI5, has the right of direct access to the Prime Minister.

The Defence Intelligence Staff (DIS)

The intelligence agencies attached to the Ministry of Defence are divided between the DIS, which is concerned with overall assessment and evaluation, and the service agencies which are responsible for their own fields (while still contributing to the former). DIS has a mixture of a military and civilian staff, and has over ninety different sections. The head of DIS is the Director-General of Intelligence, currently Sir Louis le Bailly, and his number two is the Deputy Chief of Defence Staff (Intelligence). DIS is divided into five main departments:

1. Service Intelligence
2. Management and Support of Intelligence
3. Scientific and Technical Intelligence
4. Economic Intelligence
5. Management and Support of Intelligence (Admin.)

[101] *Evening Standard*, 2 August 1973.
[102] MacDermott, *op. cit.*, p. 43. MacDermott was, prior to his retirement, a Foreign Office adviser to MI6.

MI5 and MI6 have a liaison office at the Ministry of Defence.

As the main intelligence agency of the military arm of the state, DIS (and its less sophisticated predecessors) has always had the function of keeping under surveillance a large number of the British people. All the personnel of the three services and the civilian staff of the MOD (and its many outposts) together with their families and friends have been subject to rigorous security checks; they number hundreds of thousands of people. DIS, again like its predecessors, also has a responsibility for the internal defence of the British state. Two factors have changed in the last five years. Firstly, there has been the massive military and intelligence commitment to Northern Ireland in which DIS has not been uninterested. Secondly, contingency plans for the defence of the state against internal subversion and possible insurrection underwent a major revision.[103]

Sir Kenneth Strong who pioneered multi-disciplinary assessment for the military has expressed the role of intelligence in his book as 'an organised and scientific attempt to predict the future course of events that may affect the national interest.'[104]

Finally, the MOD has its own internal security units. These are the Directorate of Headquarters Security (MOD) based at Metropole Building, Northumberland Avenue, London WC2, and Lacon House, Theobald's Road, London WC1, and the Directorate of Security (Procurement Executive) based at Castlewood House, 77–91 Oxford Street, London WC1. The former is concerned with physical security and the latter with contract-work. Both of these units are answerable to the Assistant Under-Secretary of State (Security).

Conclusion

The existence of an agency like MI5 is for some people either unproblematic or a necessity. The former view is that of Bulloch in his book *MI5*: 'MI5 today is a power in the land, but not a power of which any loyal Englishman need be afraid.'[105] A 'loyal Englishman' is one who not only does not spy for a foreign power but is not a militant trade unionist or a member of a 'subversive' organisation (any one leftwards of the Tory Party). In short, a 'loyal Englishman' is one who supports the prevailing order and who does not seek to change it whether through radical reform or revolution.

[103] See chapter 7.
[104] Quoted in *Daily Telegraph*, 26 September 1968.
[105] Bullock, *op. cit.*, p. 12.

In past times the threat to the state has been largely generated by the 'external enemy'. Today, however, the possibility of an internal threat to the continued reproduction of the state and the capitalist system brings the activities of MI5, and other intelligence agencies, into a new prominence.

Heads of the intelligence establishment

Director-General of MI5 (Security Service, DI5)

Sir Vernon Kell	from 1909
Sir David Petrie	1940
Sir Peter Sillitoe	1946
Sir Dick Goldsmith White	1953
Sir Roger Hollis	1956
Sir Martin Furnival-Jones	1965
Sir Michael Hanley	1972

Director-General of MI6 (Secret Service, DI6)

Sir Mansfield Cumming	1911
Sir Hugh Sinclair	1924
Sir Stewart Menzies	1949
Sir John Sinclair	1951
Sir D. Goldsmith White	1956
Sir John Rennie	1969
Sir Maurice Oldfield	1973

Director-General of Intelligence (DIS)

Sir Kenneth Strong (Major-General)	1964
Air Chief-Marshall Sir Alfred Earle	1966
Admiral Sir Louis Le Bailly	1973

Chairman of the Joint Intelligence Committee (JIC)

1963	Sir Bernard Burrows
1966	Sir Denis Greenhill
1968	Sir Edward Peck

Co-ordinator of Intelligence and Security in the Cabinet Office

Sir Dick Goldsmith White	1970
Sir Peter Wilkinson	1973

The usual way of representing the relationship of the agencies places the emphasis on the theoretical accountability to Ministers, and suggests a degree of control by the latter which is quite inaccurate.

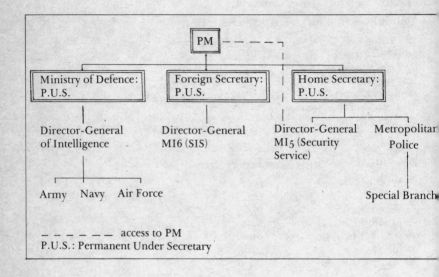

_ _ _ _ _ _ access to PM
P.U.S.: Permanent Under Secretary

A more accurate way of portraying the relationship between government Ministers and the agencies would emphasise the partial access of the former to the latter (as below).

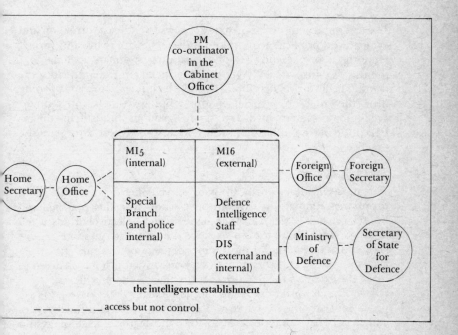

5   The Techniques of Surveillance

The techniques employed by state agencies to gather information and evidence on political activists and movements are many and varied. Here the main methods, telephone-tapping and mail-opening, and the use of informers and agents-provocateur are examined in some detail. The historical development of the legitimation of mail-opening (from the 17th century) and telephone-tapping (from the 19th century) are intimately intertwined, as the stated grounds for justifying the interception of communications rests – almost solely – on long-standing practice.

Telephone-tapping

The most insidious form of state surveillance is the practice of telephone-tapping. The eavesdropper is able to gather personal and political details which can then be recorded, selectively transcribed and stored for future use. So sensitive is the state to questions on this subject that no figures for the number of telephones tapped have been available since 1957. During more recent years much has changed to make the extent of the practice of more than academic interest.

However, a word of warning should be made at the outset, for the practice of tapping is, as yet, of limited importance in intelligence-gathering. The limitations are two-fold: the degree of technology and manpower available, and the political acceptability of the practice. Each time the practice comes to light because of some error by the agency concerned, much indignation is expressed in parliament and in the press; however, these are two bodies with notoriously short memories and the effect of an exposé is merely to cause the practice to continue a little more discreetly than before.

In 1956 the Home Secretary, Mr Butler, forestalled criticism of the Marrinan case by setting up a Committee of Inquiry, the Birkett Committee, which reported in 1957 with recommendations for future practice.[1] Understandably the Committee first sought to establish the legal

---

[1] *The Report of the Committee of Privy Councillors appointed to enquire into the interception of communications*, HMSO, Cmnd 283 (1957). The Birkett Report.

basis for the practice of telephone-tapping – a task which was to prove insoluble.

Justification was first sought in the age-old practice of opening the mail. In 1516 the monarchy created its own postal service and this was later extended to allow private individuals to use the system. By the Acts of 1657 and 1660 the Crown was given the right of monopoly over the provision of the postal service, and the 1657 Act explicitly recognised that this was the best means to 'discover and prevent any dangerous and wicked Designs against the Commonwealth'. In 1663 the procedure was regularised in a Proclamation that said letters were to be opened only on a warrant from the Secretary of State. The first judicial ruling on the practice was given by Lord Camden in his judgement on Entick v Carrington in 1765. On the question of issuing general warrants he ruled: 'If it is law it will be found in our books. If it is not to be found there it is not law.'[2] He went on to say that because the state saw fit to act in a certain manner this did not establish the lawfulness of the act. However, it appears the practice of opening the post could be justified under the Post Office Act of 1711.

When the Secretary of State issued a warrant to open the letters of an Italian revolutionary, Joseph Mazzini, in 1844, a parliamentary storm arose, and two Secret Committees of the House of Commons and the House of Lords were asked to report. Lord Campbell, a member of one committee, wrote in his autobiography that the practice was neither authorised by common law nor statute, but he added that the Secretary of State did have the authority to intercept evidence of possible criminal actions. In fact all the Post Office Acts of 1711, 1837, 1908 and 1953 recognise *the practice* of intercepting mail on a warrant issued by the Home Secretary. However, this does not confer *the legal power* to do it, and there is no legal or statutory basis for this power as exercised by the state.

Although the Telegraphy Act of 1868 gave the state a monopoly over the provision of the telephone system, it makes no mention of the issuing of warrants for interception. Up to 1937, the Post Office intercepted calls at the direct request of the police, Special Branch or MI5.[3] Then the Home Secretary decided to regularise the system by bringing tapping into line with mail-opening, and ruled it was only to be done on the issuing of a warrant by himself. The authority to do this was thought at the time to rest on the same power as for mail-opening,

---

[2] Birkett, *op. cit.*, p. 11.
[3] This was done without the authorisation of the Home Secretary.

a power which did not exist. In evidence to the Birkett Commission the Home Office expressed the view that the power stemmed from a prerogative right (of the Crown) to examine all material carried by the Crown in relation to the safety of the state and public order, and that this right extended to new means of communication not envisaged in the eighteenth century. The Committee dismissively noted this view and pointed out that no constitutional writer on the Royal prerogative had ever referred to this particular power. Given the evidence, the Committee's conclusions were no surprise. They did not doubt that the practice had been going on for several centuries, but they could find no statutory authority giving the state the power to intercept the mail and telephone conversations. Therefore they had to content themselves with affirming the existence of the practice, and suggested that letters and telephones were but different means of communication through state-controlled monopolies – and if one was justified so was the other. Anyway, as the Committee noted, the Crown Proceedings Act of 1947 gave full protection to the Post Office against any legal action for interfering with the mail and this could no doubt be extended to the telephone. This little known Act completely exempts whole areas of state action from legal recourse by the citizen, so that even if one could prove one's mail had been opened one would have little chance of a successful legal action.

The authorisation of telephone-tapping is, theoretically, the responsibility of one man, the Home Secretary.[4] This responsibility stems from the various Post Office Acts. The relevant section of the 1953 Post Office Act says there must be 'an express warrant under the hand of a Secretary of State'.[5] Reference to '*a* Secretary of State' is generally held to mean a specific Secretary of State, that is, the Home Secretary. Furthermore, all references by succeeding governments to the issuing of warrants have suggested that *only* the Home Secretary carries out this function. On the rare occasion when this is questioned it has been reluctantly agreed that, in theory, every Secretary of State could authorise warrants, but that in fact only the Home Secretary actually exercises this power.

The central question, however, remains unanswered. Do all the agencies which indulge in tapping get a warrant from the Home Secretary? Clearly the customs and excise, the police and the Special

---

[4] Warrants issued in Northern Ireland and Scotland are signed by the relevant Secretary for State.

[5] Section 58–1.

Branch do obtain warrants in most cases. But do the security service, MI5, and all the other agencies always apply to the Home Office? Apart from MI5 no reference is ever made to the tapping activities of the other agencies – no doubt we are meant to believe they do not tap telephones. MI6, which is nominally under the Foreign Office, can go to the Foreign Secretary – *a* Secretary of State; similarly, the DIS and the other military agencies can be obliged by the Secretary of State for Defence. Moreover, a warrant issued by the Foreign Secretary or the Defence Secretary is not covered by the rules laid down by and for the Home Office. The review of warrants is usually carried out by the agencies themselves and not – as in the case of the Home Office – by both the agency and the Home Office staff.

The procedure for those agencies which apply to the Home Office is to present a list of the names, addresses and telephone numbers to be monitored. Applications are first considered by the Criminal Department at the Home Office, and formally viewed by the Permanent Under-Secretary before the Minister gives his authorisation to the request. MI5 applications go via a Home Office Deputy Under-Secretary to the Permanent Under-Secretary. On at least two occasions the Home Office has seen fit to lay down the grounds for making an application. In 1950 several applications from the police were turned down by the Home Office and, as a result, the conditions were spelt out in 1951. For the police and customs there were three conditions: the offence must be serious where there is no previous conviction – normal methods of investigation must have been tried and have failed, and there must be reason to think the interception would result in a conviction.

At the same time different principles were laid down for MI5. These were that a major subversive or espionage activity likely to injure the national interest must be involved; and the information gained must be of direct use in fulfilling MI5's statutory duties (counter-espionage and subversion). In theory MI5 also have to satisfy the provision that all other methods have failed; in practice this limitation is meaningless. The Home Office is entirely dependent on the interpretation of the applying agency that all normal methods have failed and that a conviction is likely to result. In the case of MI5 the rationale is even more tenuous. They apply the 'need to know' principle as strictly to politicians and other civil servants as they do to their own men. Furthermore as the 1951 Maxwell-Fyfe directive spelt out, it was not the right of a Minister to know the details of cases involving security and subversion; in fact he is specifically excluded from having this knowledge. These two factors alone make it most unlikely that more than a small fraction of tapping by MI5 is authorised by the Home Secretary.

A further letter from the Home Office was sent to the Metropolitan Police in 1956 because of an increase, by nearly 50 per cent, in applications over the previous five years. The police responded by reducing the average duration of warrants and by setting up a weekly review procedure.

In order to allay public fears following the Marrinan case the Birkett Committee published the figures for warrants issued between 1937 and 1956, but recommended that no figures should be given in future.[6] This recommendation has been accepted by successive governments – Tory and Labour – and no figures have been announced since then. The figures for the years that were made public lumped together warrants authorised by the Home Secretary for the police, customs and the security service.

	Telephones	Letters
1937	17	335
1940	125	1,192
1945	56	90
1950	179	232
1955	231	205

After a brief dip from the wartime high, the figures again rose with the onset of the Cold War. Two reservations, however, must be noted. Firstly, warrants were often issued to cover several names and addresses (general warrants), a practice the Birkett Committee recommended should cease. Secondly, it appears that all the records prior to 1952 were destroyed. The Metropolitan Police destroyed all warrants issued between 1937 and 1952 on their cancellation, and thereafter kept a note only of the total number issued. A similar practice was pursued by MI5. Indeed MI5 became so concerned about records of warrants being held in the Home Office that in 1947 all relevant records were destroyed and only a list of the serial numbers was held. The process of reviewing the warrants in force varies according to the agency. All warrants issued to the police and customs are in theory reviewed by the Home Office and the agency every month, while the security service reviews its own warrants every three to six months. The

---

[6] See p. 205 for further details of the Marrinan case.

different time periods clearly reflect the different interests of the agencies, the police and the Special Branch being more concerned with short-term intelligence and MI5 with long-term.

As no official figures have been announced since 1956 it is only possible to make an informed guess as to the extent of the practice today. In January 1973 the *Daily Mail* published a story based on information given to an MP which suggested the number of warrants issued to the Metropolitan Police alone was 1,250 a year.[7] When this figure was raised in Parliament Mr Mark Carlisle, Minister of State at the Home Office, replied that the figure was 'ludicrously high' but refused to give the real figures as this was 'not in the national interest'.[8] This justification for refusing to release the figures 'in the national interest' is spurious, for the only result of releasing the total number of warrants would be to expose the government of the day to embarrassment and would in no way aid foreign espionage.

But was this figure of 1,250 'ludicrously high' or was it too close to the truth for comfort? A number of factors suggest the latter to be the case. Firstly, while the extent of foreign espionage in this country is probably no greater in 1975 than in 1956, the size and nature of the Left in Britain is not only quantitatively larger; it has become infinitely more complex. The large increase of Special Branch officers since 1967 is itself testimony to this fact. An increased demand for warrants in the past few years will have caused few eyebrows to rise, given the militant and 'violent' nature of political struggle in these years – the Angry Brigade and Provisional IRA bombing campaigns, letter bombs to Jews and industrial unrest. Secondly, there has been the growing emphasis on pre-emptive policing by Criminal Intelligence, the Regional Crime Squads and the Special Branch.[9] Thirdly, the abolition of general warrants has been a minor though not insignificant factor in the rising figures. Finally, there has been a great increase in drug-taking over the past six years. The use of soft drugs is exposed almost weekly as not being the preserve of a dissident few, but a social habit for many young people, regardless of class, and the demand for warrants has increased in this field. Further, the demands of the central

---

[7] This followed a *Daily Telegraph* story (19 December 1972) suggesting that there were 1200 warrants issued in 1972 and 700 in 1970.

[8] *The Times*, 2 February 1973.

[9] It has also been suggested that greater emphasis is being put on tapping and bugging by Criminal Intelligence because of the 'dangers' of police corruption resulting from the use of informers. *Daily Mail*, 29 July 1974.

computer unit – the National Drugs Intelligence Unit – has contributed to this trend. For these reasons alone the figure of 1,250 warrants issued for the police and Special Branch in London alone does not seem 'ludicrously high'.

Even if the number of warrants issued by the various Secretaries of State were known the figures would not include 'bugging' operations by the different agencies (which require no authorisation), nor the institutionalised arrangements between the agencies and the Post Office. The 'institutional' relation between the police (or CID and Special Branch) and the post offices and telephone exchanges was laid down in a Home Office Circular in 1969.[10]

This circular empowers Head Postmasters and Telephone Managers to assist the police on request in cases where the police are investigating an indictable offence, where an investigation has been authorised by the DPP or where the police are acting on behalf of a government department in relation to a document 'missing' from the said department. In each of these instances the post office or telephone exchange can assist the local police without reference to the central Post Office and without a warrant from a Secretary of State.

How do these agencies tap a telephone? The interception of telephone calls can be done in several different ways. The numbers called can be recorded on a printometer. This monitors all calls, by recording the number rung, whether a connection was made, and the length of the call. This system is used occasionally for low-level intelligence; for example, the papertape record would be checked to see if a known English political activist has been in regular contact with a known Irish militant or group. The printometer is, in fact, a primitive model of the planned computerised recording of all telephone calls that is being undertaken in the interests of providing a labour-saving system for providing telephone accounts.[11] Calls can also be recorded on tape-recorders at the exchange by the Post Office. This is the most common form of surveillance. Usually the tapes will be listened to once a week, parts will be selectively transcribed, and then this transcription will be forwarded to the requesting agency. Another method is the direct tap. This is done either by a team of men (a twenty-four-hour rota needs four to six men) sitting in a room or apartment

[10] Home Office Circular 'Consolidated Circular to the Police (1969)', s.l., paras 46ff, cited by L. H. Leigh in *Police Powers in England and Wales* (1975) p. 215.

[11] These are the new TXE2 and TXE4 electronic exchanges.

nearby, or, which is more usual, the intercepted calls are transferred directly to a central listening post.

In the case of the Metropolitan Police and Special Branch the central listening post is at Chelsea Barracks where 72 lines are available (in the early 1960s there were only 23 lines).[12] MI5, MI6, the DIS and the other agencies each have central listening posts of their own – MI5's centre is thought to be on the fourth floor of an office block in Kensington High Street. There is also the more sophisticated tap, where the telephone acts as a microphone relaying both telephone calls and conversations in the room: a simple adjustment to the household phone can turn it into an unsuspected spy. Of course not every tapped phone has this refinement; it is reserved for those thought by the agencies to be 'ring-leaders' or centres for 'subversives', otherwise examining the miles of taped conversations would present an impossible task. Yet another method is to use a 'bug'. Bugging is not covered by the issuing of warrants and can be used on the sole authority of the head of the agency concerned; moreover since 1968 internally-imposed restrictions on the use of bugs have been removed.[13]

With a direct tap straight through to the listening post all the Post Office has to do is provide the necessary link. Indirect tapping by tape-recorder at the exchange is organised by a special section of Post Office staff who receive a weekly list from the district Central Checking Exchange. As early as 1952 there was evidence of this practice. A local councillor in Slough who worked in the telephone exchange pointed out to some of his fellow councillors who were on a visit the mechanism for tape-recording.[14] Each exchange has an inspector and engineer who intercept the calls on a given line without the knowledge of the main switchboard operators. The link having been made, all the engineer has to do is to check that the recorder is working properly and periodically change the tapes. These tapes are collected by the Investigation Branch (IB) men and passed to the relevant agency for transcription. The Investigation Branch comprises officers seconded from Scotland Yard (usually from CID, Criminal Intelligence and Special Branch), former policemen employed as civil servants by the Post Office, and specially vetted GPO technicians. Their headquarters is Euston Towers in Euston Road, London, where there are a total of a

[12] *Evening Standard*, 4 July 1973.
[13] See p. 183.
[14] *Sunday Pictorial*, 30 March 1952.

hundred officers. The function of the IB men in this field is two-fold: to collect tapes and check on tapping arrangements, and to arrange for the interception of mail.

Before readers rip out their telephones and send them back to the Post Office it is necessary to consider who is most likely to be tapped, namely those involved in criminal or political action, civil servants, members of the armed forces, workers in firms with government contracts, and 'public figures' of a left-wing inclination. Technical and human limitations mean that in effect only a handful of people in these groups are under surveillance. How is the handful chosen? There are five broad categories:

1. The *centres* of politically left-wing groups and organisations are regularly tapped, often permanently, and their mail is opened. The wide catchment areas provided by a union headquarters or a left-wing information centre obviates the need to keep track of a large number of activists. By tapping the telephones and opening the mail a constant check can be kept on the activities of the group, their supporters, and new people seeking contact.

2. The *leaders* of each group, whether or not the group concerned has formal or informal leaders. Again these provide good means of keeping track of a number of people, particularly in community and libertarian groups.

3. The headquarters and 'leadership' of an *ad hoc* campaign, like the Stop the Seventy Tour, the anti-Caetano demonstrations or a legal Defence Committee.

4. Individuals such as journalists or MPs who become concerned through sympathy or work in a 'suspect' cause.

5. Civil servants who are either being Positively Vetted or are under suspicion for some reason.

In short, most political activists, in the community or industry, are not under permanent surveillance by the state. However, when they become involved in a particular campaign, picket or demonstration the likelihood of surveillance increases.

State interception of communications is not limited to telephones (and letters); it extends to telegrams, parcels, international calls and cables. Under Section 4 of the Official Secrets Act 1920 a Secretary of State can make out a warrant when it appears to be in the national interest to intercept any foreign communications. The monarchy and then the bourgeois governments of the eighteenth and nineteenth centuries considered foreign mail fair game. At the turn of this century, with the formalisation of the intelligence services, this practice was also given official recognition. The interception of cables, both incoming and outgoing, was dramatically exposed in the cable-vetting scandal of 1967 when the D-Notice Committee Secretary, Colonel Lohan, failed to stop Chapman Pincher of the *Daily Express* publishing full details of the operation. It was found to be long-standing, extensive, and to embrace far more than matters related only to espionage. It included much in the field of economic affairs at the request of the Foreign Office and the Board of Trade (now the Department of Trade).[15] This area of interception was either ignored by the Birkett Committee, or which is more likely, they were simply not informed of the practice.

The dangers inherent in telephone-tapping are not limited to the individual under surveillance. In practice they impinge on all those in communication with him or her. It was this factor which led to Mr Marrinan, a barrister, being brought before the Bar Council on evidence supplied by the police from a telephone-tap. Mr Marrinan had represented the gangleader Billy Hill at his Old Bailey trial, after which several press stories appeared suggesting that the former had obstructed the police in their investigation. The Bar Council contacted Scotland Yard to see if they had any evidence to support this allegation and the Home Secretary, Viscount Tenby, authorised the police to show transcriptions from Billy Hill's phone conversations to Sir Hartley Shawcross, the Chairman of the Bar Council, and subsequently to other members of the Council. Tenby's decision was condemned by the Birkett Committee who recommended that no information gained in this way should be handed to a body outside the state service.

However, just two years later in 1959, despite governmental assurances, another similar case occurred when Dr Kenneth Fox was struck off the Medical Register because of an association with a married patient. Evidence of the association was provided by a conversation tapped by the police. Mr Butler as Home Secretary told the Commons that no warrant had been issued for the interception of the call between Dr Fox and another woman patient, nor had he authorised the passing of the transcript to the General Medical Coun-

[15] See Hedley and *The D-Notice Affair* (1968).

cil. As the interception had been carried out (at the suggestion of the
police) with the consent of the woman patient, Butler said no
authorisation was required. The GMC had then subpoenaed the
police to produce the evidence. Thus it was revealed that no warrant
was necessary where the consent of one of the parties was given, and
quite logically Mr Butler said, 'I cannot absolutely guarantee that such
a thing will not happen' in the course of criminal proceedings.'[16] So
what had just two years previously been taken as a guarantee that taped
conversations would not be given to those outside state services was
now circumvented by the government's interpretation of the law on
which the Birkett Committee had been silent. The dangers inherent in
such a practice are obvious, for the consent of one party can be given
willingly or unwillingly, as a favour or in response to an implied threat
of prosecution.

In a more recent case, in 1971, the Manchester police bugged a
meeting between a solicitor and his client. The solicitors, Max Bitel
Greene and Co., had called a conference with their client and a potential witness. However, the witness had already made a statement to the
police, and at their suggestion had concealed a mike and a recorder in
his clothing. By this means the meeting was bugged and the tape
collected by detectives immediately the witness left the solicitor's
office. Only a guilty conscience on the part of the witness some time
later brought the matter to light. The solicitors approached the Home
Office who declined to comment, saying it was a matter for the local
police. Manchester police admitted the action but thought it justified,
'having regard to all the circumstances', and would give no assurances
that it would not happen again. The police practice of tapping conversations, whether on the telephone or with a bug, of a lawyer and his
client is the grossest invasion of the legal process, for it is the police
who prepare the charges, gather evidence and appear as witnesses in
court for the prosecution. If the defence were to employ such measures
against the police and the state prosecutors they would without doubt
be charged with conspiracy to pervert the course of justice. The law,
the historical offspring of the state, protects its own.

Nothing is more likely to raise the hackles of those guardians of our
traditional liberties, Members of Parliament, than the suggestion their
own telephones might be tapped. Surely MPs must be privileged and
their freedom of speech inviolate? Not so at all. The Birkett Committee, following the precedent of the 1844 committees, said 'an MP

[16] *News Chronicle*, 4 December 1959.

is not to be distinguished from an ordinary member of the public.'[17] However, while MPs may in theory be considered no different from everyone else, it could be expected that the practice would either be non-existent or so well concealed it would never be spoken of. But this is not the case. As early as 1950 Sir Tufton Beamish reported he was having a conversation with someone in the War Office when they were interrupted and a voice said: 'Please remember that I have been listening to your conversation. Please remember to be more careful in future.' When Labour returned to government after twenty years of opposition in 1964 Mr Wilson stopped the practice of tapping MPs' telephones. This was not revealed until 1966, and Wilson's statement to the Commons put the matter more delicately; he said: 'the balance should be tipped the other way' and that he would give instructions there should be no tapping of MPs' telephones.[18]

This statement confirmed Labour MPs' long-held suspicions that MPs suspected of being 'fellow-travellers' were under surveillance at the behest of the Tories. No doubt this was so, but three months later in February 1967, it was revealed that the Labour leadership had itself requested an investigation of some Labour MPs.[19] With the return of the Tories in 1970 Mr Heath repeated the assurance of Mr Wilson that MPs' telephones would not be tapped, although, he added, 'only with the proviso that the security of the State must be maintained.'[20] But these were exactly the grounds for tapping under the previous Tory government.

Like MPs the press enjoys no privileges. Most crime and defence correspondents know that from time to time they are under surveillance. In October 1972 the *Sunday Times* published details of a 'secret' report prepared by the Department of the Environment advocating a cut by almost a half in Britain's rail network. While public outrage was directed at the proposal, governmental outrage sought to find the culprit. It seemed the report had originated from the *Railway Gazette* and detectives, bearing a warrant under the Theft Act 1968, searched the premises of the magazine and took a statement from the editor, Mr Richard Hope. Following the visit Hope noticed 'funny things' happening on his telephone at the office and at home. Then a few days later one of the magazine's reporters was questioned at his flat

[17] Birkett, *op. cit.*, p. 27.
[18] *Hansard*, 17 November 1966.
[19] See pp. 179–180.
[20] *Hansard*, 16 July 1970.

by detectives about the source of the document and when he proved unhelpful he was told certain details of his personal life would be revealed to his parents and relatives – details that could only have been learnt by listening to his telephone calls. Scotland Yard held an internal inquiry into these charges with the result that Mr Carr, the Home Secretary, denied that telephones had been tapped.

But the matter did not rest there. Before public exposure halted these antics, detectives visited the editor of the *Sunday Times*, Harold Evans, and found him a prickly target. He was asked: 'Did you realise the document was a classified Government Paper?' Evans replied: 'If you ask me did it have a red tag on top saying "Top Secret Do Not Give To The Russians" – no.'[21] Challenged in parliament about these events Sir Peter Rawlinson, the Attorney-General, responded in the following terms: 'I repeat that nobody is immune from investigation if the police feel there is a proper matter to investigate.' But it was the government who ordered the investigation, not the police, who were merely following the orders of their political masters. An editorial in the *New Law Journal* summed up most people's feeling: the government's actions 'smacked more of the over-reaction of the banana republic dictatorship than of sensible and cool, democratic government.'[22] No prosecutions followed and the government realised the affair was beginning to look like the D-Notice fiasco for which they had heaped so much scorn on Harold Wilson.[23]

There are many examples of political activists on the left believing their telephones are being tapped. Often this results from interference on the line, crackling noises, frequent wrong numbers, ominous clickings, dead lines – which may or may not be due to tapping. An underground magazine suggested in 1969 a sure way of telling if the telephone was being tapped. They said people should dial the engineer's test number (175 or 174, followed by the last four digits of their number), to see if the connection was made then replace the telephone on the hook and wait to be rung back. If the connection was not made (dead line or unobtainable) this was because a 'tap' had been interposed. A lot of people tried the test and could not make the connection with the engineer's number, but whether this was due to the inefficiency of the telephone system or more sinister reasons is hard to judge. Certainly a telephone which over a period of weeks consistently

---

[21] *Financial Times*, 13 December 1972.
[22] *New Law Journal*, December 1972.
[23] See p. 205.

failed to respond to this test should be used with some caution.

The following experience perhaps provides more definite evidence. In a house inhabited by a number of people active in left-wing politics it was noticed the telephone was frequently completely 'dead' for about five minutes on most mornings at about 10.30 am. One morning the telephone was kept off the hook and listened to. After a short while there was a click, followed by sounds of people in an office, talking and moving about. This went on for a couple of minutes, then footsteps came much closer, there was a click and the dialling tone returned immediately. This experience was repeated twice in the following weeks. Alternatively there was the clear-cut test used by members of CND who arranged a fictitious demonstration over the telephone and turned up at the appointed time and place to find the police waiting in anticipation.

A case which illustrates the response of the authorities to charges of tapping is that of Richard Moseley in 1969. He was at that time secretary of the Southern Group of the National Council for Civil Liberties, and was living in Brighton. Early one evening in October while talking to the NCCL headquarters in London, he had finished one conversation and was waiting to be transferred to another extension when a man's voice cut in and said: 'Recording finished'. The local police hotly denied the suggestion they might be tapping Moseley's phone, and the South Eastern Telephone Region found a 'plausible' explanation for the occurrence, expressing regret the service 'had not been as satisfactory as he and we would have wished'. As a final resort the NCCL wrote to the Home Office who replied to Tony Smythe, the General-Secretary:

> 'We refuse to comment on individual allegations simply because if we were to assure correspondents that their 'phones had not been tapped in those cases where this was so, we should either have to refrain from commenting in the rare case where the telephone was tapped or admit it was: either course would clearly defeat the object of the operation. It is therefore the established practice neither to confirm nor to deny allegations of this kind.'[24]

The pattern is clear. The local police deny it, the Post Office find other explanations for the occurrence, and the government will neither confirm nor deny the charge.

A critical question in relation to telephone-tapping is the ad-

[24] Letter, 5 January 1970.

missibility of such evidence in a court of law. So far the state agencies have not sought to use evidence gained by this method in political trials – although they have attempted to use tapes from 'bugged' meetings.[25] If and when they do seek to use transcribed conversations in court, defence counsels will find that the precedent has already been well-established in criminal cases. The problems associated with the use of tape-recorded evidence abound, the more so because the courts have accepted that evidence represented by a recorded transcript is equivalent to notes made by a police officer after an arrest. However, the tape-recorder always has an advantage over the fallible human memory for it purports to include the exact wording of a conversation, and not just someone's recollection of it. The 'fallibility' of tapes may have been called into question over Watergate but it is unlikely that this memory will succeed in overturning the precedents already set in our courts on the admissibility of tapes.

Tape-recorded conversations can be altered in many almost un-detectable ways: words can be deleted, phrases changed round, passages eliminated, and questions inserted which were never asked. An expert, and particularly those skilled technicians attached to the different state intelligence agencies, can make any or all of these changes, re-record the tape and swear on oath in court that it is the original recording. Even if the defence is granted legal aid to cover the cost of employing an expert of equal calibre he may not be able to detect a dubbed tape. In the event, who is most likely to be believed in court, the prosecution backed by the recorded evidence or the protestations of the defence – based on the defendant's memory – that the recording has been doctored? One of the leading judgements given on the use of tapes was given in 1966 by the Appeal Court (R.v.Ali, 1966). A recorded conversation between two men in a Punjabi dialect in a police station provided the only substantive evidence against them on a murder charge. The Court of Criminal Appeal ruled on the question of tape-recorders that: 'the criminal does not act ac-cording to the Queensbury Rules. The method of the informer and the eavesdropper is commonly used in the detection of crime. The only difference here was that a mechanical device was the eavesdropper.' Nor is the question of Judges' Rules and illegally obtained evidence relevant in such cases, for by Kamara v R (1955) it is clearly lawful to admit evidence illegally obtained if it is relevant. It has also been es-tablished that recorded evidence is primary evidence, that is,

[25] See below.

equivalent to a witness appearing in court. This decision was reinforced in 1968 when Lord Parker ruled that because information had been gained by interfering with the public telephone service it did not make the evidence inadmissible. The implications of this judgement are highly dangerous. For example, a private security firm might be employed by an industrial company to tap the telephones of the plant union organisers with the result that they could be charged with conspiracy to cause a breach of the peace (like organising a picket). The illegality of the tapping would not affect the admissibility of the evidence against the workers concerned.

Herbert Morrison, Home Secretary in the 1945 Labour government, wrote in the post-Birkett period that in his experience the innocent had nothing to fear.[26] And on the face of it this seems a perfectly reasonable argument. But who is innocent when innocence is a purely relative concept – a concept that is determined by the changing definitions of what is 'legal' and what is 'criminal', in a country where criminality and political activity become enmeshed, and the delicate balance between freedoms of the individual and the demands of 'law and order' is in an indelicate state of disorder?

The proposition that 'doctored' evidence might be used in court may seem like scare-mongering to some and a portent for the future to others. During periods of civil disorder or when 'subversive minorities' are seen to be very active then legal niceties often appear irrelevant. The Birkett Committee expressed it thus: 'The detection and suppression of crime is essential to good government of any society, but it is not so fundamental as the security of the state itself.'[27] Equally, the Committee pointed out that the continuance of this practice rested on the premise that it can be 'exercised effectively without public unrest'.[28] Since its deliberations there has been little public unrest and the state's agencies have continually extended the practice unhindered by democratic restraints.

Opening the mail

The practice of opening the mail of those opposed to the prevailing order is as old as the postal service itself, and the monarchy, in establishing it as a public service, clearly had this intention in mind. In the eighteenth century two special departments of the Post Office were

[26] *Empire News*, 30 June 1957.
[27] Birkett, *op. cit.*, p. 32.
[28] Birkett, *op. cit.*, p. 29.

set up to intercept the mail: the Secret Office opened foreign mail and the Private Office dealt with internal letters. Later during the Chartist struggles in the late 1830s the Home Office issued many general warrants each carrying about six names, and throughout the period the letters to most of the leaders were opened and the contents transcribed. Around this time another branch of the Post Office was set up, the Decyphering Branch, concerned in particular with diplomatic messages. During the last century the work of the mail censors was facilitated by the introduction of the cheap postal rate for postcards and unsealed letters, a service much used by the working class. However it was during the two World Wars that the art of opening letters on a mass scale was perfected. The First World War heralded the initiation of MI5 in tackling foreign spies and the opening of internal and foreign mail was one of the major reasons for its success in busting German spyrings. In 1911 Captain Kell, the head of the newly-created MI5, approached the Home Secretary, Winston Churchill, who agreed that the normal rules could be cast aside. Until then a warrant was required each time letters were to be opened; Churchill agreed that letters sent to people on Kell's list could be opened on a general warrant. In all over eight thousand people were engaged in communications intelligence (including radio) and in the Second World War this rose to around thirty thousand. The techniques developed by wartime intelligence were to prove invaluable in peacetime.

As was shown in the last section, the legal basis for opening letters (as for tapping telephones) is dubious, but the longevity of the practice is not in doubt. A warrant issued by a Secretary of State is used to cover both practices and the groups indicated as being of interest to the state in the last section are identical for the purposes of mail-opening. There is, however, one additional and unnoticed power in relation to mail, the practice of returning a letter to its sender. The 1844 committee reported that this had happened in the case of seven warrants over a period of forty-five years, while in the ten years prior to 1957 this had occurred in twenty-eight cases, 'on grounds of major public interest'.[29] This procedure is mainly used in two circumstances, either to save embarrassment where a letter is sent by the children or relative of some important member of the ruling class to the headquarters of a subversive organisation, or to cause confusion to a spy or political activist.

[29] Birkett, *op. cit.*, p. 21.

Every post office has a set of cards listing the groups, individuals and companies whose mail is specially sorted for attention before delivery. About half refer to suspected criminal activities by firms or individuals of interest to the police, Inland Revenue or Customs. The other half comprises those whose political activities are of interest to the police, the Special Branch or another agency. Mail for these people is delivered in a sealed envelope by special messenger to the regional district post offices, where a special section of the GPO Investigation Branch (IB) takes over. The special messenger waits for the letters to be opened and photocopied, and then returns with the bundle – taking care not to deviate from his route because he will be sporadically tailed and admonished if found stopping for any reason, even a cup of tea.

The experience of one special messenger during the visit of Mr Kosygin in February 1967, concerned the mail of the Socialist Labour League. The messenger took a sealed packet of letters for the SLL to the Post Office headquarters in King Edward Buildings, St Martin-le-Grand and delivered the packet to an officer in Section: sub-ground 14. Three security officers checked his identity on the way down, and after handing over the letters he was led to a separate room to await his return journey. Before he left a security officer telephoned the sorting office to say he was on his way back, and when, on one occasion, he varied his route a plain-clothed gentleman approached and accompanied him for the rest of the journey.

A variety of methods are available to the Investigation Branch in eliciting the contents of a letter. The time-honoured method of using a steaming kettle is now little used, although it was the mainstay in earlier times. Today some letters are 'photographed' through the envelope; some are extracted with a 'spinning needle' which is inserted through the tiniest of holes in the flap and then the contents are wound up at great speed and extracted; or, more usually, an untraceable cut is made in the envelope down one of its joints which is later resealed.

The total number of warrants issued for opening letters in 1957 was just over two hundred for the whole country in all categories (criminal and political). However, by 1972 those issued for political mail in London alone numbered more than four hundred. This included only those individuals and the headquarters of political groups whose mail was being opened on a long-term basis, not those added for short periods because they were involved in a particular demonstration or event. In addition the 'informal' approach is often made at local level, such as when a police officer goes along to the sorting office and says

P 811X (Spl)

ADVICE OF DESPATCH & FORM OF RECEIPT
(for special items on non-financial nature only)

CPD (S.S.) Post Office,
Room 202, Union House,
St. Martin's le Grand,
London, EC1A 1DQ.

..................17 JULY 1972........19........

The.......*O/c*..

E.D.O. (R.D.) The undermentioned special items
are herewith.

~~Have been sent to you today.~~

....

.............................(6)...............................

....

....

Please acknowledge receipt below and return
this form completed to me at the above address.

....

RECEIPT

The CPD (S.S.),
Receipt acknowledged.

OFFICE STAMP | ....

....19..........

NOTE.—This form should be used where
acknowledgement is specially desired of the
receipt of items or documents of a special
or confidential nature, etc., but not for the
acknowledgement of the receipt of money
or the equivalent of money.

815/934 970947 20M 5/72 FHB Ltd. 815

5 and 6.   This form and official envelope (see facing page) were mistakenly
delivered to *Freedom*, the anarchist weekly, in July 1972. They are used by the local
post offices when handing over packets of mail for opening to the regional
offices.

No. 40

IMMEDIATE

EXPRESS

THE OFFICER ON DUTY,

INVESTIGATION DIVISION,

(SPECIAL SECTION), POST OFFICE,

ROOM 202, UNION HOUSE,

ST. MARTINS-LE-GRAND,

LONDON, E.C1.

POST OFFICE

'Got anything there for John Doe, the Inspector wants to see what he's up to now.'

Examples of this form of surveillance have come to light in two ways: either the IB men make a mistake and muddle up two sets of letters, or people employed by the Post Office have come forward with evidence. The form and the envelope delivered to *Freedom* falls into the first category, as did the mix-up in 1953 when two letters to a Communist Party member in Bristol were transposed and arrived in the wrong envelopes – a letter from the local council did not arrive in the official envelope while another personal letter did. Again, in 1973 mail for the Communist Party Headquarters in King Street, London WC2, regularly included letters addressed to Rising Free, a left bookshop and information centre in WC1. The experience of Nicholas Walter, who reported on his work as a postman, falls into the second category. 'When I worked at the Highgate sorting office in December 1954 ... the letters for Mr Andrew Rostein, the Communist writer, were separately sorted and then checked by a senior Post Official before they came to me.'[30]

Letters posted for inland delivery are not the only ones opened for inspection. Communications in and out of the country are intercepted on a larger scale. Powers available under the Exchange Control Act 1947 are exercised quite openly by the Customs and Excise, and in 1960 parliament was told that over 300,000 letters had been opened in the previous year under the Act. The total amount of 'illegal' money discovered was under £50,000, hardly a justification for such a wholesale invasion of privacy. By 1966 this figure had risen, according to a conservative estimate, to over 500,000 letters being opened.[31] It is quite obvious that the amount of currency transmitted through the post to destinations abroad is negligible – no business magnate needs to resort to such obvious tactics. On the other hand information gained by the intelligence agencies and special departments of the Department of Trade and the Foreign Office of a political or economic nature is clearly much more valuable.

A case resulting from the opening of mail from abroad arose in 1970. In January of that year two plainclothed detectives called at the offices of the NCCL and asked to see Tony Smythe, the General-Secretary, on 'a personal matter'.[32] Failing to find him there they even-

---

[30] *Hampstead and Highgate Express*, 6 October 1963.
[31] *Daily Sketch*, 28 June 1967.
[32] Told to the author by Tony Smythe.

tually called at his home at 8 am one morning, got him out of bed and attempted to enter his house to question him about this 'personal' matter. Their attempt to enter was firmly resisted – they had no warrant – so one of them drew from his briefcase a couple of packets sent from Denmark to Tony Smythe at the NCCL office. Smythe was asked if he realised it was an offence to send the enclosed publications through the post, and he replied that it was also an offence for police officers to force their way into private homes. In fact the publications had been sent to NCCL following a complaint by a Danish group, IHWO, who published a gay magazine, that letters sent to and from Britain had been opened or had never arrived. Tony Smythe, for the NCCL, had undertaken to investigate police powers in this field and had requested samples of the literature.

Other techniques of surveillance

The interception of telephone calls and letters are two common forms of surveillance, but by no means the only ones. Others include photographing, filming and tailing. Photographing individuals involved in political activity is systematically undertaken by the police, the agencies and private security firms. A police photographer, in plainclothes, is at most demonstrations, and one of the easiest ways to 'spot the cop' is to look for the photographer who carefully takes pictures of each section of a march – very few bona fide photographers bother to do this. Of course, the police and the agencies have another means of getting pictures of demonstrations, such as asking the press photographers to supply them with prints. This kind of request is often made and rarely refused. It is quite 'legal' for the police to take pictures of marchers, demonstrators and pickets, and the only means of limiting their effectiveness is to embarrass them – perhaps by taking pictures of them. The Home Office recognises this practice as a legitimate and proper one for the police to undertake in pursuance of their duties. When a young teacher complained in 1963 that pictures had been taken at a poster parade a Home Office official replied: 'I am directed by the Secretary of State ... to say that he is aware that photographs are taken by the police in the course of their duties for a variety of legitimate purposes.' Durham police took pictures of people entering a court where a drugs case was being heard, and when questioned the Deputy Chief Constable replied: 'The police took photographs of people entering the court ... There was nothing insidious about what was done.'[33]

[33] *Workers Press*, 23 October 1973.

In London the police use a portable video camera to film major demonstrations. Another form of surveillance used for traffic and crowd control are the fixed position cameras around London, notably those in Trafalgar Square (on top of the National Gallery) and in Grosvenor Square (on the roof of the Duchess of Argyll's house). Two of the other cameras are on the roof of St George's Hospital overlooking Hyde Park, and in Leather Lane, Holborn. When asked by a reporter from *The Times* whether they were used for security purposes a Scotland Yard spokesman said: 'We wouldn't be allowed to comment even if they had been used for security. I wouldn't tell you even if they had been . . .'[34] However the Duchess, less reticent when asked the same question, said the camera had been installed 'to help the police with demonstrations'.

The taking and filming of photos of political activists is a long-established practice, though since the 1968 demonstrations this has been undertaken in a more systematic manner. Activists when identified have their pictures attached to their Special Branch and MI5 files. In the industrial field the efforts of the Special Branch are supplemented by those of private security firms working on behalf of management, who increasingly keep files on key militants.

Informers and agents-provocateur

The distinction between a spy, an informer and an agent-provocateur is often a hard one to make. Here the term spy (or 'agent') is used in relation to full-time employees of the security and intelligence agencies, while the informer is often a member of the group under surveillance who may or may not be paid for his activities. Further, informers are used by the uniformed police in the criminal field, and the Special Branch and MI5 in the political.[35] An agent-provocateur is someone who attempts to entrap a person (or persons) by inciting or encouraging them to commit a crime, or political act liable to legal sanctions. The role of an agent-provocateur can be played either by a member of one of the agencies, or by a member of a gang or political group (acting on direct instructions from the police or agency). Whereas the informer provides only information, the agent-provocateur usually participates in the planning – and often the execution – of a crime or political act. The use of the informer and the agent-provocateur has a long history in our society, and their respective roles

[34] *The Times*, 31 January 1973.
[35] See chapters 3 and 4.

have been legitimised by government and courts in the struggle to maintain law and order and political stability.

Monarchy and parliamentary democracy alike have made extensive use of the spy and the informer against the threat of internal subversion. Prior to the institutionalisation of the security and intelligence functions in the early years of this century, when these theoretically became subject to parliamentary control, the methods of internal spying and informing were operated more openly.[36] During the eighteenth and nineteenth centuries magistrates paid informers to bring cases to their courts, the Home Secretary employed ex-convicts and journalists to infiltrate political groups and to report on their meetings, and the military – who were responsible for the suppression of political demonstrations – also employed a network of spies. When the Common Informers Act of 1951 was passed, it repealed in whole or in parts some forty-eight previous statutes, dating from 1382 to 1949. These various statutes were used in addition to the system of offering 'blood money' for information about crimes in general which was 'indiscriminately used by a Parliament at its wits' end to abate the volume of crime.'[37] The practice died out as magistrates came to depend on the regular police for information on which to prosecute. The 1951 Act substituted for the old provisions fines to be imposed on the offender for the various criminal activities defined under old statutes rather than public rewards for the informers. The informer is of course still used by the police but he now enjoys no legal status, which is far from saying his work is illegal.

Every member of the CID knows that one of the essential tools of his trade is the cultivation of informers, indeed he is unlikely to 'get on' without them. They are his personal property and must never be required to appear in court – despite the fact they are usually material witnesses. How is the informer recruited? Usually he or she has been sent down by the detective on at least one occasion, and their continuing relationship rests on the implied threat that the detective has something on the informer – whether real or imagined is irrelevant, for the informer will know how easily he can be 'set up' by the detective should he give offence. Other reasons are no doubt personal vendettas or the payment of small sums by the detective either from his own pocket or from the Informants' Fund. No doubt there are certain internal restraints on the detective becoming too involved with his infor-

---

[36] See Ch. 3 and Ch. 4.
[37] Sir C. K. Allen, *Queen's Peace* (1953).

mants, although when drawing money from official funds for this purpose the officer does not have to provide the name of his informant nor does he have to provide a receipt for the money handed over. Many in the police believe greater use should be made of informers: 'In these days when crime detection is a never ending uphill struggle, the Service needs to exploit the paid informer to a much greater degree than it does at the moment.'[38]

The use of informers was vividly demonstrated by two *Guardian* reporters in 1972. It concerned an ex-convict who was framed by two detectives for a job he didn't do and blackmailed by them into giving information which would lead to a conviction. The man in question had been out of prison for two months when the detectives set up an attempted robbery and threatened to do him for it unless he put the finger onto someone else. (He had originally been sent down for stealing a consignment of meat. The police arrested him, with the meat, asleep at the wheel of his car in a lay-by while making his getaway.) The ex-convict told a social worker of the threats, who in turn contacted the *Guardian*. The paper's reporters photographed the two detectives making a rendezvous with the man, and tape-recorded several incriminating conversations:

Detective: But I don't particularly want to lock you up, but I want someone.
Man: So in exchange for me . . .
Detective: I want somebody.

The detectives knew a man with a record would be easy to get convicted, for who would believe his story? In this case he was lucky; the tapes and the photos were handed over to the police for investigation— most are not so fortunate.[39]

Like the informer the agent-provocateur is used in criminal and political cases. In 1934 the Attorney-General testified before a standing committee of the Commons that he had used a 'spy' to get a copy of an obscene publication in order to carry out a prosecution: he told the committee: 'I had no difficulty in sending an agent-provocateur to obtain a copy, and I got it . . .'.[40] The real hypocrisy arises when a police-directed agent-provocateur induces a person to commit a

---

[38] *Police Review*, 9 February 1973.
[39] *Guardian*, 3 November 1972.
[40] *Hansard,* 14 June 1934.

crime he would not otherwise have committed. Such a case occurred in 1945. A police informant encouraged a man to get him some clothing coupons illegally, from a third party; then both were prosecuted. In court the police withdrew their case against the accused, and the magistrate was moved to comment: 'It is said that an agent-provocateur – thank Heaven we have no English word for it – was endeavouring to trap another person to commit an offence in order that he might inform the police.'[41]

Two more recent cases resulted in embarrassment for the police. The first, in 1970, was a drugs case. Stephen Foulder and two others were accused of possessing 3,000 tablets of LSD. They stated in court that an East End 'hoodlum' had asked them to get the tablets for a client, and when they refused he threatened and bullied them until they agreed to his request. Eventually they obtained the tablets and handed them over to the buyers who immediately revealed themselves as Detective Constable Batey and Temporary Detective Constable Norris. In court the defence contended the defendants would never have committed the crime but for the threats, which had been in-stigated by the policemen. Mr Justice McManus accepted that this was a case of entrapment, holding that the evidence had been improperly obtained. Similarly, in 1969, in the case of R. v. Macro, the Court of Appeal quashed the conviction of three men involved in a Post Office raid. An informer, who also took part in the raid, had not been charged and his role had been concealed from the court. Lord Justice Winn described the raid as a charade.

In times of emergency or war the use of agents-provocateur is always a temptation the state agencies seem unable to resist. The role of agents-provocateur against the Chartists in the 1830s and against the Hunger Marchers of the 1930s is examined in chapter three. One of the few recorded cases during the Second World War involved the entrapment of a doctor by this means. On the instructions of the police three men lied about their state of health and obtained certificates to say they were unfit for work. The case was dismissed in court and costs awarded against the prosecution. The magistrate commented that the doctor had no other course but to assume the men were telling the truth. A fellow doctor writing to the *Lancet* made two astute observations on the case: 'The use of these paid spies is condemned by all but a minority of citizens, and the Englishman still prefers to commit his crime without the assistance of the police or other agents.' He went on to attack the

increasing emphasis in medical legislation on the health of the industrial worker: 'the doctor's job, even in a nation of shopkeepers, is
to keep or get the citizen well and not merely to keep him at the lathe or
bench.'[42]

The use of the agent-provocateur against political activists differs
only in kind from that used against the criminal. Wal Hannington, one
of the leaders of the struggles by the unemployed in the 1920s and
1930s recounted an experience in his autobiography.[43] At the culmina-
tion of the great Hunger Marches of 1932 the council of the National
Unemployed Workers Movement met to plan the final stage – the
presentation of a massive petition to parliament. One of the council
members arrived late and gave Hannington an envelope which had
been handed to him for delivery outside the offices. Fortunately Hannington opened the envelope there and then and found that the letter
alluded to a conspiracy involving himself and other leaders in a plot to
undertake a terrorist campaign, including the abduction of Cabinet
Ministers. Hannington told the council members of its contents and
after some deliberation it was agreed to burn the letter. Early the next
morning their headquarters was raided by the police and Hannington
was arrested for allegedly inciting the police to disaffect.[44]

Two notable cases in recent times were the Soar Eire case in 1970
and that of Ellesmore and Conroy in 1973. In the latter case Andy
Ellesmore and Pauline Conroy were arrested and charged with conspiring to obtain firearms. Although the police claimed the arrests
came from a tip-off it transpired in court that the charges resulted
from a joint Flying Squad/Bomb Squad operation and a badly-
organised attempt to frame the two political activists. To understand
the background to the case it is necessary to look back at the events
prior to the alleged offence. Between January 1971 and January 1972
the Bomb Squad (a joint CID and Special Branch squad) carried out a
large number of raids on the homes of left-wing political activists in an
attempt to track down the people behind the Angry Brigade bombings. Among those raided were Andy Ellesmore and Pauline Conroy.
Ellesmore worked for Agitprop, a left information centre and
bookshop in Bethnal Green, which was raided four times by the Bomb
Squad in the course of twelve months under explosive warrants. In
fact, these searches showed the Squad to be more interested in

[42] *Lancet*, 4 December 1943.
[43] W. Hannington, *Never on Our Knees* (1967).
[44] See pp. 120–122 for police spies in the NUWM.

gathering intelligence information on the activities of left groups than in finding explosives. Among those who took part in these raids were Detective Chief Inspector Mold, Detective Chief Superintendent Roy Habershon, and Detective Sergeant Gilham.

Pauline Conroy was of interest to the authorities for two reasons. She had been arrested in the autumn of 1971 and charged with conspiring to cause explosions with others, who later became known as the 'Stoke Newington Eight', in the second 'Angry Brigade' trial. Her arresting officers were Detective Chief Inspector Mold and Detective Sergeant Gilham. When the committal proceedings began at Lambeth magistrate's court in January 1972 the charge against Pauline Conroy was withdrawn by the Attorney-General for lack of evidence. At the end of the commital:

'Lord Gifford, (Pauline's) counsel, made an application to the magistrates that Mold's and Gilham's superiors in the Bomb Squad – Commander Ernest Bond and Detective Superintendent Roy Habershon be bound over to keep the peace; that they be ordered to stop harrassing Pauline. It was deemed an extraordinary request by the magistrate and refused.'[45]

Prior to this Pauline Conroy had been held in custody for a number of weeks before being released on bail. The second reason Pauline Conroy was of interest was that her husband, Mike Sirros, was under threat of deportation to Turkey where he faced a two-year prison sentence for refusing to do military service. Finally, Ellesmore and Conroy had been helping the Defence Committees for both Purdie and Prescott and the Stoke Newington Eight – such an association appears, in the eyes of the state, to be tantamount to an admission of collusion in the alleged offence. So much for the background to the case.

On 23 June 1972 Ellesmore went round to see Conroy at her flat in Powis Square, Notting Hill in London, to discuss her husband's deportation case. There he learnt that Pauline was to meet an ex-criminal, one Jack Tierney, who said he had some information on the police, so Ellesmore went along too to the meeting in a pub. At the meeting Tierney left the impression he could get hold of police files on political activists and a further meeting was arranged. However, Pauline Conroy said she would be too involved in Mike Sirros's depor-

[45] *Time Out*, 1 June 1973.

tation case to attend. This meeting was observed by two Flying Squad detectives, Detective Sergeant Meyrick and Detective Constable Snodgrass. (Tierney it later transpired was an informer whom Meyrick had been using for the previous five years). These two officers had no idea who Ellesmore was and this, coupled with the fact that Conroy said she would not attend the next meeting, prompted a high-level conference at Tintagel House, the Bomb Squad HQ, between the Flying Squad and the Bomb Squad officers.

After the conference Tierney was given his orders: 'It was more or less my instructions for me to press for Pauline to be present at all meetings,' he told the court. Another result of the conference was to set up the final trap. Firstly it was decided that a woman, PC Carol Scard, should be seconded to act as Tierney's girlfriend so as to provide corroborating evidence, secondly that a 'bug' should be concealed in Tierney's clothing to transmit the conversation to a Flying Squad car outside the pub, and finally, Detective Chief Inspector Mold was sent along to see if he could identify the 'mystery' man. The meeting took place at the Burnt Oak pub on 24 June 1973. Outside Mr Mold was waiting and he discovered that their 'mystery' man was none other than Andy Ellesmore from Agitprop. Inside the pub Tierney prevaricated about not being able to get hold of the promised political files, but instead offered to get some guns 'to help the Angy Brigade out . . .' This was backed up by girlfriend PC Scard, who said : 'He means it, he can get them you know.' Ellesmore turned down the offer emphatically and said he was only interested in the files, so a further meeting was set up for the following evening. The tape-recording of this conversation was not available to the court at the Old Bailey as the police say the recording machine was not working properly.

The final meeting took place in another pub, the Princess Alexandra. PC Carol Scard was again in attendance and so was the discreet undercover car outside the pub with the tape-recorder. The conversation opened with PC Scard pressing Ellesmore to go and get Pauline Conroy. He said this was not possible. So the talk again moved to guns: 'There I was faced with this guy saying take these guns or else, so I agreed. I wanted to buy time, I thought if I agreed with him he would leave the pub and then I was going to leave,' Ellesmore told the court. They left but Ellesmore went to the toilet first, where he was arrested by Meyrick, Snodgrass and Detective Inspector Barton of the Flying Squad on a charge of conspiring to buy firearms. Twenty minutes later the flying Squad arrested Pauline Conroy at her flat on the same charge.

Before the Old Bailey trial came up Pauline Conroy left the country for Algeria with her husband, so it started in her absence. From the outset the defence maintained Ellesmore had been framed as a result of the activities of an admitted informer working with a policewoman in plainclothes who acted as an agent-provocateur. Cross-examination of the police witnesses and of Tierney established the close links between the Flying Squad and the Bomb Squad in the case, and this lent weight to the defence contention that the object of the exercise was to 'get Pauline Conroy'. Clearly the police investigation had been instigated by the Flying Squad, for Tierney was Detective Sergeant Meyrick's personal informer, but the Bomb Squad had been brought in as soon as the political implications became evident.

Before the jury left the court to consider their verdict the Judge told them that if the defence case was to be believed the police working on the case were 'wicked, wicked people'. Seven and a half hours later the jury returned and delivered a verdict of not guilty. Thus Ellesmore evaded the trap deliberately laid for him and Pauline Conroy, and so joined the others whom the police – and particularly the Bomb Squad – have failed to substantiate charges against.[46]

In April 1974 Kenneth Lennon visited the offices of the NCCL and in a six-hour interview recorded a statement in which he alleged that he had been recruited by the Branch to infiltrate Irish groups in Britain. This interview was given on 11 April and two days later Lennon was found shot in the back of the head in Banstead, Surrey. After his death the statement Lennon made to NCCL was made public and the Home Secretary commissioned an internal police investigation into the relationship between Lennon and the Branch.[47] Many questions were left unanswered by this police inquiry which exonerated the actions of the Branch officers involved.

---

[46] Pauline Conroy and Chris Allen were both arrested in 1971 and held in custody only to be released in January 1972 for lack of evidence. Ian Purdie was acquitted in December 1971. Four of the eight defendants in the Stoke Newington Eight trial were acquitted. All had been charged with conspiracy to cause explosions after Bomb Squad investigations.

[47] *Report to the Home Secretary from the Commissioner of Police for the Metropolis on the actions of the police officers concerned with the case of Kenneth Joseph Lennon*, HMSO, 31 July 1974.

Firstly, the Report alleges that Lennon offered his services to the Branch, while Lennon's statement and subsequent inquiries suggest that he was blackmailed into becoming an informer and agent-provocateur.[48] Certainly by the Report's own admission Lennon was a valuable source of information. His tip-off led to the arrest and imprisonment (for 10 year sentences) of three fellow-Irishmen (the Luton Three) in 1973. After this Lennon was given £20 a month from the Metropolitan Special Branch Information Fund.[49] Secondly, on 6 January 1974 Lennon was arrested with a 19 year-old Irish lad Patrick O'Brien outside Winson Green Prison, Birmingham, where the Luton Three were being held. Lennon and O'Brien were then charged with conspiring to effect the escape of the Luton Three. The official report, together with investigations by Geoff Robertson of the *New Statesman*, show that critical information about Lennon's background and his relationship with the Branch were withheld from the trial. This knowledge was communicated to the office of the Director of Public Prosecutions prior to the trial by Detective Superintendent Cooney, of the Birmingham police, and Commander Rodgers, the head of Branch operations. After the committal for trial the Report records that 'it was confidently anticipated by Mr Jardine (the DPP's Assistant Director) and the senior Prosecuting Counsel that on the weight of evidence there was little likelihood of the jury returning a "Guilty" verdict against Lennon.'[50] Robertson, after examining the trial transcript, interviews, and statements, concluded that

'The trial of Lennon and O'Brien was an exercise in unreality, designed to dispatch a bewildered boy to prison and to release a reluctant Judas. Kenneth Lennon's NCCL statement implies that the DPP, the Special Branch and the Birmingham police conspired to rig his trial, to turn serious criminal proceedings into a charade to fool the IRA.'[51]

Lennon was duly acquitted and O'Brien sentenced to three years in prison, but subsequent to Lennon's death and the publication of his statement O'Brien successfully appealed against his conviction and

[48] *Sunday Times*, 21 April 1974.
[49] *Report to the Home Secretary, op. cit.*, p. 6.
[50] *Ibid.*, p. 9.
[51] *New Statesman*, 14 June 1974.

was released from prison. As a postscript to the whole affair a new precedent was established in law on the use of agents-provocateur by the state. At the appeal by the Luton Three Lord Widgery, the Lord Chief Justice, ruled that it was not a defence to show that the accused would not have committed the offence without the assistance of a police spy.

Another area where the police use agents-provocateur is that of public order, a practice of long-standing in British history. There are many examples. During the Hunger Marches of the early 1930s London was besieged by demonstrators from all parts of the country. As Kidd, the Secretary-General of NCCL, put it: 'Hunger Marchers have come to London and used their age-old right to demonstrate on an empty stomach.'[52] The authorities were so scared by the immense numbers taking part that the march was halted by a series of baton charges in Whitehall and on the Embankment. Kidd recounts how he saw two men, dressed in workmen's clothes, haranguing and inciting the crowd to charge the police cordon. 'I was just about to step on the pavement at the Whitehall Theatre when these two roughly-dressed men drew regulation police truncheons from their hip pockets, laid about them and arrested two other men.'[53] Protests after the event by Kidd and a journalist who both swore out affidavits detailing the police action brought only a brush-off from Lord Trenchard, the Metropolitan Police Commissioner.

More recently all the big demonstrations – on Vietnam in 1967 and 1968, Rhodesia in 1971, the Mangrove march of 1970, and 'Bloody Sunday' march in 1972 – were attended by large numbers of police in plainclothes. They included both Special Branch and CID officers and uniformed police in plainclothes for the day. Each group plays a distinctive role. The Special Branch officers present watch the activities and note the speeches of those considered to be the 'ringleaders', if necessary pointing them out to other policemen who usually attempt to arrest the 'leaders' if an affray occurs. Provocation during a demonstration is all too easy for the police, leaving the observer confused as to who actually started the punch-up. One sight remains in my memory, of an inspector at the 1971 Rhodesia demonstration in the Strand restraining his men from attacking press photographers who insisted on recording the behaviour of the police. (At this demonstration a *Time Out* photographer, Jeff Katz, who was chased by a

---

[52] Kidd, *British Liberty in Danger* (1940) p. 150.
[53] Kidd, *op. cit.*, p. 146.

policeman for over a hundred yards, fell over the kerb breaking his wrist. As a result of representations by the NUJ an apology was elicited from the police.)

There remains to be considered the attitude of the courts to the use of agents-provocateur. In some cases an acquittal can result from inconsistencies shown up in the prosecution case. But where this has not happened, what has been the courts' reaction to charges of entrapment? After the case of R. v. Macro[54] where an informer had taken part in a robbery but was not himself charged, the Home Office sent out a confidential circular to Chief Constables on the use of informers, ostensibly seeking to limit their use to 'appropriate circumstances'; but details of the circular were not made public. The judgements of the courts however do act as guidelines as to what the state agencies know they can get away with. In law there is no defence of entrapment as there is in the USA, so several other approaches have been suggested by defences. Firstly, it has been suggested that the agent-provocateur is an accomplice in the alleged offence. A 1848 ruling that such a person was not to be viewed as an accomplice was confirmed in an Appeal Court judgement given by Lord Parker in 1967. Therefore, whether the agent-provocateur was an observer of the offence, incited it, or was a full participant, his evidence is held to be admissible. Secondly, it has been suggested that evidence from informers and agents-provocateur should be excluded on the grounds that it is illegally or unfairly obtained. This position was tested in a Court Martial Appeal in the case of 'Murphy' in 1965. The defendant in this case was convicted of giving information of the security arrangements of a Northern Ireland barracks to some men he believed to be members of a subversive group operating in the South. The men turned out to be police officers. The defence appeal rested on a 1964 judgement given by Lord Parker which suggested evidence should be excluded, at the judge's discretion, if the evidence had 'been obtained oppressively, by false representations, by a trick, by threats, by bribes, by anything of that sort.' The Court Martial Appeal said the deception (police passing for what they were not) did not constitute a trick, and anyway the question of the constable appearing in plainclothes had been judged to be fair long ago. And, the Court suggested the gravity of the charge had to be taken into account, a view confirmed by Lord Parker in 1967, when he said: 'No doubt action of this sort should not be employed unless it is genuinely thought by those in authority that it is necessary having

[54] See p. 221.

regard to the nature of the suspected offence or the circumstances in the locality.'[55] The legitimacy of such action is clearly viewed as a matter for the state to decide, not the courts.

In each of these approaches the case for the defence sought to establish by one means or another the defence of entrapment, and each has been rejected. The only marginally hopeful sign was given in a case in 1969 where on appeal a sentence was reduced because of the participation of agents-provocateur. The appellant had planned a robbery while still in prison. On his release a police informer had approached him, and later introduced a police officer as 'a top criminal from London'. Cars and an imitation pistol for the robbery were supplied by the informer and the police agent-provocateur, thus ensuring the execution of the offence. At the appeal the sentence was reduced but the conviction stood.

There is no defence in the British courts against entrapment by agents-provocateur, whether they be policemen or persons acting on police instructions. Their evidence is both admissible and substantive. If the legitimacy of these methods is to be determined by the state, as the courts have ruled, then they will be used where and when the state's agencies lack sufficient evidence to get a conviction on the actions of the accused alone. Freedom in this sense, as has been seen in Northern Ireland, is determined not by some concept of inalienable rights but by the state. If the reader has been surprised in this section by references to criminal cases, as distinct from political, it should be pointed out that the practice of the state in using informers and agents-provocateur has never been solely limited to political cases. Further, when facing trial in a court of law the political activist will find that his future hangs on the established precedent set in criminal law by the judiciary over hundreds of years.

[55] Sneddon v. Stevenson (1967) 2 All E.R. 1277.

6   The Private Security Industry

The agencies considered so far have been concerned with policing in the community; however, there is another area which affects many people in their everyday lives. This is 'policing' at work, carried out not by the police but by the firms themselves or by companies hired for this purpose. The security industry mushroomed in the 1960s into a major industry in its own right. The explosion in consumerism in the late 1950s, and the consequent rise in the volume of money and goods involved, led in turn to an increase in theft, shoplifting, and the robbery of wage-money. The new industry at first concentrated on providing services geared to the physical security of goods, premises and money, but it was not long before more sophisticated wares were being designed to ensure the loyalty and honesty of those employed (or about to be employed). With the beginnings of the economic recession in the mid-1960s profits also became vulnerable to industrial 'unrest' and strikes.

The security industry offered a means of maximising profits, and technological products developed for policing (both in the United Kingdom and the United States of America) have been applied with alacrity to the private security field. It is interesting to note that the brunt of the security industry's attention is directed at the productive sector of the economy rather than at the commercial, administrative or financial sectors. Although strictly speaking private security firms do not fall into the category of 'political police', they are included here because their activities are relevant in the wider context of this book.

The most familiar aspects of the private security industry are the cash-carrying armoured vehicles and property guards. It is estimated that over 700 firms operate in this field in Britain today with more than 250,000 uniformed men, and over 10,000 armoured vehicles. Three companies dominate this part of the industry: Securicor, Group 4 Total Security (the trade name of Factoryguards Ltd) and Security Express.

Securicor dates back to 1935 and a firm called Night Watch Services with fifteen guards on bicycles patrolling expensive London homes. After the war the name was changed to Security Corp. – a good 'army' name befitting the military character and image that security firms have always encouraged. After protests, however, the Home Office suggested the name be changed again in case the firm be mistaken for a regular army unit and so Securicor was born. In the 1950s the firm employed seven hundred trained guards and was even then the largest company supplying day- and night-time guards for offices, factories and building sites.

Thanks to the British workers' suspicion of banks, wage-carrying security prospered. In the United States 80 per cent of the adult population have bank accounts; in Britain it is estimated that fewer than 30 per cent have.[1]

In the 1960s the industry expanded rapidly. Securicor was taken over by Associated Hotels and later acquired a fleet of cash-carrying armoured vehicles when it took over Armoured Car Services Ltd. Today Securicor has 300 United Kingdom branches and 60 overseas; 18,000 staff in the United Kingdom and another 8,000 overseas; a total of over 3,000 armoured vehicles and nearly 1,000 guard dogs. It claims to carry 'at least' £20,000 million cash annually and makes up 48 million wage packets each year, totalling £1,300 million. With at least 35 security depots around the country, its staff keep in touch via 70 transmitter stations. Besides cash-carrying, and hiring out of 'static' and patrolling guards, Securicor, and the other firms, provide a courier service for the transportation of anything from confidential documents, valuable goods, and computer programmes to vital pieces of machinery.[2] In addition it will provide commercial firms with advice about security arrangements and equipment at their factories, and undercover agents against 'pilfering'.[3] Securicor also runs a sophisticated system to protect long-distance lorries from hijackings. Called HELP – Haulage Emergency Link Protection – it covers 3,000 vehicles linked to Securicor HELP radio stations throughout the country.

[1] Stated at the Cropwood Conference on 'The Security Industry in the United Kingdom' (1970) organised by the Cambridge University Institute of Criminology who later published a report of the proceedings.
[2] Each week in Shetland a helicopter lands at the local airport with research documents from one of the oil rigs. This is handed over to Securicor whose guards take the papers a few yards to the waiting British Airways flight.
[3] A firm called Wansdyke Security has a nuclear bomb-proof store for industrial records and secrets in an old limestone mine 100 feet underground in a small village near Bath. Many large British companies store their essential or top secret records there.

The second largest company is Group 4 Total Security, the trade name for the Swedish-owned Factoryguards company; it also has a subsidiary company, Store Detectives, specialising in supplying agents to check for shoplifters and on shop staff. Another, smaller firm is Security Express which has a fleet of several hundred armoured trucks and specialises in bulk cash transport for banks, unlike Securicor which does most of its business transporting 'small' sums between bank branches or delivering wages to firms. The sudden upsurge in robberies from bulk cash-carrying vehicles a few years ago hit the firms badly. There are also several hundred smaller companies providing guards, ranging from those with a staff of a hundred down to one man and a dog concerns. Other firms, such as Chubb, have branched out of their traditional safe and lock interests into supplying guards.

A major worry of security firms is infiltration by criminals. All staff in the more reputable companies are screened before they are taken on. A driver for a bullion-carrying truck, for example, will be thoroughly investigated, whereas an applicant for night-guarding will have only a routine check. The large firms like to present an image of efficient screening of their night guards. However those who occupied the building Centrepoint, in London, early in 1974 gained entry by infiltrating a supporter into the Burns security firm who were responsible for guarding the building. The demonstrators commented on the lack of checks and the ease with which it was possible to get on the payroll. But in other cases the smaller the firm is the more cursory the check. Wages for night guards are not good and the work is boring.

The supplying of guards is highly competitive. Many firms think of security and guards as an unnecessary expense required only because of the insurance companies' insistence. Firms are therefore often reluctant to pay for reputable guards, who would be relatively expensive, although the guard from a small firm may be inefficient, too old, or a criminal himself. Security firms do not look for 'intelligent' people, expecting people of 'average intelligence', as they put it, or the relatively old, to apply.

At higher levels the industry attracts many ex-policemen, or those who might have considered joining the police. The detective departments of large firms are staffed almost entirely by ex-CID officers. These departments carry out work similar in many ways to the CID, with their own network of contacts. The boardrooms of security firms are well-represented by retired high-ranking policemen.[4]

[4] See pp. 239–240.

Most of the companies mentioned have been primarily concerned with the 'protective' side of the security industry, like guards, safes or alarms. On the other side of the industry are those firms offering 'detective' services – the private detective and the specialist security consultants. Security consultants (as they like to be known) are often ex-members of one of the state security or intelligence organisations. They provide a variety of services including the screening of employeess and the investigation of information leaks and cases of industrial espionage; they offer equipment such as speech-scramblers, paper-shredders and de-bugging devices. Private detectives undertake an even wider variety of jobs, many of which are outside the scope of this book.

The Younger Committee on Privacy had great difficulty in finding out how many private detectives were operating in Britain.[5] They quoted estimates ranging from 1,000 to 20,000 and eventually settled on a 'reasonable' estimate of 3,000. Many regard this as a conservative estimate – the true figure could be at least double. Most private detectives are 'former policemen, solicitors' clerks or ex-servicemen with experience of security work'.[6] And as there are no legal controls of licensing, 'there is nothing to stop criminals who are at large from becoming private detectives.'[7] Many agencies claim not to undertake illegal or 'unethical' assignments, but some will accept any work, including industrial espionage and they frequently use bugs and telephone-tapping equipment.

For instance, in 1968 the Christopher Roberts agency admitted investigating the activities of the Anti-Apartheid Movement in Britain.[8] This surveillance, which several MPs believed was carried out for the South African government, including infiltrating an agent into the Movement's voluntary staff, photographing supporters and reporting on meetings. Two years later the same agency was hired by an unnamed MP to investigate the use of parliamentary services by MPs sympathetic to the Anti-Apartheid Movement.[9]

The growth of the security industry from the early 1960s focussed attention on the weapons and uniforms of security firms. Seeking respectability, the industry became sensitive to accusations of uncontrolled

[5] *The Younger Committee on Privacy*, Cmnd 5012 (1972).
[6] *Ibid.*
[7] *Ibid.*, p. 129.
[8] *Sunday Times*, 3 November 1968.
[9] *The Times*, 14 March 1970 and 7 May 1970.

growth of private police forces. To forestall this criticism the large cash-protecting, guard and alarm firms established the British Security Industry Association (BSIA) early in 1967 to act as an unofficial controlling body. By 1971 only 18 of the industry's 500 firms belonged to the Association but these firms represented over 90 per cent of the total business of the industry; the figures remain roughly the same today. Encouraged by the Home Office who were, and still are, reluctant to give any official recognition to the industry, the Association set about improving the image of security through a code of standards for members. The Association also acts as the co-ordinating body for contact with the insurance industry, the police, the Home Office and its various crime prevention projects.

The members of BSIA in 1975 included:[10]

Abel Alarm Co.
AFA-Minerva (EMI) Ltd.
Brocks Group of Companies
Chubb Alarms Ltd.
Chubb and Sons Lock and Safe Co. Ltd.
Gardner Security Co. Ltd.
Granley Products (London) Ltd.
Group 4 Total Security Ltd.
Lander Alarm Company (Scotland) Ltd.
Modern Automatic Alarms Ltd.
Safes Ltd.
Securicor Ltd.
Security Express Ltd.
Shorrock Security Systems Ltd.

The present Chairman of BSIA is Lord Hayter, the Chairman of Chubb & Sons since 1957. Up to his death in April 1974 the Chairman of Securicor, Keith Erskine, was the BSIA's Vice Chairman, and J. A. Shepherd-Barron, the Chairman of Security Express, was the Association's Treasurer. The Secretary of BSIA is Peter Hamilton, an ex-military and colonial intelligence officer who is now security adviser for Chubb and one of the industry's leading theoreticians. In 1971 the Association started a new body, the National Supervisory Council for Intruder Alarms, in an attempt to control the increasing number of small firms which were moving into the alarms business. Like the BSIA, this is an independent body with no official Home

[10] BSIA press handout, 22 January 1975.

Office recognition, but observers from the Home Office, Association of Chief Police Officers and the Metropolitan Police attend meetings of the Council. BSIA is also represented on related Home Office committees.

Until recently public discussion of the private security industry centred on such details as the uniforms and weapons of cash-carrying or property guards rather than on the overall role of the industry. Most firms use police or military-style uniforms. For the larger firms these help to establish a corporate identity: for all firms the wearing of uniforms makes their guards stand out and give them an aura of authority and respectability. Often they are designed to be similar to police uniforms but sufficiently different to avoid prosecution under the 1964 Police Act, which makes it an offence for any person to wear 'any article of police uniform in circumstances where it gives him an appearance so nearly resembling that of a member of the police force as to be calculated to deceive.'[11] In another section of the Act an 'article of police uniform' is defined as any article of uniform, any distinctive badge or mark or document of identification usually issued to the police or having a similar appearance to something issued to the police.[12] In May 1973, Labour MP Stanley Clinton Davis (later a Junior Minister) attacked security firms for trying to imitate police uniforms and added that some police forces had had to change their uniforms to make them distinctive from private security uniforms.

A recent case concerned a guard from Thames Security Services who had dressed in a cap similar to those issued to Essex policemen (but without the constabulary badge), a blue shirt, black tie, black police-style trousers and a truncheon strap. Initially the magistrates dismissed the charges because they were satisfied the guard was not, at the time, trying to pass himself off as a policeman. The prosecution appealed and took the case to the High Court where Mr Justice Shaw said that the words 'as to be calculated to deceive' in Section 52(2) of the Act meant 'likely to deceive or reasonably likely to deceive', and that in this case there was every likelihood of the public thinking the guard was a police officer.[13] He sent the case back to the magistrates with a direction to convict. Given this ruling it seems that the only thing preventing more prosecutions of security firms is the sympathetic attitude of senior police officers.

[11] Police Act 1964 Section 52(2).
[12] Police Act 1964 Section 52(4).
[13] *Security Gazette*, September 1973. Turner v. Shearer (1973).

During the early 1960s guards protecting bullion or large quantities of bank notes were armed with firearms. In December 1961, an armed bank-guard shot a robber during a raid on a bank van. This incident led security firms to stop issuing firearms to their guards and to criticise the use of armed guards by banks. Scotland Yard admitted that firearms' certificates were 'occasionally' issued to employees of firms 'engaged in the transport of certain valuable consignments'.[14] The BSIA, formed five years later, still holds the view expressed then that 'while the British policeman remains unarmed, the British security guard will remain unarmed.'[15]

Firms have tried other weapons, such as nerve gas aerosols or other noxious sprays, but none of them are in use today. The standard weapon that has been used by security guards is the 'stick' or truncheon. Occasionally security guards with truncheons have been prosecuted for carrying offensive weapons. A reported case, which might be thought to have outlawed truncheons occurred in July 1973,[16] when the Court of Appeal upheld convictions for carrying offensive weapons against three guards from White Star Securities in the Isle of Wight. Lord Justice Megaw ruled that the carrying of a weapon should not be treated as a matter of routine or as 'part of the uniform'. He said the law did not sanction the constant carrying of offensive weapons even by people who might be under threat of attack. Defendants might be able to prove 'reasonable cause' for carrying an offensive weapon if they were 'in immediate danger of attack'. This ruling, however, did not stop the use of truncheons by some firms. Two months later the Police Federation, in a protest to the Home Office, said: 'we have been concerned with the open display by members of private security organisations of offensive weapons in public. We are aware that there have been prosecutions by the police but this does not appear to deter its continuance.'[17]

The Police Federation, which represents policemen below the rank of Superintendent, has always been suspicious of private security and supports the introduction of legislation to control the industry by a licensing system, whereas the Association of Chief Police Officers supports the Home Office line of encouraging the industry to operate its own watchdog organisation through the BSIA. While enjoying the

[14] Tom Clayton, *The Protectors* (1967) p. 79.
[15] *Op. cit.*, p. 77.
[16] *Daily Mail*, 24 July 1973.
[17] *News of the World*, 2 September 1973.

Home Office's unofficial stamp of approval, BSIA itself wants to see an official licensing system introduced by parliament.[18] Many politicians also support this view as does the legal profession. In 1973 the *New Law Journal* in an editorial strongly supported a licensing system adding that 'it is now high time that the Home Office took notice of the increasing public concern about a situation that is rapidly getting out of hand.'[19] The Home Office has always rejected the idea of a licensing system except as a last resort, preferring to support the industry's attempts at self-regulation through the BSIA.

In 1971 the Cambridge University Institute of Criminology organised the Cropwood Conference on the security industry which was attended by senior policemen (including Sir John Waldron, then Commissioner for the Metropolis and Mr Williamson, HM Inspector of Constabulary); top executives from the security industry and senior civil servants (including Mr D. H. J. Hilary, the Assistant Secretary in the Home Office Police Department). Hilary argued strongly at the Conference that his department would support legislation only if 'a clear need could be shown to exist' which, he argued, had not been done. 'The security industry', he is reported as saying, 'unlike the police, had not been given any special powers: it only possessed the powers of the ordinary citizen'. Other delegates to the conference disagreed with him, arguing that 'whatever the legal position may be, the industry had *de facto* been given special rights.'[20]

Since the conference the security industry has been given more 'special rights' by the state. Argument by the Home Office that legislation and licensing would tend to give the industry some kind of 'stamp of approval or authority' seems irrelevant: the state has already given *de facto* recognition to the industry. The industry still believes that official recognition by the Home Office will only be a question of time. As the demands of the police increase but the problem of shortage of manpower remains the scope of private security firms will increase to such a point that it is assumed the government and senior police officers will have to give official recognition through legislation. For the last two years, in his annual reports, Sir Robert Mark, Commissioner of London's police, has highlighted the serious shortage of manpower, adding that unless the situation improves he will increasingly have to decide between policing priorities, even to the ex-

[18] They would like this official control to be operated by the BSIA.
[19] Report in *The Times*, 7 September 1973.
[20] Report on the Cropwood Conference.

tent of the 'partial abandonment of what are the conventional and accepted forms of policing'.[21]

This point was picked up by Robert Traini, crime correspondent of *The Sun* in his regular monthly column in *Security Gazette*:

> 'in the disposition of the available manpower he (Mark) has to decide on priorities. And it is this matter of priorities which poses the dilemma and, in my opinion, puts the spotlight on the urgency and inevitability of officially defining an area of activity in which the private security company must be given and must accept responsibility.'[22]

However, links between the industry and the state are already so strong that official recognition would do no more than rubber-stamp what is now happening.

The Security industry and state agencies

One of the more obvious links between the industry and the police exists in the crime-prevention operation of burglar alarms. Here the police are directly involved in advising on the installation of alarms and answering alarm calls. The most inefficient method of alerting the police is the alarm-bell outside outside the premises set off by an intruder. Beside being intended to frighten off the intruder (and wake the neighbourhood) the bell, it is hoped, will attract passing policemen or a civilian who will call the police. An increasingly popular form of alarm is that linked to a Central Alarm Station run by a security company. Here security staff monitor alarms and inform the police when one is set off. The most direct system is when an alarm is linked directly to a police station by post office land-line.

In 1971 it was estimated that there were at least 110,000 alarms in the United Kingdom of which 76,000 were linked directly to the police.[23] By 1976 the number of alarms linked to the police is expected to be 140,000. A major problem of burglar alarms, whatever type, is the high incidence of false calls, illustrated by these figures from the Metropolitan police area:[24]

---

[21] *Annual Report of the Commissioner of Metropolitan Police for 1972*. HMSO (1973).

[22] *Security Gazette*, August 1973.

[23] Figures given by Dr D. Dring, Managing Director, Chubb Alarms, at the Cropwood Conference.

[24] Given by Commander E. Matthews, Head of Communications Branch at Scotland Yard at the Cropwood Conference. Alarm calls to the police via a private Central Alarm Station have an even higher proportion of false calls.

Year	Known alarms linked to police	Total calls received	Total false calls	Break-ins	Arrests as % of all calls
1968	21,364	70,511	67,737 (96%)	757	0·4
1969	23,605	82,296	78,887 (96%)	1,122	0·4
1970	26,850	94,214	90,214 (96%)	840	0·2

If each of these false calls occupied two policemen for half-an-hour then in 1970 there were 90,000 police man-hours wasted by false alarm calls in London alone. The National Supervisory Council for Intruder Alarms is very concerned to improve the efficiency of alarms and cut down false calls. The police have introduced a procedure whereby owners of alarms that persistently give false calls are first warned and then have their alarm disconnected from the police station or told that no more alarms will be answered.

The Police Federation has often complained at the number of officers leaving the force to join one of the sections of the security industry or alternatively, the apparent ease security firms have in attracting staff when the uniformed police is under-staffed. Many, if not most, of the industrial security officers are ex-policemen, and over half the private detectives and security consultants are ex-policemen; the rest are from other state or military intelligence agencies. The detective departments of firms like Securicor or Group 4 are mainly staffed by ex-policemen. The industry also creams off the senior police officers who move either onto the boards of private firms or into senior security posts. Below is a small selection of the people who have left either the police or another state agency to join a private company or one of the security firms:

Name and police rank	*New job*[25]
E. Field: Chief Superintendent York and N.E. Yorkshire police. Retired 1973.	Now Security Adviser to Shepherd Construction Ltd.
Sir Philip Margeston: Ex-Assistant Commissioner of London's Police.	Ex-Chairman of BSIA and President of Securicor.

[25] People listed here may not hold these positions now. The list is intended to show the range of jobs into which ex-police or intelligence officers move rather than to provide a detailed guide to the current situation.

Tom Paul:
Crime Prevention Office Somerset   Alarms Manager for South
and Bath Constabulary. Retired 1973.   West Alarms Ltd.

Peter Brodie:
Ex-Assistant Commissioner (Crime)   Security Consultant
in London.   AFA-Minerva.

H. Hannam:
Ex-Detective Chief Inspector.   Retired 1974 as Security
                                       consultant to McAlpines.

Sir Richard Jackson:
Ex-Assistant Commissioner in London   Director of Securicor
and Ex-President of Interpol.   and subsidiary firms.

Peter Hamilton:
Ex-Army Intelligence.   Secretary of BSIA and
                                       Advisor for Chubb.

Sir Percy Sillitoe:
Former Head of MI5.   First Chairman of Security
                                       Express when company formed.

Sir Ranulph Bacon:
Former Assistant Commissioner in
London   Director of Securicor.

Sir Ronald Howe:
Former Assistant Commissioner in
London   Director of Factoryguards.

Richard Chitty:
Retired 1974 as Deputy Assistant   Security Adviser to Curzon
Commissioner in London.   House casinos.

Harold Hudson:
Retired in 1974 as Deputy Assistant   Security Adviser to
Commissioner in London.   Ladbrokes.

Ernest Millin:
Retired in 1974 as Deputy Assistant   Security Adviser to
Commissioner in London.   Casanova casinos.

Roy Yorke:
Retired 1974 as Commander in London.   Security Adviser to
                                       Playboy.

Sir Martin Furnival Jones:
Former Head of MI5. Retired 1972.   Head of Security for
                                       Playboy.

Sir John Nott-Bower:
Former Commissioner in London.

Director of Associated
Fire Alarms and Security
Guards Ltd.

Eric Oliver:
Ex-Detective Superintendent.

Security Adviser to
Unilever.

John Wilson:
Ex-Detective Chief Inspector in Leeds.

Security Officer
Yorkshire Imperial Metals.

Ron Bullock:
Retired in 1972 as Detective Chief
Inspector

Set up own security
consultant firm
Carisbrook Consultants.

Eric Gregory:
Retired in 1973 as Assistant Chief
Constable for Thames Valley.

Special Security Officer
to British Leyland.

At boardroom level the value of these people to private security is twofold: firstly, they have the experience of working in similar fields and often have proven detective ability; secondly, their presence lends authority and encourages both customers and government to have confidence in the firms. Ex-policeman, ex-intelligence or security officers and ex-civil servants also take with them into private industry the knowledge and contacts built up through years of public service. Securicor, for example, not only has Sir Philip Margeston and Sir Richard Jackson, both ex-Assistant Commissioners of Police in London, on its board, but also Ray (now Lord) Gunter; two ex-Home Secretaries, Henry (now Lord) Brooke and Robert Carr; ex-Minister Lord Thorneycroft (now also with Pye, Pirelli and Trust House Forte); and lastly, but not least, Sir Charles Cunningham, an ex-Parliamentary Under-Secretary of State at the Home Office.

The presence of so many ex-policemen within the industry has led to a close relationship with state agencies. This, in turn, helps firms gain access to official records by use of the 'old boy network'. Officially, of course, these records are available only to serving police officers but the fact that, with the right contacts, the files have been accessible to others is admitted by almost everyone except the Home Office.

The managing director of Group 4 Total Security, Mr Philip Sorensen, said in 1971 that 'there is no doubt that there is an old boy's network which sometimes helps us to discover whether a man has a criminal record but it is wrong that we should be placed in this situation.'[26] At the time Mr Sorensen was proposing to the Home Office that the Continental practice of issuing 'honest' people with police certificates stating they had no criminal record should be adopted in Britain to prevent criminals being employed by security firms.[27] Two years later the British Legal Association wrote to the Home Secretary expressing concern at how easily CRO information could be obtained. This followed reports[28] that Air France's London office, with a staff of 600, had actually printed a special form to process requests to the Criminal Records Office about applicants for jobs.[29] These forms were handed to the British Airports Authority police who have access to criminal records at Scotland Yard. The airline confirmed the report but added that they did not realise they had done anything wrong. The police had apparently not told the airline that the information was not available, but accepted the procedure.[30]

Firms who do not have access to criminal records through their security officer may use private detective agencies, many of whom have openly advertised their ability to check criminal records for a few pounds. But criminal records are only one piece of confidential information on individuals required for pre- or post-employment surveillance. Bank balances, tax records, driving licences, medical records, vehicle registrations and ex-directory telephone numbers are some of the items available at a price. In July 1973 three employees of the Ace Detective Agency pleaded guilty to conspiring to procure confidential information from government departments including the Inland Revenue and Criminal Records Office. One of the defendants was an ex-policeman, another an ex-employee of the Inland Revenue.

In January 1973, four detectives from the Christopher Roberts agency were brought to trial on similar charges. It was claimed that two of the defendants who owned the detective agency, Ian and Stuart Withers, had previously boasted of their ability to get criminal records or other confidential information, and John Cornish an ex-policeman, also one of their employees, allegedly obtained information from criminal files.

[26] *The Times*, 11 March 1971.
[27] Security firms are not interested only in whether people have criminal records, but in other police information that might show a prospective employee to be untrustworthy, a political militant, etc.
[28] *Guardian*, 22 November 1973.
[29] *Guardian*, 19 November 1973.
[30] The Legal Association also mentioned an unidentified security executive who said, during a commercial radio 'phone-in' programme, that firms had access to CRO files through their local police.

A serving police officer, Detective Sergeant John Josiah, stationed at Farnworth, a witness at the trial, admitted that he had known Cornish when he was in the force and had continued their friendship after Cornish left. In evidence it was said that Mr Cornish had written a report on the police record of a man called Christopher H. T. Clarke. The day before this report was written, Sergeant Josiah had drawn Clarke's file from the Criminal Records Office. However, he denied passing any confidential information to Mr Cornish. Evidence was also given about obtaining information from the Ministry of Defence, a bank, a building society and about car registration and driving licence details.

All the defendants were found guilty and given suspended prison terms, but the House of Lords, in an extraordinary decision in November 1974 quashed their conviction, leaving a vast loophole in the criminal law allowing intrusion into citizens' privacy. This prosecution was the first brought under a government-ordered police investigation into leaks of confidential information. Several other detectives have been charged but not yet tried. However, the prosecution of the Withers brothers (who have since re-opened their agency under another name) and others does not in practice place an effective brake on the security industry's access to criminal records and other confidential personal information. Those who have been prosecuted are often from the smaller 'cowboy' firms while the 'respectable' ones carry on more subtly and undetected.

In a large number of firms the criminal records and personal background of staff are officially investigated. These are the firms with government contracts which involve wholly or partly classified information, material or work. In 1972 there were 4,500 firms with defence contracts each worth over £5,000 and thousands more with contracts from other departments, many involving classified work.[31]

MI5 is the agency responsible for security on all government classified contracts; security is not the responsibility of the department placing the contract. MI5 sends a 'security aspects letter' to firms before a contract is signed which defines the classification of the work and the outline security provisions MI5 wants the firm to introduce. As every contract includes a security clause, any firm which fails to meet MI5 standards or is lax in its security precautions could find its contract terminated. MI5 has a team of Special Advisers who visit a firm when a contract has been signed and advise on all aspects of security. Afterwards they keep in contact with the firm's Security Officer and are

---

[31] Answer to parliamentary question. Reported in *The Times*, 5 July 1973.

always available to help with problems. They also send out Security Manuals and run special courses for security officers and higher management personnel.

The standard security provisions of these contracts gives MI5 the right to inspect all security arrangements, to control the placing of sub-contracts, to be given full particulars of anyone handling or having access to classified information – or anyone in close or regular contact with these people.[32] MI5 also has the right to demand the 'exclusion from access to classified information of any person who does not need such access for the proper performance of the contract, or who (unless the Department specifically consents) is an alien or is not the servant of the contractor, or whom the Department has required to be excluded.'[33] The 'purge procedure' and Positive Vetting system also apply to a firm's employees with a classified contract.[34]

The state employs at least fifteen security companies to guard and patrol government department (and, at one time, police) buildings.[35] The Departments of Agriculture, Defence, Employment, Trade, Health, Energy and the Home and Foreign Offices all have contracts with private firms. Several companies are also involved in security at our air and sea ports. Securicor is employed to 'detain' immigrants refused entry to Britain at Heathrow. A director of Securicor explained that the immigrants 'were not under arrest, but were held' until their deportation.[36] Securicor holds the contract for security at all British Airports Authority airports and other firms, such as Burns International at Heathrow, have contracts with individual airlines. Since the summer of 1973 guards employed at airports have had the statutory power to search passengers and their luggage under the Protection of Aircraft Act. This Act was introduced to implement the provisions of the international Montreal Convention held earlier to discuss hijacking and aircraft safety. In certain circumstances, when the threat is assumed to be serious, private guards also have the right to detain people, and use force to do so if necessary. Several Labour MPs, the Police Federation and the National Council for Civil Liberties were

[32] Not only would they have a firm's personnel records, but their own and Special Branch information on employees' political activities.

[33] *Security Procedures in the Public Service*, HMSO, 1962.

[34] See Ch. 4.

[35] Parliamentary answer, 6 February 1974. Firms included Securicor, Security Express, Burns, Group 4. The Ministry of Defence said their list would take too long to provide, as they employed so many security firms.

[36] Sir Randulph Bacon, at the Cropwood Conference.

among those who complained bitterly at the inclusion of private security guards in this Act and its extension of their powers. The Act was passed in both Houses without a division.

The security industry and the labour movement: Reds under the bed

'The purpose of security in its widest sense is to protect a way of life.'[37] This simple definition, by Chubb executive and security theoretician, Peter Hamilton, illustrates the rationale of the security industry. It is seen by the security theorists as complementary to the role of the uniformed police in protecting the economic and social system which is under attack by, they believe, forces seeking to destroy capitalism and 'western democracy'. These forces are seen as the paid agents of communist or other foreign governments and those acting from within the system to sabotage industry and subvert the workforce. Economic warfare is the tool of communism that the security industry believes it must fight. Like Kitson, a counter-insurgency theorist, who believes that society is at war against subversion, Hamilton argues that industry is at war on the shop-floor.

Peter Hamilton has spent his whole life in security, initially for the military and since the early 1960s for private industry. He spent three years 'fighting communism in Malaya both in the intelligence and combat senses'.[38] He was then appointed government security adviser in Cyprus (1957–1960) and later, in 1960, adviser to Edgar Whitehead, the Prime Minister of Southern Rhodesia. Since 1962 he has been Security Adviser to Chubb, is secretary of the BSIA and on the editorial board of the magazine *Security Gazette*. Hamilton is highly respected within the industry and is to be found at many of its conferences. Today he articulates the prevalent attitudes of the industry. Society, he argues, is under attack by espionage and subversion which 'are moral, if not always legal, crimes and both are concerned with gain and redistribution of wealth.'[39]

The security industry does not appear to accept that there could be any 'home-grown' revolutionary movement, or that trade union militants are not directly or indirectly in the pay of Moscow. Workers may have what they believe are legitimate grievances, but they will be 'manipulated by sinister outside forces to twist and distort facts so as to

[37] *Security: Attitudes and Techniques for Management*, p. 123 (published in 1968 by Hutchinson for Chubb on their 150th anniversary).
[38] Peter Hamilton, *Espionage and Subversion in an Industrial Society* (1967).
[39] Hamilton, *op. cit.*

cause industrial unrest and to wreck all attempts by legitimate trade union officials to negotiate with management.'[40] In industry the main danger is posed by 'passive sabotage ... (which) connotes industrial action such as strikes, go-slows, work-to-rule, and other forms of deliberate industrial disruption.'[41] Sabotage includes industrial action 'aimed to hamper some legitimate national purposes such as ... vital economic measures'.[42] The man who strikes, goes-slow, or works-to-rule is seen as a 'social criminal' whose actions are likely to lead to violence. Commenting on the unofficial strikes which followed the sacking of Lord Hall as Chairman of the Post Office, Hamilton argued that, 'from this to actual destruction of telephone exchanges or the dislocation of vital services, including burglar alarms, is but a short step.'[43]

The 'battle' is not just confined to the shop-floor. Those who are attacking or seeking to demolish 'established values' are also seen as being guilty of subversion and sabotage. 'The new threats posed by espionage and subversion occur in the vacuum which appears to be resulting from the accelerating withdrawal of the great social binding forces of feudalism and its more liberal developments in recent times.'[44]

The industry still maintains that the major threat is from 'communism', which it sees as any political action that holds up or stops production and hence limits profits. It also maintains that the communist bogey disguises its interest in legitimate trade union and political activity. The security industry believes that industrial espionage is increasing rapidly. It is not possible to say whether this is in fact true, but security firms and consultants have flourished by convincing industry that it is. They argue that industrial espionage is mainly the work of communist agents – in fact much industrial espionage appears to be between commercial competitors. Increasingly commercial firms are demanding 'intelligence' about the market and their rivals. The line between industrial espionage and what is known as 'competitive intelligence' is very thin. Industrial espionage is often referred to as 'aggressive market research', and is mainly the result of industry's drive for higher profits, if possible at lower costs.

[40] Paul Slee Smith, *Industrial Intelligence and Espionage* (1970) p. 121.
[41] Hamilton, *op. cit.*
[42] Hamilton, *op. cit.*, p. 37.
[43] *Security Gazette*, January 1971.
[44] Hamilton, *op. cit.*, p. 79.

Though it claims otherwise, the activities of the security industry are contrary in many respects to the interests of workers. Its task is to help select employees, ensuring that there are no communists, trouble-makers, criminals, drunks, homosexuals or whatever, whose employment is believed to be against the best interests of the company. Management must then keep their employees loyal and contented, which helps efficiency and production. As Peter Hamilton has written: 'Management on whom our future power and prosperity primarily depend cannot be effective without a loyal and contented staff and labour force.'[45]

Initial information on applicants for executive posts is sought through interviews and questionnaires which, besides requesting information directly relevant to the job, can ask searching questions about the applicant's personal life. An applicant's reading material, religion, hobbies, financial affairs, sex-life, social life, relatives and friends are all areas covered by many application forms in certain sections of industry. Then checks will be made on previous jobs, often by personal visits to personnel or security officers. Police records may be checked, unofficially, especially if the job is in somewhere like a bank.[46] Inquiries are made of credit-rating agencies to see if there is a record of bankruptcy or financial trouble. If the prospective employer considers the post highly 'sensitive', he may order a complete background check by the firm's security staff or by a private detective agency.

The first stage of pre-employment checking on industrial workers is detailed application forms and contact with past employers. Within industries the security or personnel staff of different firms will often know each other or a mutual acquaintance, which helps with the inquiries. A telephone call or letter will soon find out what previous employers thought of an applicant's work, politics and attitudes. There is no protection for the worker against half-truths or rumours being told about him. He is completely vulnerable to the efficiency or inefficiency of a company's records and the personal or political prejudices of the security or personnel staff.[47]

A refinement or extension of this informal network between firms is the gathering of information about workers by employers' trade

[45] *Ibid.*

[46] See James Rule, *Private Lives and Public Surveillance* (1973).

[47] In his book, *Private Lives and Public Surveillance*, James Rule adds that 'some (police) forces and criminal record offices routinely review lists of seasonal employment applications at resorts and holiday camps in order to screen out those with convictions.' p. 163.

organisations. In some key industries these federations or organisations compile 'blacklists' of political troublemakers, of people convicted or suspected of theft, or those who have annoyed past employers for one reason or another. Then there are several organisations outside industry which specialise in intelligence work against 'extremists' and draw up blacklists for industry.[48]

The largest and best known of these groups in Britain is the Economic League, which acts as a clearing house for employers' experiences and troubles with workers and trade unions. Its stated aim is 'exposing the experiences, the intentions and strategy of subversive organisations and providing positive education to combat misrepresentation by industrial agitators.' In 1973 the League received over £400,000 in subscriptions and donations from member companies. Its list of supporters and of the 31 directors contains most of the large industrial, commercial and banking concerns in the country. Among the donors to the League in 1973 for example, were British Leyland (£3,000), GKN (£1,500), Slater Walker (£2,500), Trafalgar House Investments (£2,100), Midland Bank (£4,070) and the National Westminster Bank (£4,625). The League employs a total of 163 staff (no doubt only after careful screening) and among its activities during 1973 was the printing and distribution of more than twenty million leaflets on the dangers of subversion. By monitoring trade union and left-wing publications, attending meetings and gathering information provided by member firms and sympathetic right-wing trade unionists, the League has built up a vast index, or blacklist, or 'subversives', their tactics and future plans.

Because of the secrecy that surrounds organisations such as the Economic League, hard evidence of blacklisting is rare. Indeed, the attitude of the right-wing groups at least equals that of most left-wing organisations. One indication that blacklisting takes place on a large scale is the response of senior management or security personnel when asked to justify the practice. Usually there is no denial that blacklisting occurs. Instead the justification is given that all employers have the right to full details of an employee's past so that only 'honest' people are employed: 'Surely that is fair enough?' is the general attitude. One

[48] Don Madgwick and Tony Smythe in their book, *The Invasions of Privacy* (1974) quoted a 1970 *Newsweek* report that private, corporate-backed, American Security Council, had files on 6 million 'subversives'; The Church League of America claimed 7 million files on anti-Christian or anti-'American way of life' people.

company which donates to the League told the *Observer* that the League 'does a hell of a lot of security vetting for us on political grounds.'[49]

In 1973, however, specific evidence of the League's blacklisting activities arose out of an industrial dispute in southern England. Strachan's, an engineering factory near Southampton, had a strike in 1973. Up to the time of the occupation of the factory by the workers in 1974 when redundancies were announced, the Special Branch maintained regular contact with the firm's management. The Branch told the firm that the local International Socialist group had 'picked' the factory for industrial unrest, and the Branch were kept informed of certain workers' activities by a member of management. The Special Branch, however, was not the only interested party to what was happening at the factory; nor was it the only organisation passing information to the employers. Before the occupation of the factory, one of the workers had been told by management that he would not be considered for promotion because they had discovered he had been a communist candidate in the 1963 local government elections.[50] Later he and a union official discovered that the management had been telephoning a 'secret' number, giving a code number (520) to ask for information about workers at the factory. The workers rang the number, gave the code, and asked for information on the worker who had previously been denied promotion. After a short time they were told that he had been a communist candidate in 1963 and had also written articles for the Communist Party's daily paper, the *Morning Star*.[51] When the *Guardian* newspaper telephoned the number they were told it was an Economic League ex-directory telephone number.[52]

The Economic League is not the only organisation fighting to preserve Britain's 'way of life' from subversives.[53] Industrial Research and Information Services – IRIS – circulates to industry the names of militants and warns of the dangers of employing subversives. It was very active in the mid-1960s, especially during the 1966 seaman's

[49] *Observer*, 19 October 1969.

[50] Elections provide a good source of information. Every candidate needs ten people to sign the nomination papers, so fifty Communist Party candidates would reveal 500 supporters.

[51] The information, according to the worker concerned, was completely wrong.

[52] *Guardian*, 11 May 1974.

[53] For more information see *Big Business and Politics* published by the Labour Research Department (1974).

strike. Ray Gunter, ex-Labour Government Minister and director of Securicor, was a director of IRIS from December 1968 to October 1970 and was chairman during 1969. Common Cause is a similar organisation. Its aims are to act 'as advisers . . . to any company . . . (regarding employees and assist) in the screening of those . . . (who) might reasonably be expected to be engaging in activities detrimental to the welfare of the state.'[54] British United Industrialists (BUI) received a total of £248,939 in 1973 for its support of capitalism and its work investigating 'front' organisations and subversive groups.[55] Its aims are 'the promotion, preservation and protection so far as legally practicable of the principle of free enterprise in trade and industry.'[56] Aims of Industry restricts itself mainly to propaganda against nationalisation and the threat of socialism (via the Labour Party), although it has recently set up an intelligence department. Its official annual income from its 4,000 member companies is usually just over £100,000 except in election years when it leaps to £300,000 or more.

The Institute for the Study of Conflict, which usually concerns itself with military issues and closely follows the theories of Kitson, circulated a document in 1974 called 'Sources of Conflict in British Industry'.[57] This suggested the blacklisting and sacking of communists and subversives.[58]

Within the security industry there are commercial firms who also supply blacklists (of mainly non-political information) or who will undertake background investigations of job applicants. At the Old Bailey trial in 1973 of the four employees of the Christopher Roberts private detective agency, on charges of conspiracy to obtain confidential information, it was revealed that the firm had been employed to check on workers' political activities. Besides being employed by banks, solicitors, insurance firms and individuals, this and other detective

---

[54] Aims and Objects, Common Cause Ltd. (Companies Registry file).

[55] BUI ceased to be a limited company in 1968 to maintain secrecy over its activities and to escape revealing details of its activities to Company's House. In 1973 BUI Director, Col. Hobbs, admitted BUI had donated to the Monday Club.

[56] Aims and Objects, British United Industrialist Ltd. (Companies Registry file).

[57] *Source of Conflict in British Industry* (1974). The then-Director of the Institute for the Study of Conflict, Brian Crozier, was at the same time Chairman of the US Central Intelligence Agency's London propaganda operation 'Forum World Features'. *Time Out*, 20 June 1975.

[58] *Ibid*.

agencies had frequently been engaged by non-unionised companies to investigate the background of prospective employees to make sure that their labour force was not 'infiltrated' by union members.

Lodge Services is the largest organisation in Britain supplying store detectives to catch shoplifters and check on shop staff. It is estimated that £1 million a day is lost by retail firms – but only a small proportion, about 20–25 per cent is through shoplifting by customers. Fiddling or theft by staff account for the rest.[59] In one three-month period several years ago Lodge claimed its detectives discovered over 350 dishonest staff.[60] Lodge had a blacklist of between 12,000–20,000 names of people sacked or suspected of theft or dishonesty, which is open to any of their customers. Securicor was embarrassed in 1963 when one of its subsidiary companies, Complete Security Service, was found to be offering investigations on companies' employees. The firm widely circulated a letter offering, among other services, 'the screening of prospective employees, a search into their antecedents and background'.[61] Securicor, after much adverse publicity, announced that Complete Security Service were withdrawing the letter. Another security firm that offered screening services was Management Investigation Services founded in 1965 by Ralph Matthews, ex-Military Intelligence Officer and once on the staff of the Directorate of Military Intelligence at the Ministry of Defence. His firm, which usually specialises in industrial counter-espionage, operated a blacklist of people with criminal records or who had been 'sacked for breaches of trust'. It also offered to check on job applicants including contacting police criminal record offices, although it stated that 'this is a strictly unofficial procedure'.[62]

While management want workers to be 'happy', they often display a profound distrust of their workers – and here again the security industry plays its part. In the eyes of security staff even satisfied workers can easily be turned into a disloyal liability:

> 'Many factors can contribute towards a lowering of moral standards: political associations, emotional background, mental instability, drink, sex perversions, drugs etc. There can be no doubt that political associations play a significant part in influencing the

---

[59] Including shops' own security officers or hired detectives.
[60] Anthony Thompson, *Big Brother in Britain Today* (1970) p. 151.
[61] Letter circulated by Complete Security Services Ltd, dated 1 June 1963.
[62] *Sun*, 10 January 1968.

course of actions to be taken by the employee intent on "hitting back" at his employers.'[63]

'Aftercare' is the word given to the employer's task of keeping an eye on his workers. Management is encouraged by 'thinking security' to get to know their workers and encourage and participate in social, recreational or extramural activities.[64] 'Opportunities should be taken to have off-the-record talks with staff and workers about prospects, conditions of work, problems arising from work, etc.'[65] Information gained this way should be used to build up a 'behaviour pattern' together with security and personnel records which are all part of a firm's internal intelligence network. Such a network 'can be made palatable to the "usual channels" by tact, the establishment of good personal relations and by demonstrating its usefulness to them as well. If they have nothing to hide they will have nothing to worry about, and if they have, an intelligence service is even more justified.'[66] If a firm's intelligence service uncovers untrustworthy workers or subversives they should be sacked 'discreetly and quickly without giving any grounds for saying they have been victimised.'[67]

Further surveillance is directed against trade unions, and political organisations with members inside the factory or working in the surrounding community. Here, industry has a common interest with the Special Branch and MI5 whose jobs are to maintain security in firms with government contracts, and to spy on political 'extremists' or subversive groups, either by surveillance, or the infiltration of undercover agents or through specially recruited workers acting as informers.

While bugging and tapping of union offices and phones is not unknown, the practice does not seem widespread. But surveillance could be carried out in other ways. In 1973 the chief security officer for Guest, Keen and Nettlefolds (GKN) Birmingham factory had installed in his office a special machine that enabled him to listen in on any call being made over the firm's internal telephone system (and interrupt if he wanted to). When workers found out about this they successfully demanded its removal. GKN's Administrative Director said the

[63] Paul Slee Smith, *Industrial Intelligence and Espionage* (1970) p. 115.

[64] Securicor's 'mutual company' scheme and their 'care' for their workers is designed to ensure loyalty and an identification with the firm among staff.

[65] Slee Smith, *op. cit.*, p. 119.

[66] Peter Hamilton, *Espionage and Subversion in an Industrial Society* (1967) p. 126.

[67] Slee Smith, *op. cit.*, p. 121.

machine had been installed to allow the security officer to contact his staff: 'His men are trained in First Aid, for instance. They might have been needed for that purpose. The fact that the phone enabled the security chief to listen in on all our phones was coincidental.'[68]

A few years ago a director of the Essex firm, Wilep Bruch, employed Barry Quartermain's Southern Provincial Investigations agency to put a bug in the firm's offices. A spokesman justified this by saying that 'it was the only way of finding out what happened after hours.'[69] In 1973 car manufacturers Chrysler's admitted that during a strike at their Stoke plant hidden 'spy' cameras had been used to photograph the picket lines and identify outside 'left-wing militants' who had 'infiltrated the picket'.[70] Three years earlier, in 1970, it was revealed that security staff at Rootes Motors' (now part of Chrysler) had been reporting on outside political activity in Coventry.

When students at Warwick University occupied the administrative buildings and gained access to university files among the letters they found was one to the Vice-Chancellor from a director of Rootes. With it was a copy of the following report by Rootes' 'Legal Adviser':

'Accompanied by Mr T. Norton, Security Officer, Stoke, I duly attended a meeting of the Coventry Labour Party at its offices . . . The guest speaker, Dr Montgomery spoke, to an audience of eight people . . . I think that one member of the audience may have been Mr Bob Mitchell, one of the left-wing students at Warwick University. The remainder included Mr H. Finch, whom [sic] I understand is a shop steward at Dunlops; with the exception of a shorthand writer who is on Norton's staff there were no other Rootes employees present. After Dr Montgomery had finished, three members of the audience, including Mr Finch, paid markedly lukewarm tribute to the speech. These three were strong supporters of the All Trades Union Alliance . . . (and) are dedicated subversives.'[71]

Another letter to the Vice-Chancellor was from the Deputy Managing Director of Automotive Products Ltd:

[68] *Sunday People*, 7 January 1973.
[69] R. Payne, *Private Spies* (1967) p. 85.
[70] *Daily Telegraph*, 18 June 1973.
[71] E. P. Thompson, (ed) *Warwick University Ltd.* (1970) p. 107. Rootes were donors to the University funds.

'Further to our conversation, I enclose the documents referred to. The only additional information I can give is: 1) The smaller document was distributed outside our works on 31 January 1969 by people that we believe to be students of the University. 2) We sent a representative to the meeting on 3 February, at Coundon Road, which was attended by only twenty-eight people . . . 4) We are not proposing to send anyone to the next meeting because we do not wish to draw attention to our interest in what is going on.'[72]

The surveillance of workers can also include the infiltration of under-cover agents onto the shop-floor or into union organisations by employers or employers' organisations. Paul Slee Smith in his book, *Industrial Intelligence and Espionage*, explains why this is done:

'In this way top management is able to gauge the true feeling of their employees, be forewarned about the issues likely to be raised in industrial disputes and the attitudes of union officials, shop stewards and unofficial strike leaders. The possession of this kind of intelligence enables management to plan ahead, to formulate proposals that have a reasonable chance of being accepted and makes possible an intelligent, anticipated approach to labour problems.'[73]

Possession of information on a potential strike situation can enable managements to plan for this eventuality and thus try to ensure that sufficient stocks of materials are on hand prior to the outbreak of a strike.

To obtain information from a supplier's factory the main firm can station its own agents or informers inside the sub-contractor's workforce; or the sub-contractor may pass on information from his own spies; in addition agents or informers for an employers' organisation may also pass relevant information to firms. Commercial security firms have also provided agents to spy on workers. Complete Security Service Ltd., the Securicor subsidiary whose blacklisting activities were mentioned earlier, was one of these firms.[74] In a letter to companies, sent on 1 June 1963, they pointed out that pilfering occurred in every factory and they 'specialise in preventing this unwarranted sharing of

[72] *Op. cit.*, p. 109.
[73] Slee Smith, *op. cit.*, p. 106.
[74] See p. 251.

7. A *Workers Press* photographer arouses the interest of the Eurotec detectives outside the National Industrial Relations Court.

your profits'.[75] Among the services offered were, 'the supplying of undercover agents – a man planted among your employees to provide you with a complete appraisal of any unauthorised happenings. The following of vehicles used by employees during the course of their work. Reporting on any person who may be suspected of causing dissension or inciting employees to defection.'[76]

In a case reported in 1963, an undercover agent employed by security staff at the British Motor Corporation in Scotland seems to have overstepped the mark. 'Tried on a charge of attempting to frame a number of his workmates by planting machinery on their lorries, he was found guilty and sent to prison.'[77] A more recent case concerned the imprisonment of the 'Pentonville Five' in 1972 for contempt of the National Industrial Relations Court. The Midland Cold Storage Company's container depot in east London had been picketed by members

[75] See footnote 61.
[76] *Ibid*.
[77] Thompson, *Big Brother in Britain Today* (1970) p. 148.

of the Transport and General Workers' Union for five weeks in contravention of an order by the Industrial Court. The Company eventually hired the private detective agency, Euro-Tec, ('investigators extraordinary'), to 'ascertain the names and addresses of the persons regularly in the picket line at the gates of the company, to ascertain the affiliations of such persons in any organisation and to report on the activities of such persons in the picket lines.'[78] Three detectives were used for the surveillance, including Euro-Tec's principal Garry Murray (who started the firm in 1969 after leaving military intelligence). They observed and photographed people on the picket, noted who spoke to them, followed the dockers to their houses and other places and talked to the dockers' wives, pretending to be 'freelance news researchers'. Euro-Tec also hired a van and one of their agents drove it up to the picket lines and recorded his conversations with the pickets.[79]

[78] *Workers Press*, 8 July 1972; *Time Out*, 14–20 July 1972.
[79] *Ibid.*

7 Counter-revolutionary Preparations

Unlike the previous chapter this one is not concerned with the practice of a particular institution or agency but rather with the reaction of the state as a whole in moments when it perceives internal revolution to be on the cards. The state's response is examined historically; in the immediate past; and in relation to its present preparations should a major internal challenge develop inside Britain.

A history of internal defence 1916–1960

The fear of revolution in Britain was never greater than in the period immediately after the October Revolution in 1917. The war in Europe was grinding on, strikes were breaking out in critical areas of the economy and the socialist movement was taking on a new impetus from the Russian example. Prior to the First World War there had been many long and bitter strikes. The ruling class employed all the means at its disposal through the agencies of the state to meet the challenge of the Labour movement between 1918 and the General Strike in 1926. At no time since 1926 has the possibility of a major internal conflict been greater than at present – the economic recession faced by Britain in the mid-1970s could become worse than that of the 1930s. An examination of that earlier period will show the origins of the state's planning to counter revolution.

The plans laid for national emergencies have gone through several phases. Prior to the First World War a foreign enemy was the dominant concern; in the post-war period it was a 'domestic enemy'. During the late 1930s the state again reacted to an external threat, and this continued after the Second World War with the start of the Cold War and the possibility of nuclear warfare. In the 1960s, the state's attention was focused yet again inwards; however, the steps taken for countering the 'enemy', whether internal or external, have been in many ways similar in their basic approach.

The first plans to co-ordinate all the agencies of the state on a national basis were laid in preparation for the First World War. The duties to be carried out by each Ministry and agency were specified in the War Book which was prepared in 1913.[1] The War Book contained, for example, instructions to local police forces on billeting, the requisitioning of vehicles (and horses), mobilisation, the protection of buildings, and intelligence-gathering. Another task was the drawing-up of lists of aliens to be interned at the outbreak of hostilities – 30,000 aliens were interned in camps jointly administered by the War Office, the Home Office and the Local Government Board. The outbreak of strikes, rebellions by soldiers and socialist protests at the continuation of the war in 1918 served to give the Lloyd George Coalition govern-ment notice of the troubles to be expected. Early in 1919 a committee of the Cabinet was appointed and met regularly under the chair-manship of the Home Secretary to consider plans for countering major strikes. The committee proposed that a special organisation should be set up to co-ordinate the activities of all Ministries and agen-cies. The Coalition government accepted this proposal and set up the Supply and Transport Committee under the chairmanship of Sir Eric Geddes. Geddes had been the member of the War Cabinet responsible for transport. The task of the Committee was to draw up plans to en-sure the maintenance of supplies in the event of a national strike – that is, to subvert the efforts of the strikers by the use of state agencies operating under the umbrella of the law. The Geddes plan proposed the division of the country into sixteen Districts – in practice there were only eleven – each of which was to be under the command of a Junior Minister, called 'District Commissioner', a title borrowed unashamed-ly from colonial practice. Food Controllers were to be given additional powers under the Defence of the Realm Act (DORA), and army and police operations were to be co-ordinated. The first stages of the plan were put into operation during the short rail strike of September 1919. In addition to the army, the police and the Special Constables, the government called on loyal citizens to enrol in a 'Citizen Guard' and more than 70,000 joined up.

The organisation of the government at this time, although more formal than in the pre-war period, operated with greater informality than today. The Cabinet secretariat had been set up on a permanent basis in 1916 and Sir Maurice Hankey was appointed to be Secretary to the Cabinet. He was also secretary to the Committee for Imperial Defence, which was suspended as such during the war. But on the dis-solution of the War Cabinet in November 1919 it was revived. It was a

[1] A similar manual exists today and would contain plans for dealing with every kind of emergency.

Prime Minister's committee and the Commander-in-Chief of the General Staff regularly attended the meetings concerned with industrial struggles. While the detailed planning for handling strikes was done by the Geddes committee, policy decisions were taken by a conference of Ministers rather than by the full Cabinet. This conference was supplied with intelligence reports from the Home Office, the War Office and the Ministry of Transport and in addition by Sir Basil Thomson, the Director of Intelligence, at this time head of an independent Special Branch.[2]

On 2 February 1920, there was a special conference of Ministers to discuss threatened industrial action and the likelihood of a revolution.[3] The meeting was at first concerned with the availability of the Army, and Winston Churchill and the Chief of the General Staff considered the country to be nearly defenceless. Even the new Air Force could keep only a hundred planes in the air at a time, though 'The PM presumed they could use machine guns and drop bombs'.[4] G. H. Roberts, one of the Labour MPs in the Coalition government, warned of sabotage at the beginning of a strike. 'There are large groups preparing for Soviet government', he told the meeting, while W. H. Long, Minister for the Admiralty, exclaimed:

> 'The peaceable manpower of the country is without arms. I have not a pistol less than 200 years old. A Bill is needed for licensing persons to bear arms. This has been useful in Ireland because the authorities know who is possessed of arms.
> *Shortt* (Home Secretary): The Home Office had a Bill ready but in the past there have always been objections.
> *Bonar Law* (Privy Seal): All weapons ought to be available for distribution to the friends of the government.
> *Lord Iverforth* (Minister for Munitions): We have a surplus of all kinds of munitions. We have been selling them to the Baltic States.[5]

Sir Robert Horne, Minister of Labour, suggested that secret lists of reliable supporters should be prepared by the Chief Constables and

---

[2] See Ch. 3.
[3] Some of the inner deliberations of the Cabinet in this period are revealed in the *Whitehall Diary* which contains the notes of Thomas Jones – the Deputy Secretary to the Cabinet until 1930. There are three volumes, published in 1969; Volume 1, 1916–1925; Volume 2, 1926–1930; Volume 3, Ireland. Oxford University Press.
[4] T. Jones, *Whitehall Diary*, Vol. 1 (1969) p. 99.
[5] *Whitehall Diary*, Volume 1, p. 100.

Geddes suggested a briefing meeting for Mayors – but this suggestion was withdrawn because there were some Labour Mayors. Towards the end of the conference Geddes asked to be relieved of the chairmanship of the Supply and Transport Committee as he did not want to see the Ministry of Transport labelled as a strike-breaking department: 'Nonsense', protested several ministers:

> '*Churchill:* It is not strike-breaking, it is feeding the people.
> *Chamberlain:* It is really defence of the foundations of civilisation.'[6]

Later in 1920, on 16 October, the miners did go on strike, though by 28 October the threatened railway sympathy strike was called off and the miners returned to work with the award of interim pay rises. The government however took the opportunity to replace the wartime Defence of the Realm Act (which was expiring) with the 1920 Emergency Powers Act.[7] By 1921 the short-lived post-war boom had disappeared, unemployment was running at over one and a half million and the economy was extremely sensitive to a major stoppage. In March 1921 two events coincided. The miners' interim pay rise ran out and the mines were due to be handed back to the private owners (after the wartime nationalisation). The mine-owners proposed new agreements which meant a cut in wages; the miners rejected this and went on strike on 31 March. The Triple Alliance of the three big unions – the railwaymen, the transport workers and the miners – sought to bring out the train drivers and transport workers in sympathy. On 31 March the government declared a state of emergency under the 1920 Act and on 1 April the mine-owners started a national lock-out.

The conference of Ministers met on 4 April and considered intelligence reports on the strike. The discussion was particularly concerned with the availability of troops. Sir L. Worthington-Evans, Minister at the War Office, said: 'We need eighteen battalions to hold London';[8] but of the eighteen available seven were Irish and were not thought to be reliable in the situation. Worthington-Evans therefore proposed to bring troops home from abroad. A long debate ensued on where the battalions should be taken from and it was agreed that two could come from Malta, and two from Egypt; but there was disagreement over the possibility of recalling four from Silesia. The Foreign Office were worried about repercussions. Mr Chamberlain (Leader of

---

[6] *Op. cit.*, p. 102.
[7] See Ch. 1.
[8] *Whitehall Diary*, Vol. 1, p. 135.

the Commons) declared: 'I am all for holding British coalfields rather than Silesian.'[9] Other Ministers were more concerned that loyal citizens should have a rallying point, and Lord Birkenhead, the Lord Chancellor, declared: 'We ought not to be shot without a fight.'[10] Three days later there was another conference of Ministers on the state's preparedness. Geddes reported that the District Commissioners were appointed together with a Chief Commissioner, and that a letter of appeal from the Prime Minister to local councils was in bank safes in each of the eleven Districts. The meeting then moved on to consider other ways of conducting propaganda against the miners' cause. Sir P. Lloyd-Greame MBE, Secretary of the Overseas Trade Department, was authorised to '. . . spend money [£1,000] on sending men to Scotland to work up the Government case in the local papers from inside – e.g. *Edinburgh Evening News*, *Glasgow Bulletins*, etc.'[11] When someone suggested that the government should issue leaflets in non-mining areas to gain public support, Lloyd-Greame said that the point of propaganda was to conceal its origins, for example during the last strike, when 'the government was sending out matter to 900 newspapers via Coalition and Unionist organisations, etc., and the local political organisations were paid, and the public suspected little or nothing.'[12] This admission meant that during the 1920 miners' strike the government paid local Tory and Coalition Liberal constituency associations out of state money (taxes) to distribute propaganda without any reference to parliament.

The next day, 8 April, the conference met again and Geddes presented an intelligence assessment distilled from the daily reports sent in by the District Commissioners. 'Things are getting worse, incipient disorder spreading in Scotland and beginning to get to England', he told the assembled Ministers.[13] Lord Curzon, Leader of the Lords, reported that in addition to the Army and police there were available the reservists, the new Defence Force (a volunteer citizen organisation) and the Special Constables. And Chamberlain suggested, with classic bourgeois naïveté, the drafting of 'an appeal to the miners to save property.'[14] All these preparations were, however, to prove unnecessary for on 15 April – 'Black Friday' – the Triple Alliance

[9] *Whitehall Diary*, Vol. 1, p. 136.
[10] *Op. cit.*, p. 135.
[11] *Op. cit.*, p. 139.
[12] *Ibid.*
[13] *Op. cit.*, p. 140.
[14] *Op. cit.*, p. 143.

called off the national strike and the miners struggled on alone until June.

After the 1922 General Election returned the Tories to power under Bonar Law, the emergency plans were re-vamped. John Davidson, the Chancellor of the Duchy of Lancaster, became the Minister responsible for emergency planning and the chairmanship of the co-ordinating committee was given to Sir John Anderson, the Permanent Under Secretary at the Home Office. Anderson reported to the Cabinet in July 1923 and proposed few changes – the old District Commissioners were now to be called 'Civil Commissioners'. Nor did the advent of the first Labour government under MacDonald in 1924 bring any changes: '. . . far from being destroyed by the Party which led the Labour Movement (the emergency plan), was preserved and even used by the Party which was so anxious to prove itself "fit to govern".'[15] Josiah Wedgwood, the Labour Chancellor of the Duchy of Lancaster, was made responsible for emergency planning. In March 1924 a strike by tram drivers in London was to be supported by a sympathy strike of Underground workers and the Labour government declared a state of emergency on 31 March. Fortuitously the strike ended quickly and forestalled a confrontation between the Labour government and the labour movement.

The Tories returned to power again in October 1924 and Baldwin gave the responsibility for emergency planning to the Home Secretary, Sir William Joynson-Hicks; Sir John Anderson remained the chairman of the committee. By July 1925 the miners again prepared to go on strike against the mine-owners' new proposed cut in wages, and the General Council of the TUC issued instructions for a national embargo on the movement of coal.[16] The prospect that at last the unions could act together to bring the country's economy to a standstill caught the government unprepared, for the emergency planning was not up to a widespread and prolonged confrontation. In the words of Sir Lloyd-Greame, then Minister for the Board of Trade, 'We are not ready.'[17] To buy time a Royal Commission was set up under Sir Herbert Samuel and the government agreed to a state subsidy of £23 million, spread over nine months, to make up the miners' pay packets.

[15] Walter, *The RSG's* (1963) p. 8.
[16] The Triple Alliance of the 'big three' unions had by 1925 become defunct and the General Council of the TUC thereafter 'represented' the trade union movement in talks with the government.
[17] *Whitehall Diary*, Vol. 1, p. 325.

The miners rejected the Samuel Report in March 1926 and the state subsidy of wages ran out in April. On 30 April the government declared a state of emergency and the strike began on 3 May. The General Council of the TUC called off the strike on 13 May, having surrendered unconditionally the day before. Many reasons have been offered for the ending of the General Strike – it was not effective; the state's plans for running services were effective; the common sense of the British worker prevailed; the declaration by Sir John Simon, Liberal MP, that the strike was illegal, etc. The real reason was more deep-seated: the TUC was afraid of its own position between the bosses and the rank-and-file workers: 'It was not fear of a breakdown, but fear that the strike might get out of their own hands that primarily moved the most influential members of the General Council.'[18] The strike was, in fact, massively effective and only minimal services were operating despite the state's preparations; moreover it would have been impossible for the state to have reached and maintained anything like an effective service over a sustained period without a major out-right conflict with the working class as a whole.

Action against the strike proceeded on two levels. The unofficial 'Organisation for the Maintenance of Supplies' was set up by patriotic members of the ruling class and produced a rallying point for tens of thousands of like-minded citizens. The President was Lord Harding of Penshurst, an ex-Viceroy of India, and most members of its council were friends of the government who had retired from public affairs. Of more importance was the committee under Sir John Anderson, which moved into top gear in 1925. This became the official Emergency Committee on supply and transport, and co-ordinated all state agencies and services. The Chief Civil Commissioner, Sir William Mitchell-Thomson, the Postmaster-General, and the eleven Civil Commissioners were all appointed by the end of 1925. In November 1923 the Ministry of Health circular 636 had outlined the duties and powers of the Commissioners to each local authority – that is, to the Clerks of the Councils, not the elected Councillors. The powers of royal prerogative which could give additional legal authority to the Commissioners were backed by a series of Regulations (made by Order in Council) under the 1920 Emergency Powers Act.[19] The government

---

[18] J. Symonds, *The General Strike* (1957) p. 211.

[19] One regulation made on 11 May but never implemented was to prohibit banks from paying out money to anyone 'acting in opposition to the National Interest'.

called upon all the supposedly 'neutral' institutions of the state – the law, the Army, the police and the administration – to come to the defence of capitalism:

> 'The government saw the issue almost totally in terms of con-stitutionality versus illegality and the threat of revolution . . . the real problem from the government point of view was not that the miners were receiving a pittance but that millions of men were refusing to work for their employers.'[20]

The division between the TUC leaders and union membership was never greater than on 13 May 1926. Disbelief greeted the news that the strike was to end and it was several days before the men returned to work and normal services were resumed. The miners continued the strike alone until hunger forced them to settle for increased hours and reduced wages on 26 November 1926.

The destruction of labour movement solidarity by the betrayal by the TUC leaders in 1926 was indeed fortunate for the ruling class, for the world-wide recession in the capitalist world was only just begin-ning to bite. Unemployment was to reach nearly three million in the early 1930s and British capitalism underwent a major crisis.

During the 1930s the need to resist an external threat again reasserted itself as the priority with the rise of fascism in Germany and Italy. After the German occupation of Austria in 1938 Sir Warren Fisher and Sir Maurice Hankey (in his capacity as secretary to the Committee for Imperial Defence) drew up a plan called 'Civil Defence Emergency Scheme Y'. The plan closely mirrored that of the 1920s (for internal purposes) with eleven areas now called 'Regions', not Divisions. The wartime Regional Commissioners were appointed in 1939 and at their head was none other than Sir John Anderson, now a Tory MP (after a spell as governor of Bengal); he became the new Minister of Home Security. The Ministry of Home Security was effectively the Home Office under a wartime name. Anderson was later succeeded by Herbert Morrison.

In 1940 when the German invasion of southern England seemed imminent, plans were laid to establish a network of cells which would remain behind enemy lines and conduct guerrilla activities. One of the agencies working on this idea was MI6 (SIS) whose Section D was responsible for subversion and sabotage behind enemy lines. With the usual audacity of secrecy-minded agencies Section D set about getting

---

[20] Bob Dent, *Lessons of the General Strike* (1973) p. 9.

up a store of arms and recruiting agents all over Britain, without informing anyone else. MI5 became quite alarmed when it started receiving reports of Section D's activities and several of their agents were arrested as spies before the truth was discovered.[21]

After the Second World War it was the first majority Labour government under Attlee which had to cope with the adjustment to a peacetime economy and a new world in which Britain's former supremacy was visibly passing away. There was no revolution in the air as there had been in 1918 but there were several major strikes – mainly involving the dockers. The Labour government did not hesitate to send in the troops on many occasions to unload ships and to run power stations. And on 29 June 1948 the Labour government, using the 1920 Emergency Powers Act, declared a state of emergency over a dock strike. This strike ended quickly but in July 1949 a state of emergency was again declared and strike-breaking troops poured into the docks – the numbers on strike then increased from 10,000 to 15,000 as other workers refused to work alongside the troops. To plan for eventualities an Emergency Committee was set up under the chairmanship of Sir Arthur Maxwell, a former Permanent Under Secretary at the Home Office. The strike had arisen over a call by the Canadian Seamen's Union to black several ships and it ended when they too ended their strike ten days later.[22]

As World War Two ended so the planning started for World War Three. The Cold War had set in by 1946 and the Labour government passed the Civil Defence Act in 1948. However, it was the Tories returning to power in 1951 who took matters seriously and set about building a network of underground Regional Seats of Government at an estimated cost of £1,400 million.[23] These safe hideaways were not of course for the people but for those in government, the state agencies and a few selected local dignitaries. No-one would have heard much about these schemes had not the organisation Spies for Peace published details of the network on 11 April 1963.[24]

[21] Section D was axed after this debacle. See Page, Leith, Knightley, Philby (1959) p. 154.

[22] For an account of strike-breaking by the Attlee Government see The Labour Government v. The Dockers, *Solidarity* pamphlet No. 19, 1965 (Reprint) p. 10.

[23] Laurie, *Beneath the City Streets* (1972) p. 245.

[24] For the tale of how 'Spies for Peace' obtained the full details of the RSG's see *Inside Story* No. 8, March/April 1973. See also *The RSG's* by Nicholas Walter, a *Solidarity* pamphlet (1963) and Laurie, *op. cit.*

By the late 1960s the likelihood of a nuclear war was receding and few other than military planners believed that there was any protection against ICBMs (inter-continental ballistic missiles) and the like. In the 1970s the emergency plans were being seen yet again as a means to confront the internal enemy as the spectre of revolution and disorder rose out of the major economic recession facing Britain and other capitalist countries.

Interlude

Since the mid-1960s Britain has been experiencing the effects of the long-term economic recession which is now openly recognised to exist in the advanced capitalist countries of the world. More recently, politicians, academics, and military men have been speculating as to whether the recession will reach such proportions that the liberal-democratic structure of society will effectively break down, and they pose the likelihood of a more authoritarian system being a necessity in these circumstances. Capitalism, the underlying economic system, is taken for granted as a given premise in their arguments. The alternative is, apparently, chaos.

The task, as they see it, is therefore to defend the status quo at a time of economic difficulty when the increasing competition over the fruits of industry sharpens the social conflict.[25] Their response is an attempt to pre-empt any possibility of the overthrow of capitalism by making counter-revolutionary preparations.[26] The problem is thus construed not as capitalism's inability to provide a stable economic system, but as a matter of 'law and order'. During the 1972 miners' strike more than 250 miners and their supporters were arrested. Soon after the end of the strike a reporter from *The Times* interviewed a Brigadier on the General Staff at the UK Land Forces Headquarters, who said:

'The whole period of the miners' strike made us realise that the present size of the police force is too small. It is based on the fundamental philosophy that we are a law-abiding country, but things have now got to the state where there are not enough resources to deal with the increasing numbers who are not prepared to respect the law.'[27]

[25] This competition is one between capital and labour over the distribution of wages and profits, and of increased state expenditure. See Glyn and Sutcliffe, *British Capitalism, Workers, and the Profits Squeeze* (1972).
[26] See also chapters 3 and 4 for the ongoing role of the Special Branch and MI5 in this connection.
[27] *The Times*, 23 May 1972.

Moreover the conflict in Northern Ireland, the only extended civil war in the Western World, was never far from people's thoughts and now presented itself to military men, politicians and the Left alike as a foretaste of Britain in the late 1970s.

Lord Chalfont, one of the more articulate exponents of the emerging consensus that bourgeois democracy faced a serious challenge, wrote in 1974 of the 'subtle internal threat to political freedom' represented by 'the wide spectrum of political forces which seek, by methods ranging from outright subversion to legitimate political activity, to change fundamentally and irreversibly our existing political system.'[28] Chalfont postulated a wholesale attack on society expressed both externally and internally, which is 'part of a generalised attack on the political system of the free world – a system of which Britain is an integral if increasingly fragile part.'[29] By the 'free world' is meant the Western capitalist countries and (sometimes) third world satellites.

The external attack on the Western political system is a reality. The capitalist countries face a continued and extended challenge to their imperialism in the Third World, while the internal economic recession creates increasing tensions at home. The seriousness of the situation may have dawned slowly on the consciousness of politicians and media commentators, but it has clearly been in the minds of the military for quite some time. Brigadier Frank Kitson wrote in 1971 in his book, *Low Intensity Operations*, that

> 'if a genuine and serious grievance arose, such as might result from a significant drop in the standard of living, all those who now dissipate their protest over a wide variety of causes might concentrate their efforts and produce a situation which was beyond the power of the police to handle. Should this happen, the army would be required to restore the position rapidly. Fumbling at this junction might have grave consequences, even to the extent of undermining confidence in the whole system of government.'[30]

Today the military tacticians make a distinction between three kinds of defence planning. There is a defence against the external enemy in foreign lands; 'home defence' for measures taken to resist the attack of an external enemy on the homeland; and 'internal' defence which

[28] *The Times*, 22 July 1974.
[29] *The Times*, *op. cit.*
[30] F. Kitson, *Low Intensity Operations* (1971) p. 25.

refers to the suppression of an internally-generated insurrection. Internal defence is conceived as the measures necessary to counter three stages in the progression to civil war (revolution). Firstly, the presence or escalation of subversive activities; secondly, an armed insurrection by a section of the community; and lastly, an outright civil war in which the country is divided into two warring camps. Kitson also provides a distinction between subversion and insurrection (which is close to Chalfont's position):

> '*Subversion*, then, will be held to mean all measures short of the use of armed force taken by one section of the people of a country to overthrow those governing the country at the time, or *to force them to do things which they do not want to do*. It can involve the use of political and economic pressure, strikes, protest marches, and propaganda, and can also include the use of small-scale violence for the purpose of coercing recalcitrant members of the population into giving support. *Insurgency* will be held to cover the use of armed force by a section of the people against the government for the purposes mentioned above.'[31]

The problem, for liberals, with this definition of subversion is that it includes activities which, at least hitherto, have been accepted as 'legitimate' political activity. But the best way to avert insurrection and civil war, it is suggested, is to combat subversion in its infancy, before the potential of 'subversive' ideas can gain adherents and wide support.

By the autumn of 1973 the predictions of Mr Heath – made to the United Nations General Assembly in 1970 – that internal rather than external conflict could be the concern of the decade seemed to be a self-fulfilling prophecy.[32] How much Heath and his fellow Ministers contributed to what then seemed an impending confrontation between the state and the unions is not easy to determine. The loss of the 1974 election, the reluctance of the voters to give a mandate for

---

[31] Kitson, *op. cit.*, p. 3. My emphasis.

[32] Speaking to the UN General Assembly in 1970, Mr Heath said: 'Moreover, today we must recognise a new threat to the peace of nations, indeed to the very fabric of society. We have seen in the last few years the growth of the cult of political violence, preached and practised not so much between states as within them. It is a sombre thought, but it may be that in the 1970s, the decade which faces us, civil war, rather than between nations, will be the main danger we face'.

further confrontation, indicated perhaps that the Tories had gone too far.

Confrontation was a consistent theme under the 1970–74 government. In July 1970 the government declared a state of emergency over the dock strike and five months later, in December, a second emergency was declared in response to the electricity strike. After these two emergencies the government and the state agencies made plans for a prolonged struggle. In February 1971 two separate initiatives were taken.

A working party of the Defence Scientific Advisory Committee was set up to investigate the technical equipment available to the intelligence agencies; to examine the new equipment for crowd-control produced for Northern Ireland; to see what re-equipment of the police should take place.[33] It was also announced in the February that:

'A special committee to co-ordinate the use of police and troops in the event of civil disorder in Britain has started meeting in London . . . Its members are Sir Robert Mark, Deputy Commissioner of the Metropolis, who was a member of the advisory body concerned with the re-organisation of the Royal Ulster Constabulary, and Home Office and Ministry of Defence representatives.'[34]

A third state of emergency was declared for the first miners' strike in February 1972, and the fourth for the dock strike in August. Early the next year, in March 1973, the Home Secretary, Mr Carr, confided to crime reporters that a permanent National Security Committee (NSC) had been set up under the chairmanship of Lord Jellicoe. (Later, after the 'Lambton affair', Lord Carrington took over.) The NSC included representatives from the military, the intelligence agencies, the police, the Home Office and the Department of Trade and Industry. It was serviced by a full-time staff in special offices and given a large budget.[35]

In preparation for the long-threatened miners' strike in 1973 the NSC undertook the preparation of several contingency plans which in-

[33] *Daily Telegraph* magazine, 15 July 1973, and *Daily Express*, 12 January 1973.
[34] *Sunday Times*, 7 February 1971.
[35] In the spring of 1973 the Conservative Political Centre produced a pamphlet, *In Defence of Peace*, with a foreword by Lord Carrington, the Minister of Defence. In a section headed 'Internal Security', three steps were proposed: 1) to have a well-manned and equipped army; 2) to carry out a study of the techniques of terrorism and to evolve methods of counter-terrorism; 3) to 'pay more attention to our Intelligence services'.

cluded the building up of coal stocks at strategic power stations. At the same time the Home Secretary announced plans to stop so-called 'flying pickets' from other regions coming to the aid of power-station pickets. This measure was designed to prevent a repeat of the miners' success at Saltley, Birmingham, during the 1972 strike. There, picket lines were being broken in order to take coke out of the storage depot, but many miners came from all parts of the country to support their comrades and were joined by other trade unionists in the Birmingham area. The massed pickets came into direct confrontation with the police and by sheer weight of numbers kept the lorries out. In November 1973 it was announced that 'flying pickets' were to be intercepted while *en route* by the police. 'An intelligence bureau has been set up at Scotland Yard to give police forces throughout the country early warning of when industrial unrest may turn to violence.'[36] The Home Secretary, Mr Carr, speaking at Leicester, was more explicit: 'We want to stop the masses forming to start with.'[37] The fifth declaration of emergency started in November 1973 and lasted for more than four months – the longest ever, apart from that during the General Strike. And by January 1974 not only were 900,000 fully unemployed, but thousands were on part-time work as a result of the three-day week.

The war in Northern Ireland, IRA bombings in England, and hijackings by Arab guerrillas all contributed to an increasing paranoia, which before long became institutionalised and commonplace. For example, plans had been laid, it was reported, to counter terrorist attacks on the Channel Tunnel;[38] the Home Office requested the British Standards Institution to prepare a bullet-proof glass for internal use;[39] a spokesman for the Institution thought the following would be likely customers:

> 'embassies, army recruiting centres, barracks, messes and soldiers' recreation centres, airline offices, national tourist offices, head offices of companies trading with politically sensitive countries, certain churches, party headquarters, even the private homes of people connected with such organisations.'[40]

[36] *The Times*, 13 November 1973.
[37] *Guardian*, 13 November 1973.
[38] *Daily Mail*, 13 September 1973.
[39] British Standard 5051.
[40] *Guardian*, 4 January 1974.

Following the explosion in the Westminster Hall annexe early in 1974 the Security Co-ordinator of the House of Commons drew up a three-phase plan, Phase One being normal security, Phase Two requiring searches and closer inspection of identity cards, and Phase Three, the banning of the public from parliament with only MPs and those on essential business being allowed entry.[41]

Meanwhile back on the industrial front the business papers and magazines forecast not only gloom and despondency for their readers but predicted that violence would spread to the factory. *The Economist* in June 1974 commented: 'it is strange that some people think that a lot more redundancies, which are probably coming, will cool this temper. It is much more likely that some of the redundant will stage sit-ins, workers' occupations, riots or kidnapping of executives.'[42]

The state's response was to increase its readiness with contingency plans to maintain essential services. In the event these plans were not activated; but at another level, the confrontation that began in 1972 between the government and the miners was now seen as a precursor to a wider and deepening crisis that has yet to come.

Preparing for confrontation

Where the internal security of the state is threatened, by insurrection or revolution, it is necessary to consider the future role of the military in Britain. The structure and practices of the police, the Special Branch, MI5 and the military intelligence agencies have been covered in previous chapters, in which their contribution to long-term preparations has been noted. This section concentrates on the role of Britain's armed forces. Two aspects are taken up here: the laws available to the state together with the legal restraints on the military acting in aid of the civil power, and secondly, military planning for such an eventuality on a major scale.

In the initial stages of disorder the state would immediately have at its disposal the many laws relating to public order already in existence. Two laws come immediately to mind – the Emergency Powers Act 1920 and the Public Order Act 1936.[43] Both of these laws, however, have their limitations. The latter would be effective in combating small-

---

[41] *Guardian,* 21 June 1974.

[42] *Economist*, 15 June 1974.

[43] For the Emergency Powers Act see pp. 51–57; for the Public Order Act 1936 and related laws see Brownlie, *The Laws Relating to Public Order* (1968).

scale marches and meetings but would be ineffective in containing well-organised mass demonstrations. The former is geared to counter threats to national services (like electricity and transport) and to the movement of supplies (like coal and food), but it does not extend outside these fields. So, for example, special legislation might have to be passed to legitimise internment, to suspend the right to trial and bail, and to impose restrictions on travel. Of course in Northern Ireland this is what the government has done. By the Detention of Terrorists (N.I.) Order 1942 (1972 No. 1632 [N.I. 15]) made under the Northern Ireland (Temporary Provisions) Act 1972, internment was introduced, and there is no doubt that this would serve as a model should preventive detention be introduced in England, Wales and Scotland. Other laws which would be available for use against mass political opposition are the Incitement to Disaffection Act 1934 and the laws on sedition.[44] The historical use of law indicates that if the existing laws failed to accommodate the immediate situation, the government would not hesitate to pass new and more effective laws, as in the case of Northern Ireland. At the outbreak of the Second World War the Emergency Powers (Defence) Act 1939 was quickly passed and this gave the state sweeping powers in many areas of life.[45] Not the least of these powers was the authority to amend any previous Act of parliament. Although this Act was repealed in 1959 it stands as a model for future legislation.

What becomes of interest in a situation of potential confrontation is the 'legal' uses to which the civil power can put the military. The present law offers no guide to the powers that might be given to the military in rapidly changing circumstances – a better guide would be the powers and tactics assumed in combating the guerrilla movements of the old Empire. However, it is important to define the present state of the law in order that any changes can be seen for what they are – as preparation for a potential class war. One of these changes could be seen in the combined use of troops with police at Heathrow Airport.

In 1974 Heathrow was occupied by police and the military four times – in January, June, July and September, once under the Tories and three times under Labour. On the first occasion, in January, it was suggested that intelligence sources reported an attempt would be made by Palestinian guerrillas to shoot down a plane with a SAM-17 missile. Most of the press dutifully recorded this explanation, but some rightly pointed out that a SAM-17 shoulder-launched missile

[44] See pp. 28–40.
[45] See Kidd, *British Liberty in Danger* (1940), chapter 7.

8. Joint police-military exercises at Heathrow airport in 1974, a portent for the future?

could be fired anywhere in London (e.g. from Hampstead Heath which is under some flight paths). The missile, which has a range of over two miles, only has to be pointed in the direction of a plane's flight-path and fired – the infra-red target finder does the rest by homing in on the plane's exhaust and detonating on impact. So why were the troops guarding the airport? One or two commentators cut through the facade and declared that the joint military/police exercise had nothing to do with guerrillas and missiles. It was '. . . basically a public relations exercise to accustom the public to the reality of troops deploying through the high street.'[46]

In June the reason offered for the joint exercise was that it was for the protection of delegates arriving for the Socialist International Conference, although the delegates knew of no threat having been made. Moreover, a previous conference in November 1973 attended

[46] *Guardian*, 8 January 1974; see also Chapman Pincher in the *Daily Express* on the same day.

by Mrs Golda Meir (then Israel's Prime Minister) warranted no such precautions. The next two exercises in July and September 1974 brought forth no specific reasons and the press were left to speculate. The Home Office and Scotland Yard were non-committal, so it was reported as being part of a continuing programme in police/military liaison. By the fourth time it was becoming accepted as 'normal' – which was probably the intention in the first place.

Several questions arise as to the legality of the use of troops in the Heathrow exercise. The law relating to the use of troops in aid of the civil power in times of peace rests on the precedents set during the nineteenth century when the army was used extensively in suppressing demonstrations and insurrections. It is worth considering who can ask for the aid of troops. According to the law it must be a written request from a magistrate. This question is not of academic interest only, for unless the source of the request can be shown, who is to be held accountable? (The originator of the request is accountable in law and not to parliament.) Was sufficient cause shown to justify the employment of troops? Was the presence of force – machine-guns and armoured cars – excessive?[47] Lord Wigg raised these same questions in the House of Lords after the first exercise in January 1974. The government's case was put by Lord Colville, Minister of State at the Home Office, who replied, on the first point, that 'The Commissioner of Police for the Metropolis sought government authority to put into operation the contingency plans for the use of police and troops to defend Heathrow against terrorist attack.'[48] At the end of the debate Lord Wigg said he found Lord Colville's reply 'entirely satisfactory'.[49]

It is clear that Lord Colville's answer was correct. The law states that it is for the civil authority to call for the aid of troops – but who is the 'civil authority'? This is laid down in Queen's Regulations as being the Commissioner of the Metropolitan Police in London, and outside of the capital, a magistrate or mayor (who is automatically a JP).[50] The legal authority thus rests with a Justice of the Peace. The Commissioner has been a JP since the post was instituted in 1829; however, in April 1974 a new law was brought into effect which removed the status of Justice of the Peace from the Commissioner (and the five

[47] See Brownlie, *op. cit.*, pp. 210–213 for the extract from the *Report on Featherstone Riot, 1893*.

[48] *The Times*, 17 January 1974.

[49] *Daily Telegraph*, 17 January 1974.

[50] Queen's Regulations, 1955, para. 1164.

Assistant Commissioners). This was the Administration of Justice Act 1973, Section 19. It is therefore pertinent to ask just who made the request for troops to go to Heathrow in June and July, 1974, after this Act came into effect? Many people are under the impression that the government of the day can order troops about the country, but this is not so, for the law relating to the employment of troops in aid of the civil power gives no such authority.[51] Other questions also remain: was sufficient cause shown for the operations in June and July, and was excessive force used? Unless and until there is a challenge in the courts, these questions will remain unanswered.

There are also additional authorities as to the direction of troops in case of internal disorder. Firstly, the Crown has a prerogative power to direct the use of troops although this is considered to be limited since the advent of parliamentary government; it nonetheless remains an option should the liberal-democratic mechanism fail to act.[52] Secondly, there are the common law duties of the military, which are to maintain law and order and uphold the authority of the state. *The Manual of Military Law* defines five situations in which the military may be called to aid the civil powers: a) a national emergency (under the Emergency Powers Act 1920); b) where there is intimidation of workers (under the Conspiracy and Protection of Property Act 1875, as amended by the Trade Disputes Act 1906); c) where there is an unlawful assembly; d) where there is a riot (under the 1714 Riot Act); and e) where there is an insurrection.[53] With regard to the first two categories, those connected with trade disputes and industrial unrest, the *Manual* states:

> 'The merits and demerits of such disputes or unrest are of no concern whatsoever to the soldiers, who are solely concerned with the duty and obligation common to all citizens of assisting the civil authority in the maintenance of law and order, and in those situations their principal duty will be the protection of persons and property.'[54]

The *Manual* also defines the last category, an insurrection, as involving 'an intention to "levy war against the Queen"', as it is technically

---

[51] Professor Claire Palley has noted that the law in relation to the military contains no mention that the Cabinet can direct the military. See *The Times*, 13 February 1973.

[52] Halsbury, *Law of England* (1954) Vol. 7, pp. 260–261.

[53] Ian Brownlie, *op. cit.*, p. 198.

[54] Ian Brownlie, *op. cit.*, under Part II, Section 6, para. 7 of the *Manual of Military Law*.

called, or otherwise to act in general defiance of the government of the country.'[55] In other words the military would have a duty to act, under law, in these situations whether or not ordered to do so by the government of the day. Finally, there is the situation where the military, independently, at the behest of the monarch, or at the request of the government, suspends normal law and institutes martial law – that is, where the final authority rests with the military and not the democratic machinery (this having failed to cope).

The concept of martial law is somewhat obscure. It could be conventionally defined as 'a state of affairs where normal legal administration is impossible and the only authority left is the military commander.'[56] Wellington told the House of Lords in 1851 that 'martial law meant no law at all', and Lord Grey, in the same debate, declared it to be 'setting aside all law and acting under the military power'.[57] On the other hand, Brownlie finds that 'in the United Kingdom emergency powers are now based upon statutory power.'[58] In reality it would make little difference, should this situation be reached, if martial law were legitimised by some ancient monarchical right or by a fresh piece of legislation. It would mean the suspension of normal legal procedures (which do offer some limited rights to the individual), in favour of arbitrary state power.

The National Security Plan

For many years now it has been apparent that, with the granting of political independence to the colonies, the sphere of operations for Britain's armed forces has become increasingly limited. But to take the view that the army, having lost the Empire as a field of operations, eagerly took the chance to become engaged in Northern Ireland is to put the cart before the horse.

When the situation in Northern Ireland arose, for its own specific historical reasons, the army was available to act swiftly. Once engaged, the army lost little time in adapting the techniques of the colonial experience to part of the motherland. By the late 1960s something else was also happening: the military strategists began a major revision for their plans to counter internal disorder. Long term contingency plans

[55] *Manual*, *op. cit.*, Part II, Section 6, para. 22.
[56] *The Times*, 16 August 1974. Article by Charles Douglas-Home.
[57] Quoted in Radzinowicz, *A History of English Criminal Law* (1968), Vol. 4, p. 144.
[58] Brownlie, *op. cit.*, p. 125.

were made to deal with a declaration of a state of emergency, a general strike, an insurrection in one region of the country, and ultimately, a general insurrection leading to revolution. The reasons for this planning lie not in the desire of the military to find a new playground, nor from its intrinsic authoritarianism. The underlying factor, as already suggested, is the general deterioration in living standards and the consequent confrontations and, above all, a recognition that this situation could become significantly worse by the late 1970s. The 'enemy', instead of being black and foreign, has become British people themselves, more specifically, the working class, for it is they who bear the brunt of the fall in standards of living through inflation, and it is they who are the first to swell the already large dole queues of a recession.

Perhaps it was the publication of Brigadier Kitson's book in 1971 which really signalled to outsiders that the state's plans were in earnest.[59] Between 1971 and 1975 there were many events and reports which confirmed the preparations being made. Among these were joint police/military exercises, combined police-military-academic seminars and conferences on the subject of guerrilla warfare in an urban society, and the plans laid for the 1973–1974 winter emergency. By bringing together the events of these three years with evidence of the historical practice it is possible to construct a reasonably informed picture of the state's current preparations.

The state's planning for all likely contingencies is laid down in the National Security Plan (NSP). The NSP has been evolved over many years, and today incorporates not only military factors, but also political, legal, sociological, psychological and ideological ones as well. It is a plan born of Britain's colonial experience and it is sobering to remember that Britain's armed forces have been engaged in more than fifty counter-insurgency operations since the end of the last war. Only two operations in this period could be termed conventional warfare – Korea and Suez.

An outline of the NSP, which is directed at an internal rather than external enemy, became known with the publication of extracts from the Army's own working Manual – Land Operations Vol. III: Counter-Revolutionary Operations.[60] The six requirements for counter-revolutionary operations were as follows:

'(a) the passing of emergency regulations to facilitate the conduct of a national campaign;

[59] Kitson, *op. cit.*
[60] *Time Out*, 10 January 1975.

(b) various political, social and economic measures designed to gain popular support and counter or surpass anything offered by the insurgents;

(c) the setting up of an effective organisation for joint civil and military control at all levels;

(d) the forming of an effective, integrated and nationwide intelligence organisation without which military operations can never be successful;

(e) the strengthening of indigenous police and armed forces so that their loyalty is beyond question and their work effective. This is often easier said than done;

(f) control measures designed to isolate insurgents from popular control.'[61]

In three of the areas mentioned – unified command, intelligence organisation, and reserve forces – plans are already well advanced, while the remainder relate directly to an actual confrontation and remain, for the moment, well-hidden from public view. The Manual sets out four levels of involvement, each representing an escalation of their commitment in maintaining law and order – internal security, counter-insurgency, anti-terrorist operations and a limited war. The first level, internal security, is plainly spelt out and would involve:

'(1) dealing with civil disturbances resulting from labour disputes, racial and religious antagonism and tension or social unrest;

(2) dealing with riots and civil disobedience, with or without the political undertones which savour revolt or even rebellion;

(3) countering terrorism by individuals and small groups in the form of sabotage and assassinations particularly in urban areas.'[62]

While this document outlined the requirements of a NSP in general evidence is available which indicates the extent of the state's planning for foreseeable situations arising here in Britain.

The overall plan provides for a unified command control bringing together the police, the military and the administration at national and regional level. The country's 800 police stations are, in addition to having telephone and teleprinter facilities, linked into the emergency communications system to Strike Command. And the military have their own secure communications system linking every regional district

[61] *Ibid.*
[62] *Ibid.*

HQ, regional centre, air force base, and naval base. Moreover, military districts 'under the overall command of the United Kingdom Land Force Headquarters at Wilton, near Salisbury, are responsible for drawing up plans to meet all foreseeable contingencies affecting internal security that might require the military to take action in support of the police.'[63] Co-ordination of regional and administrative and legal functions would be via regional and sub-regional controls. Given an all-out emergency, effective power would rest with the Regional Commissioner (appointed by the government, probably a Junior Minister), the Chief Constable (for the police) and the District's General Officer Commanding (for the military).

The strength of the plan lies in the many levels of contingency allowed for, from a temporary outbreak of disorder in one city or region to a more prolonged confrontation. Contingency plans cover a strike limited to one or two essential services (e.g. coal and electricity); a general strike; insurrection in one or more regions; and finally, a general insurrection over a large area of the country (e.g. Scotland and the North of England).

Four aspects of emergency planning should be considered: intelligence-gathering; 2) military-police-academic co-operation; 3) the forces available for emergencies; and 4) the new role of Civil Defence. The information currently held by the intelligence agencies (including the intelligence side of police work) serves on the one hand to provide a response to immediate and on-going situations; on the other hand it would provide a substantial base on which to build an even more sophisticated system should rioting and fighting break out. The NSP calls for a unified intelligence system so there would have to be liaison between the army and police at local level.[64] Michael Elliott-Bateman, a lecturer in military studies at Manchester University, outlined what this would entail:

'It would mean a lieutenant or even a sergeant with links to the local police station and an elaboration of the existing army command system down to a district level. Then the army man can be in the picture of crime in the area – dubious organisations and the like. If any kind of crisis arises, then he's ready to go. If you believe political violence is on the increase then preparation has to be made – and it can't be done overnight.'[65]

[63] *Daily Telegraph*, 9 January 1974.
[64] See p. 278.
[65] *Guardian*, 8 January 1974.

9. Mock village on the Dungeness peninsula in Kent which was constructed for realistic military training in Northern Ireland and urban areas.

Once a conflict has actually broken out, say within one region of the country, then the lesson of intelligence gathered in Northern Ireland may well come into operation. Given a unified military-police-administrative command structure then all kinds of detail about people's lives can be gathered. In Northern Ireland 'an estimated 40 per cent of the adult and juvenile population . . . now have their names and family details on an intricate system of card indexes built up by the army. Some cards even give the colour of a family's wallpaper and a description of the picture hanging on the walls.'[66] These card files are apparently up-dated by random checks, house and street searches, and information from informants. The card file data-base was later disclosed to have been transferred to a £500,000 computer centre in Lisburn, Co. Antrim. This computer, run by the Army Intelligence Corps, not only logged details of resistance but also the movement of cars within the province and across the border. The latter refinement resulted from a trial experiment by the Army on unsuspecting motorists in England. 'The system,

[66] *The Times*, 18 April 1974.

the most advanced to be adopted by a security force in northern Europe, was given a trial run elsewhere in the United Kingdom, apparently in England, during which private motorists unknowingly had their car numbers monitored and recorded by computer.'[67]

It might be asked if these lists have already been prepared in anticipation for England, Wales and Scotland? Two categories are known to be kept by the local police – Communist Party members and aliens.[68] It is also known that the police submit reports on all local political events to the Special Branch together with the names of the 'leaders' concerned.[69] One of the duties laid down for police war duties is 'Taking special measures to maintain internal security, with particular reference to the detection or restriction of movement of politically subversive people.'[70] Compiling lists of 'politically subversive people' would have to be done in advance. Much information is already held by the police, the Special Branch, MI5, and the Defence Intelligence agencies. Moreover it is a standing responsibility of the Home Office to have available lists of those who would be interned (or have their movements restricted) should hostilities break out with a foreign power. It was with the aid of these prepared lists that people of German origin were quickly rounded up at the start of both World Wars. And no doubt there has been a list to hand of Communist Party members and sympathisers since the end of the Second World War. A similar list prepared for the eventuality of an internal insurrection would not only include the latter but thousands of socialists in the labour movement and outside. It does not take much imagination to reason that if Northern Ireland-style house-by-house lists are not already compiled it would not take long to do so.

Evidence of planning in this field has come from Brigadier P. Hudson, CBE, the deputy director of Army Staff Duties, who told a Royal United Services Institute seminar that:

'As far as the police are concerned, I think we are getting closer together slowly. If you start from the top, in the last year there has been a lot of streamlining of the organisation in Whitehall to deal with this situation, a great deal more understanding between various departments and ministries in Whitehall. If you go to the regions and districts of the UK, this is where contact begins and is needed. There is much more liaison, for instance, than there was

[67] *The Times*, 5 December 1974.
[68] See Ch. 2 and Ch. 3.
[69] See p. 141.
[70] Laurie, *Beneath the City Streets* (1970) p. 143.

last year. If you go down the line, there are many cases where police have taken part in study periods, exercises and also in courses at schools.'[71]

A conference of a more high-powered gathering took place in April 1974 at a North-West District Senior Officers Study Period held at Lancaster University.[72] The conference was attended by twenty-six Army officers, nearly all above the rank of Major, and included the General Officer Commanding North-West District, Major-General C. V. B. Purdon, CBE, MC; nine senior police officers from the regions including three Chief Constables; two officers from the Navy; four from the Air Force; nine academics from Lancaster University including six professors; and five more academics from other universities. The programme was called 'A Seminar on Revolutionary Warfare' and aimed 'to promote discussion between civilian thinkers and serving officers on the academic and practical problems involved in understanding revolutionary warfare.'[73] According to reports of the conference frequent references were made to industrial guerrillas' (i.e. militant trade-unionists), 'terrorists', and student activists.

The role of the military in Britain in maintaining internal order faded out during the late nineteenth century as the police increasingly assumed this job. Nevertheless the military have always remained available as the ultimate force should the state be seriously threatened. During each of the emergencies in the 1920s units of the three services were assigned to specific locations around the country and were held at the ready in case the situation escalated. Similarly during each of the five emergencies declared under the Heath government the services were slotted into the national emergency planning. The role of the military when disorder threatens clearly increases as the situation escalates. To date no emergency has led to the prolonged use of troops in the streets. The first level of involvement for the military forces would be to ensure the maintenance of supplies and services, that is, the movement of coal, food and other supplies. Contingency planning during the 1973–74 winter crisis called for the

'use of troops in the event of a national emergency arising from strikes in key industries such as coal, the docks and transport.

[71] RUSI seminar paper entitled 'The Role of the Armed Forces in Peacekeeping in the 1970s'. 4 March 1973.

[72] See *Socialist Worker*, 20 April 1974; *Workers Press*, 9 March 1974; and the list of participants published by *Mole Express*, Manchester.

[73] *Workers Press*, 9 March 1974.

(Plans) include the use of the armed forces in an internal security role and as a substitute for civilian labour. The former could include helping the police deal with illegal picketing and providing escort for transport drivers and others engaged in carrying out essential services.'[74]

The military used in this way would act as a strike-breaking force armed both with lethal weapons and the backing of the law through Emergency Regulations. Troops were used in a limited way to carry out these roles in the General Strike and in the post-1945 dock strikes, though in almost every case it tended to increase the solidarity of the strikers rather than weaken it. The essential feature at this level of confrontation is that the role of the military remains basically defensive, that is, they would not be seeking out and destroying the 'insurgents'.

It is often held that Britain has such small armed forces that they would be incapable of resisting a sustained confrontation. The total of Britain's military strength is some 354,000, comprising 170,000 in the Army, 103,000 in the Air Force and 81,000 in the Navy. Of the Army's total strength some 55,000 are based in West Germany in fulfilment of the NATO commitment, and a further 35,000 are also based abroad in Asia and the Mediterranean. In addition, there are 15,000 troops based in Northern Ireland. The number of troops assigned to the UK Land Forces is 20,000 though a further 40,000 on leave or in training could be quickly recalled in an emergency. On the face of it therefore it would appear that only some 60,000 troops, plus the home-based Air Force and Navy would be available. The strength of the military however lies not in the standing army but in the reserves and volunteers it would be able to call on. During the General Strike and in wartime the military might of the state was massively expanded. These historical precedents suggest that the following would constitute the forces available by the opening of 'hostilities':

The Army	60,000
The Army Reserve	110,000
The Navy	48,000
The Navy Reserve	30,000
The Air Force	80,000
The Air Force Reserve	32,000
The Territorial Army Volunteer Reserve	55,000
The police (inc. Scotland)	113,000

[74] *Daily Telegraph*, 28 January 1974. News story by Brigadier W. F. K. Thompson.

The Special Constabulary	200,000+
Emergency Army Reserve	100,000+
Emergency Police Reserve	100,000+
The 'Citizen Guard'	300,000+

The first eight forces represent those permanently available to the state, while the last four are those recruited specifically for, and immediately prior to, the expected confrontation. The Special Constabulary has historically been employed to place 'loyal' citizens in uniform and under the direction of the uniformed police.[75] The Citizen Guard, or some similar title, was used during the 1920s to provide a rallying point for those prepared to undertake jobs to ensure the maintenance of communications, supplies and transport. Thus prior to the actual outbreak of an insurrection or major threat, the state could mobilise over a million men and women. And the channelling of volunteers into one of the four emergency forces would ensure that the state controlled and directed all those in support of its cause.

One of the more critical aspects for the military planners when envisaging a prolonged situation of insurgency would be to have a totally secure communications system while at the same time denying this facility to the 'enemy'. In this context it is not without significance that in 1973 the Minister of Defence ordered a new military communications system from Plessey called Ptarmigan, at a cost of £100 million.[76] This is the largest and most secure (that is, not open to interception), communications project undertaken in Britain. The principle of the Ptarmigan system is that it provides for the ultimate in flexibility. Instead of having one computer centre which could be destroyed in an attack, the system employs a number of computer nodes (about fifteen), each of which is capable of taking over should one or more be captured or knocked out. The system also has a number of other features: users can be linked by telephone or radio from any part of the country; it can provide conference and broadcasting facilities; and it is totally secure. To understand the full implications of this system the reader will have to picture a possible future. Suppose a region of the country rises in insurrection against the state. In this situation it would be possible for all private telephones to be cut off with the exception of state services like hospitals, fire stations and government departments. The police and the military on the other

---

[75] See pp. 94–98.
[76] *Guardian*, 13 September 1973.

hand would have their own secure and exclusive system of communications. By this means an insurgent force would find itself with no telephones, no mail and state-controlled news on the radio and television. Only direct personal communication would remain as an option and this would entail the use of the public highways where patrols could stop and search at will.

Justification for much of the state's planning rests on the confusion created by the fact that many aspects of the military and police in Britain serve a dual purpose. For instance 'home defence' plans are made for an attack by a foreign country on Britain, while 'internal defence' refers to the defence of the state against an internal insurrection. Major General W. G. H. Beach, A Defence Fellow at Edinburgh University, wrote: '*Internal Security* (para. 127). Although the function of support for the local authority in the maintenance of law and order in peace is quite distinct from Home Defence it would be disingenuous to overlook that in practice a close connection normally exists between them'.[77] Certainly there have been long periods in British defence history when the external enemy has been the main concern of the state. However, this is not so today when the importance of the two roles is reversed and internal considerations are to the fore.

The situation concerning Civil Defence is a similar one, since Civil Defence is a protection for the personnel of the state against both nuclear attack and internal insurrection. Laurie in his book *Beneath the City Streets*, makes this point well:

'Although powerless to give people at large effective protection from attack, civil defence nevertheless fulfills its real purpose, which is as a defence *against* civilians: it protects the government from its people. And this it will do equally in time of war or of insurrection. Both problems are the same.'[78]

The responsibility for Civil Defence lies with the Home Office. In the period after the Second World War the Home Office oversaw the complex preparations taken to ensure the continuation of the state in the event of nuclear war. All through the 1950s this aspect of Civil Defence predominated, though by the middle 1960s the easing of the Cold War meant less attention and money was devoted to this end.

[77] 'The Springs of Policy', by Beach, p. 54 in *European Military Institutions – a Reconnaisance*, published by The Universities Services Study Group, Edinburgh University, 1970–1971 Report.

[78] Laurie (1972) p. 257.

In 1968 the Labour government, as part of a series of economies, substantially cut the Civil Defence programme and abolished the Civil Defence Corps together with the Auxiliary Fire Service. The Tories re-vamped Civil Defence on their return to office in 1970 though their new plans came into effect only on April 1974 – by which time Labour were back again. The new policy was outlined in a 1972 Home Office circular on Emergency Services sent to all local councils. This circular placed three contingencies under the heading of Emergency Services – a wartime emergency, peacetime emergency and disasters:

'The keystone of the government's policy is to ensure that the preparedness of local government to meet a war emergency is substantially improved. It is considered that there is much common ground between war planning and the preparations required for and the organisation appropriate to a major peacetime emergency or natural disaster. Accordingly there are many advantages in creating a closer relationship than hitherto in local planning for different emergencies of peace and war.'[79]

The effect of this new policy was not to reconstitute the old Civil Defence Corps but instead to place the responsibility on the county and metropolitan county councils. Since April 1974 these councils have appointed Emergency Planning Officers, to head what is known as the Emergency Planning Team comprising executive officers, clerical and secretarial staff.[80] In London, for instance, this meant that the Greater London Council's (GLC) Home Defence and Emergency Planning Team was expanded from one executive and a secretary to thirty-six full-time staff. The staff of the Emergency Planning Teams have all undergone training courses at the Home Defence College at Easingwold in York, which was set up in 1973. Here members of the teams join with other civil servants, police, and executives from the nationalised and private industries in seminars and tutorials. A year after the creation of the Emergency Planning Teams some councils had not implemented the Home Office recommendations. This fact caused the principal of the Home Defence College, Air Marshal Sir Leslie Mavor, to observe that in relation to the dangers of subversion and sabotage 'the full possibility of the present internal threat is only just sinking in.'[81]

[79] Home Office circular No. ES/1/1972, dated 22 March 1972.
[80] *Guardian*, 15 January 1974.
[81] *Guardian*, 12 June 1975.

Other aspects of the new plan are worth noting in this context. Each council was asked to nominate an emergency headquarters in one of its central buildings and also to name a standby HQ in another part of the region. These HQs 'irrespective of the degree of protection' against nuclear attack are 'linked by line and radio to Sub-Regional Controls'.[82] Finally, the long-term nature of state planning becomes evident:

> 'Since 1968, where county, county borough or London councils were erecting new office accommodation and they sought Home Office advice, they were advised to incorporate any wartime requirements in the new building. Where new accommodation was provided with adequate protection, grant has been paid or promised on the notional rent of the space occupied by communications, and associated equipment, linking the headquarters to the sub-regional control.'[83]

If it is asked: 'Whose is the responsibility for the internal security of the state?', it would be difficult to draw a line and say where that of the Home Office (and the police) ends and that of the Ministry of Defence starts. In the initial stages of a confrontation the police would be to the fore with the military in reserve, but there would come a point when the roles would be reversed where the Home Office (and the police) act in aid of the military. In a confrontation the reversal of roles would represent a massive escalation in the state's response, and would mean in effect that the state and the ruling class were playing their ultimate card in defence of capitalism.

To hear some of Britain's military strategists speaking lends weight to the theory held by many on the Left that what is happening in Ireland today will happen in Britain tomorrow: the chairman of the RUSI Defence Studies seminar[84] said after referring to the bombs at Aldershot barracks and the Old Bailey:

> 'what happens in Londonderry is very relevant to what can happen in London, and if we lose in Belfast we may have to fight in Brixton or Birmingham. Just as Spain in the 1930s was a rehearsal for a wider European conflict, so perhaps what is happening in Northern Ireland is a rehearsal for urban guerrilla war more widely in Europe, and particularly in Great Britain.'[85]

[82] Home Office circular, *op. cit.*
[83] Home Office circular, *op. cit.*
[84] RUSI Seminar. See footnote 71.
[85] *Ibid.*

The experience of the British Army in Northern Ireland together with the new weapons evolved for crowd control and urban guerrilla warfare may be used against the working people of England, Wales and Scotland. It is not inevitable that an ultimate confrontation, of the kind the state is prepared for, will occur as a result of the current economic recession. Time and again in British history the ruling class, with the full extent of its preparations hidden from view, has demonstrated an uncanny ability to survive major crises. The resort to the use of armed force has been the last option. But each historical moment brings forth its own conditions. If a major confrontation does occur – which will almost certainly be a class war – the state will be prepared to use all the means available in defence of the capitalist system.

8 Conclusion

The approach adopted in this book has attempted to bring out those aspects of the working of state agencies which the liberal tradition denies. This approach extends to a whole range of attitudes which affect an understanding of the contribution of the past to the present. In particular the notion that the elected government controls the institutions of the state is shown to be false (as an historically practised reality), as is the belief that it is possible to treat the various institutions of the state as independent (according to the idea of the 'separation of powers'). Given this, it is possible to see the interdependent nature and totality of the practices of these state agencies in relation to the dominant interests in society as a whole, namely those of capitalism. The historical development of the police, the military, the Special Branch, MI5, and the law, demonstrates the class interests explicitly present in their creation and imbued in their later practices.

It is precisely this perspective that liberal treatments of these agencies fail to account for or choose to ignore. Of course this is not surprising because the liberal-democratic tradition does not question the capitalistic nature of British society, but treats it as an underlying presumption. In this vein Critchley, a police historian, seeks to explain the development of the police as a progression from anarchy to civilisation: 'Total freedom is anarchy, total order tyranny. The police, who represent the collective interests of the community, are the agency which holds a balance somewhere between.'[1] Far from representing the 'collective interests of the community' the police act in the interests of a particular class. It is true that the police may act in the interests of individual members of the working class, but they have historically opposed, and do contemporarily oppose, the interests of the working class as a whole. In this respect the totality of the historical record speaks for itself and denies the foundations of the liberal-democratic position.

The historical record also aids an understanding of the present in another respect. It is clear that the state (and its agencies) has played an

[1] Critchley, *A History of the Police* (1967) p. xiii.

increasingly aggressive role in Britain since the early 1960s. This is apparent from an examination of the new and more sophisticated practices in each of the agencies considered when compared with the preceding period. The reasons for the newly prominent part played by state agencies in everyday life cannot be accounted for by attributing an over-determining significance to particular individuals or to technological innovations. The underlying causes are located in the general crisis faced by British capitalism which, although centred on economic instability, produces equally serious political and social dislocation.

Britain is not alone in experiencing the increased attention of the state's repressive agencies – informed by many years of colonial and imperialist counter-insurgency – being turned inwards towards the people themselves. All the countries of the advanced capitalist world, most of whom have liberal-democratic political systems, are each in their own way reacting to the global challenge confronting capitalism. Thus although the particular reactions of the British state to the present recession will be determined by its historically-evolved practices, the general context is provided by the on-going and world-wide struggle for survival by the dominant capitalist interests in the USA, Western Europe, and Japan.

Faced by a serious challenge to its power and authority the ruling class in Britain has historically responded by resorting to the use of force against the people – there is nothing to suggest that this will not happen again. Moreover, next time it will be a challenge faced in common with other capitalist nations: 'The internal contradictions still make for the collapse of capitalism, but a fascist totalitarianism based on the vast resources under capitalist control may well be a stage of this collapse.'[2] Again the form will differ from country to country. The uncanny ability of the British ruling class to ride through situations of internal crisis suggest that the form taken will be one of a slow transition, over many years, to a more authoritarian way of life, rather than its sudden imposition which may occur in countries where the socialist tradition is either weak or divided.

[2] Marcuse, *Counterrevolution and Revolt* (1972) p. 56.

Postscript

Since finishing the main body of this book there have been some developments which should be noted. There were two events that related to the law and its application.[1] The first event was when the Prevention of Terrorism (Temporary Provisions) Act 1974 was presented to parliament for renewal in May 1975; the Home Secretary, Roy Jenkins, told MPs: 'I am also prepared to tell the House that unless in November I feel able to recommend the dropping of substantial parts of the Act, I shall not ask the House to proceed by order.'[2] In November Mr Jenkins asked the Commons for a four months' renewal of the Act in order that a new Bill could be introduced. This was the Prevention of Terrorism (Temporary Provisions) Bill, which far from dropping 'substantial parts' contained only two minor changes and was now renewable yearly, not six-monthly. All the criticisms of the old Act hold for the new one. Moreover, the figures released for the first year of its operation confirmed that the use of the Act by the police and the Special Branch was more to gain intelligence on the Irish community in Britain than to apprehend bombers. A total of 1,174 people had been held under the Act in police custody for periods up to seven days, and only 61 of these had subsequently been charged with an offence. Of the 61 charged with offences many were of a trivial nature and only a handful had anything to do with bombing activities. In effect, all could have been detained under existing laws while the thousand Irish people who were detained and then released had been subjected to interrogation, fingerprinting, and in most cases had been photographed.

The second event was the case brought against fourteen supporters of the British Withdrawal from Northern Ireland Campaign (BWNIC) who were charged under the 1934 Incitement to Disaffection Act as a result of the distribution of a leaflet entitled: 'Some Information for

[1] At the beginning of the parliamentary session 1975–76 the government announced their intention to put forward legislation on official secrets following the report of the Franks Committee. See p. 22 ff.

[2] *Hansard*, 19 May 1975. See p. 54.

Discontented Soldiers.'³ The fourteen were charged together with conspiracy to contravene the 1934 Act, although arrested at different times and in different parts of the country. Some of them did not even know each other. Twelve were also charged with the possession of 'seductive' documents, and two – Gwyn Williams and John Hyatt – were charged with helping deserters contrary to the Army Act 1955 (they both pleaded guilty to this charge and were fined £100 and £50 respectively). During the eleven-week trial Ronnie Lee, one of the fourteen defendants, summed up the nature of the charges:

> 'You have heard unhappy soldiers, you have seen the glossy and misleading army literature, and the conspiracy which has been revealed has not been a conspiracy by the defendants to breach the Incitement to Disaffection Act, but a conspiracy by the British state to use the court and an inappropriate law to prosecute its political opponents and to endeavour to silence a campaign it does not like.'⁴

On 10 December 1975 the jury brought in a verdict of not guilty on 31 counts after a trial which had cost the state an estimated quarter of a million pounds.

Another recent development that should be noted is the organisation of two special groups to combat hijackings, sieges, and the like. The first is an armed para-military squad of the Metropolitan Police formed with officers from D.11 section.⁵ The squad is comprised of twenty men – a chief inspector, inspector, three sergeants, and fifteen constables – dressed in blue battle-smocks and dark-blue berets bearing the Metropolitan Police badge. They are armed with the standard British Army rifle and 0·38 Smith and Wesson revolvers. When they are not on duty or stand-by they work with the Special Branch on intelligence-gathering. The other specialist group is a section of the army's Special Air Service (SAS). Their main base is at Bradbury Barracks in Hereford, but they also have other centres in major cities. Although it is an army unit, the SAS operates in civilian clothes, is armed, and uses Range Rovers and Rover 3500 cars for transportation.

The National Security Committee (NSC) formed under the Tory government in 1972 was re-organised as the Civil Contingencies Com-

³ See p. 31 ff.
⁴ *Peace News*, 19 December 1975.
⁵ The official duties of D.11 section are: police war duties; civil defence; firearms and telecommunications training.

mittee in 1975.[6] Like its predecessor it includes representatives from the Home Office, the MOD, the police, intelligence agencies and the military. The Civil Contingencies Committee is concerned both with short- and long-term planning, from combatting armed terrorism to the employment of the military to maintain services and supplies during a major strike. Lastly, it was announced in the *Daily Express* in December 1975 that Sir Maurice Oldfield, head of MI6 since mid-1973, was to retire early in 1976.[7]

An understanding of the state and its agencies is only of use if their practices continue to be monitored. With this in mind, if any readers of this book know of anything that could lead to an improved second edition – if there is one – I would be very grateful if they could get in touch with me (via the publisher), as long as they do not contravene the Official Secrets Act in so doing.

1st January 1976   TONY BUNYAN

---

[6] See p. 269. After the 1972 miners strike the NSC authorised a major revision of the National Security Plan. This was the first comprehensive re-think since the early 1950s when plans were laid for defence against nuclear weapons. Then the threat to the state was external, in 1972 it again became an internal one.

[7] *Daily Express*, 15 December 1975.

Appendix: Capitalism, the state and liberal-democracy

It is sometimes assumed that the modern state is a relatively recent development; in fact the main features of the modern state – the army, the police, the judiciary, the prisons, the administration and the government – were all present under monarchic government and were inherited and adapted in the transition to the liberal-democratic system.[1] Indeed, by the time capitalism started to emerge in the sixteenth century the British nation-state was already well established. Britain was then both the leading trading nation and the dominant naval power, and this alliance of state power (navy) and private enterprise (mercantilism) was the precursor of British imperialism. From the sixteenth to the eighteenth century several competing modes of production developed. Merchant capital marked the first phase of the accumulation of capital, and after the Civil War the new agricultural capitalists came to supplant the old feudal landowners.[2]

Alongside agricultural capital, two other modes emerged – manufacturing and industrial capital. 'Manufacturing' is here used to denote the coming together in workshops of independent artisans and craftsmen, whose products were marketed by the entrepreneur (the manufacturing capitalist). On the other hand, the introduction of primitive machines capable of mass production in factories saw the employment of large numbers of unskilled labourers, particularly those displaced from the land. This was industrial capitalism, which was based on the wage-labour relationship, and led to the birth of two new classes – the bourgeoisie (the owners) and the proletariat (those depending for subsistence on selling their labour for wages). The ruling class, drawn from

---

[1] See Kropotkin, *The State* (1897) for the development of the nation-state prior to monarchic government.

[2] In the expropriation of communal land from the peasants between 1709 and 1869 nearly eight million acres were seized.

these various modes of production, was not monolithic, but comprised several competing and complementary fractions (groupings). These fractions were the merchants, the agricultural capitalists, the small manufacturers, and the new industrial bourgeoisie. In this period of competitive capitalism it was the merchants and the landed aristocracy who effectively controlled parliament and the state. Only later, in the 1830s, when industrial capital became dominant in the economic field, did the bourgeoisie begin to challenge the other fractions for control of state power. It was during this struggle between the competing modes of capitalist production in the eighteenth and nineteenth centuries that the foundations of liberal-democracy emerged (well prior to an equal voice being accorded to labour). The ideas of the neutrality of the state and its institutions were fashioned in this period, less for reasons of democracy than as a means of arbitrating between the warring capitalist fractions and combatting working-class demands.

In the latter part of the last century capitalism began to move from the competitive to the monopoly stage and the twin pillars of its current foundations emerged. One was monopolistic industrial capitalism and the other centralised bank capital. The system survived intact throughout the First World War, the General Strike, the Depression, and the Second World War. But by 1945 two changes had occurred. Firstly, Britain's position as the dominant imperialist nation was fast being eroded both through the challenge from the USA, and by the countries of the Empire demanding, and getting, political independence. The second change was in the structure of capitalism. Out of the recession of the 1930s came the final fusion of bank and industrial capital into corporate capital (finance capital). Today the ownership of the means of production is concentrated in fewer hands than ever before, with corporate capital dominating the economic life of the country. The markets of multinational corporations now encompass the West and most of the Third World; moreover, their interests are backed by military alliances formed not just in response to the initiatives of the Soviet Union and China but also against the demands for liberation by the peoples of the Third World. In Britain the inequalities of power and wealth between the classes remain largely unchanged despite attempts by political theorists and bourgeois sociologists to suggest otherwise.[3]

[3] See *Social Trends*, no. 4 (HMSO), 1973, table 56. In 1971 the top 10 per cent owned 52 per cent of personal wealth and the top 25 per cent owned 72 per cent. At the other end of the scale over 54 per cent of people possess no capital at all.

II

The apparent constitutional independence of some of the state institutions can be related directly to the period when representative democracy finally had to take into account working-class voters and then, later, Labour MPs. The four major extensions of the franchise after the 1832 Reform Act (which gave the vote to the bourgeoisie) were in 1867, 1884, 1918, and 1928. In 1872 the doyen of constitutional authorities, Walter Bagehot, expressed the strategy of the ruling class. They must oppose, he said, the potential unity of the 'lower classes':

'They must avoid, not only every evil, but every appearance of evil; while they still have the power they must remove, not only every actual grievance, but, where it is possible, every seeming grievance too; they must willingly concede every claim which they can safely concede in order that they may not have to concede unwillingly some claim which would impair the safety of the country.'[4]

When the vote was conceded it was given to the working class section by section and the immediate beneficiary was the Liberal Party, which competed with Labour for this vote well into the 1920s. By 1900, when the Labour Party was founded, six million men were entitled to vote – some 27 per cent of the population over 21. The biggest extension in the franchise came through the Reform Act of 1918 when the electorate rose from 7 to 21 million – 78 per cent of those aged over twenty-one. This included all men over twenty-one and women over the age of thirty. Full adult suffrage did not come until 1928 when more than 4 million women between twenty-one and thirty were finally enfranchised.[5]

Thus it was not until the 1920s that the working class – men and women – had the vote, and this was not to be translated into an absolute majority for Labour until 1945 – some 113 years after the first Reform Act. Labour's two brief periods of minority government (1924 and 1929–31) did little to encourage a belief in their ability to govern. MacDonald's premierships and his participation in the 1931 National Government did much to discredit the Labour Party and to destroy the infusion of class culture and consciousness into parliamentary socialism. And when the Labour Party did assume full governmental

[4] Introduction to the second edition of Bagehot's *The British Constitution*.
[5] D. Butler and J. Freeman, *British Political Facts 1900–1967* (1968).

power in 1945, whatever revolutionary aspirations had gone into its making were long gone. The parliamentary representation of the working class now operated in government by accepting the boundaries of liberal-democracy, which carried with it the implicit assumption of upholding the capitalist system.

The representational organisation of the working class thus gained governmental power for the first time only after the Second World War. The implications of this fact are not without significance in the field of law and order. In Britain the law of the land is made up of judicial decisions (common law) and parliamentary legislation. In effect most law was made during the time of ruling-class governments, that is, over several hundred years up to the Second World War. Only in the latter years of this period did the Labour Party's presence in parliament occasionally ameliorate the class nature of legislation. Furthermore, the origins of state power and the fundamental practices of state institutions such as the judiciary, the army, the prisons and the police also date from this earlier period.

Everyday assumptions about these institutions in the 1970s rest on an acceptance of them and respect for them. Yet the major contribution of the past in the make-up of the present testifies to the class nature of their origins and functions. This acceptance and respect itself rests on the belief that these institutions are the result of the collective efforts (with commonly agreed amendments) of our antecedents, that is, by the British people as a whole. Historical reality shows the institutions to be the product of the collective efforts not of the people but of the ruling class. This is not to say that they resulted from the unmitigated desires of this class, but, in the sense of Bagehot's stricture, the ruling class retained power while making reluctant concessions – short of power itself. In this way the British ruling class learnt to rule *through* the political system and *via* the state institutions. The historical astuteness of this process was summed up by Kropotkin, when talking with Emma Goldman in 1895:

'The British bourgeoisie has good reason to fear the spread of discontent, and political liberties are the best security against it, they have always seen to it that the political reins should not be pulled too tightly. The average Britisher loves to think he is free; it helps him to forget his misery. That is the irony and the pathos of the English working classes.'[6]

[6] Emma Goldman, *Living My Life*, Vol. 1 (1970), p. 169.

The process of decision-making has also undergone a fundamental change. Whereas in the ruling-class parliaments of the nineteenth century the debates in the chambers of parliament were often decisive, and power could rightly be said to reside substantially in this 'democratic' institution, today parliament is a side-show – the formal acting out of theory in defiance of practice. Moreover, in the last century the Cabinet operated with great informality: no minutes were taken, few papers were circulated, and matters of state were openly considered in the bars of parliament and the clubs of London – there was in reality an assumption of shared values by all concerned. Although new state activities greatly increased the scope of governmental power from the 1870s, this did not in itself lead to the formalisation of decision-making, which did not occur until the First World War when Lloyd George created a Cabinet secretariat and started the recording of minutes. However, once started, this practice of more formal Cabinet procedures began to usurp the decision-making role of parliament and in the inter-war years the Cabinet became the effective base of executive power. In the Second World War Winston Churchill as Prime Minister assumed executive power for this office and the practice continued thereafter. So in the forty years when the Labour Party was very slowly coming to governmental power, that power shifted from parliament to the Prime Minister and his Cabinet. Similarly the state administration, which for most of the nineteenth century relied on ministerial patronage and the purchase of posts, was reformed in the 1870s. Thenceforth the administration was removed from direct governmental control.

Such a structure had its consequences for the party of 'permanent' opposition when it attained power. The reliance of Ministers on the permanent administrative apparatus is formidable and the possibilities for action are limited all too often to the marginal. The rhetoric of Labour in opposition is quickly cut down to size by the accumulated historical practices of state institutions, while the latter's daily decision-making is left unhindered by the formal democratic process.

If decision-making in general has been removed from the democratic process, then it can be argued that the state's repressive agencies have never been significantly subject to liberal-democratic control. By the time working-class representatives came into parliament, the key agencies – the police, the armed forces, the Special Branch and MI5 – were all formally outside parliamentary control.

III

The incorporation of the representative institutions of the working class into liberal-democracy was critical to the survival of capitalism, because 'The decision to achieve socialism through the parliamentary road meant accepting rules evolved by generations of the ruling class.'[7] The acceptance of liberal-democratic means of achieving change through the Labour Party and the trade unions carried with it the implicit assumption that they would play their part in the reproduction of capitalism.

But did the activities generated in and around the Labour Party represent the sum total of working-class political action? Historians have generally treated this as unproblematic or as a question of law and order in the context of an onward march towards a civilised way of life. Certainly it is possible to demonstrate how the representative in-stitutions of the class became incorporated into the system of liberal-democracy. What remains unexplained is the totality of political action, for while institutions may become incorporated the class as a whole can-not. Prior to the granting of the franchise the political activities of the working class were completely extra-parliamentary, and this remained largely the case until the 1920s. In fact much political action was directed towards the attainment of liberal-democratic rights, like the vote and the recognition of trade unions. From the early reform movements through to the struggles of the suffragettes any change in the *status quo* was resolutely opposed by the use of state force, for the historic fear of the British bourgeoisie was that the working class – the overwhelming majority of the people – would rise in revolution against the capitalist system. The base for such a revolution lies in extra-parliamentary working-class organisations which could not (because they had no vote), or did not, subscribe to the parliamentary road to socialism.

As it is today, the coercive power of the state in everyday life has been largely legitimised and the marginal violence of the workers often stigmatised as criminal and unlawful. Police histories place much emphasis on the violence of the 'mob' in the period prior to the creation of the new police forces from the 1830s. Historical evidence does not support this position:

'From my (no doubt) incomplete and imperfect record of the twenty-odd major riots and disturbances taking place in Britain

[7] Frank Pearce, *Writing on the Wall*, no. 2.

between the Edinburgh Porteous Riots of 1736 and the great Chartist demonstration of April 1848 in London, I have totted up the following score: the crowds killed a dozen at most; while, on the other side, the courts hanged 118 and 630 were shot dead by troops.'[8]

At the same time the violence of capitalist production against the people passed unpunished. For example, between 1850 and 1920 the number of miners killed by pit disasters was 8,520 (3,179 of which were in South Wales); but the law was silent where the rapacious demands of capitalist expansion were concerned and no mine-owner found himself in prison.[9]

Even during the 1920s and 1930s, the political activities of the working class were only partially directed through the Labour Party. And fear of movements outside the liberal-democratic system was not limited to members of the bourgeois parties and their class – it extended to the leaders of the parliamentary Labour Party and the newly-formed Trade Union Congress. The contradiction for the working class was (and is) between organising for better conditions under the wage-labour relation of capitalism, and on the other hand, working for the abolition of this very relation and thus of capitalism itself. While the former objective alone remains reformist (and in practice, economistic), the latter on its own is adventurist (and idealist). Only the unity in struggle of these two objectives could match the real interests and needs of the working class.

What becomes clear from the historical practice of the British state is that its repressive agencies have been overwhelmingly directed against the extra-constitutional movements of the working class and their revolutionary potential. This is no less true of the present than of the past. The various institutions and personnel of the state that are the subject of this study – the law, the police, the army and the intelligence agencies – play their part in the reproduction of the prevailing order which entails the incorporation, containment or elimination of any political movement threatening capitalist dominance.

[8] G. Rude, *Paris and London in the 18th Century* (1970), pp. 27–28.
[9] In 1913 an underground explosion occurred in Senghenydd pit in the Aber Valley in Wales and 439 miners died. Through the due process of law the mine-owners were prosecuted and fined £24.

IV

The authority of the state rests on the duality of force and consent, but at different historical moments one or other tends to predominate. During the first half of the nineteenth century this authority relied primarily on the use of overt force, but with the emergence of liberal-democracy, it came to rest increasingly upon consent. Today the state's authority derives from the consent given to it by the majority of the people, and the groups who withold consent by active opposition are disciplined by the agencies of state.

The need to establish the legitimacy of state action is all important: 'Indeed the attempt is always made to ensure that force will appear to be based on the consent of the majority, expressed by the so-called organs of public opinion (politicians, media, etc.)'[10] In Britain today the legitimation of the actions of the state, together with the perpetuation of the values and beliefs of everyday life that support it, have not only the appearance of consent, but have the actual consent of the majority of people in a society where the dominant historical and present-day interests are those of the capitalist class.

The nature of this 'consent' must be understood. It was gained from the working class by a combination of violence and ideological attrition – against the political movements of the class and against its individual members, both in the factory and outside in daily community life. There is no way, however, in which this consent can ever be assumed to prevail automatically – for no amount of mystification can veil the real nature of the wage–labour relation or the revolutionary potential of that class. The reactions, to specific events, of the working class, are often hard to find in conventional histories and the media today, but they are nonetheless real despite the fact that bourgeois commentators seek to exclude them from the historical record. When the October Revolution occurred in Russia in 1917 the British ruling class recoiled in horror and sent in troops and agents in an attempt to pre-empt it. A different reaction was recorded by Aneurin Bevin in 1951:

'I remember so well what happened when the Russian revolution occurred. I remember the miners, when they heard that the Tzarist tyranny had been overthrown, rushing to meet each other in the streets with tears streaming down their cheeks, shaking hands and saying: "At last it has happened." Let us remember in 1951 that the revolution of 1917 came to the working class of Great Britain, not

[10] A. Gramsci, *Prison Notebooks* (1971), p. 80.

as a social disaster, but as one of the most emancipating events in
the history of mankind.'[11]

The movement from the old hegemonic order of the feudal monarchs
(with their allied aristocracy) to the new bourgeois order did not pass
without a major crisis occurring, and continuity was only possible
through the exercise of force. Slowly, however, the preconditions of the
new bourgeois hegemony emerged with the adaptation of the old institutions into a liberal-democratic form. Central to this process was an
acceptance of the form of government and of the rule of law. The first, as
has been shown, came through a recognition of the representative institutions of working-class power – the Labour Party and the formal
structure of the trade unions – and their incorporation into the liberal-
democracy. This involved their acceptance of political action within the
legal–political framework as the only legitimate means of bringing
about change. Concomitant with this was obedience to the rule of law
which was effected through a process of attrition, which not only defined
the limits of political action but also served as a shield for the property
rights of the bourgeoisie. Ideas or actions, whether individually or
collectively expressed, that were perceived as a threat to the rule of law,
were declared to be illegitimate or 'criminal', to be punished on behalf
of society as a whole.

The development of the liberal-democratic system from the overt class
institutions which preceded it provides the underpinnings of today's
practices: the co-option of the representative institutions of the working
class through their acceptance of the liberal-democratic system; the
removal of power from parliament to the executive and the state administration; and the virtual non-accountability of the state's repressive
agencies. These all combine to provide the British state with a hidden
strength almost unparalleled in the liberal democracies of the West.

[11] *Labour Party Annual Conference Report*, 1951, p. 194.

Bibliography

Aitken, J., *Officially Secret* (Weidenfeld & Nicolson, London, 1971).

Alderson, J. C. & P. J. Stead (eds), *The Police We Deserve* (Wolfe, London, 1973).

Allen, Sir C. K., *The Queen's Peace* (Stevens and Sons, London, 1953).

Allen, Sir C. K., *Law and Orders* (Stevens and Sons, London, 1945).

Bordua, J. (ed.), *The Police: six sociological essays* (Wiley, N.Y., 1967).

Bowes, S., *The Police and Civil Liberties* (Lawrence and Wishart, London, 1966).

British Parliamentary Papers: Crime and Punishment: POLICE, Vol. 5. (Irish University Press, Dublin, 1968.)

Browne, D., *The Rise of Scotland Yard* (Putnam, London, 1956).

Brownlie, I., *The Law relating to Public Order* (Butterworths, London, 1968).

Bulloch, J., *MI5* (Barker, London, 1963).

Chandler, F. W., *Political Spies and Provocative Agents* (pub. by author, Sheffield, 1933).

Chester, L., S. Fay & H. Young, *The Zinoviev Letter* (Heinemann, London, 1967).

Clayton, T., *The Protectors* (Oldbourne, 1967).

Cloward & Piven, *Regulating the Poor* (Tavistock, London, 1972).

Cockburn, P., *The Years of the Week* (Penguin, Harmondsworth, 1971).

Coote, A. & L. Grant, *The NCCL Guide* (Penguin, Harmondsworth, 1972).

Cox, B., *Civil Liberties in Britain* (Penguin, Harmondsworth, 1975).

Critchley, T. A., *A History of the Police in England and Wales 900–1966* (Constable, London, 1967).

Deacon, R., *A History of the Secret Service* (Muller, London, 1969).

Dilnot, G., *Scotland Yard* (Geoffrey Bless, London, 1929).

Driver, C., *The Disarmers* (Hodder & Stoughton, London, 1964).

Dukes, Sir P., *The Story of ST25* (Cassells, London, 1938).

Firmin, S., *Scotland Yard* (Hutchinson, London, 1951).

Franklin, C., *The Third Degree* (Robert Hale, London, 1970).

Frow, R. & E. & M. Katanga, *Strikes* (Charles Knight, London, 1971).

Glynn, A. & B. Sutcliffe, *British Capitalism, Workers and the Profits Squeeze* (Penguin, Harmondsworth, 1972).

Goldman, E., *Living My Life, Vol. 1* (Dover, U.S.A., 1970).

Gramsci, A., *Prison Notebooks* (Lawrence & Wishart, London, 1971).

Hamilton, P., *Espionage and Subversion in an Industrial Society* (Hutchinson, London, 1967).

Hannington, W., *Never on Our Knees* (Lawrence & Wishart, London, 1967).

Harrison, R., *The CID and the FBI* (Muller, London, 1956).

Hart, J., *The British Police* (Allen and Unwin, London, 1951).

Hedley, P. & C. Aynsley, *The D-Notice Affair* (Joseph, London, 1968).

Howard, G., *Guardians of the Queen's Peace* (Odhams, London, 1953).

Howe, Sir R., *The Story of Scotland Yard* (Barker, London, 1965).

Howgrave-Graham, H. M., *Light and Shade at Scotland Yard* (John Murray, London, 1948).

Humphry, D., *Police Power and Black People* (Panther, London, 1972).

Jackson, R., *The Case for the Prosecution* (Barker, London, 1962).

Jennings, Sir I., *The Law and the Constitution* (University of London Press, London, 1959).

Johnson, F. A., *Defence by Committee* (O.U.P., London, 1960).

Jones, J., *Whitehall Diary*, Vols 1 and 2 (O.U.P., London, 1969).

Keir, Sir D. L., *The Constitutional History of Modern Britain* (A. & C. Black, London, 1966).

Kidd, R., *British Liberty in Danger* (Lawrence & Wishart, London, 1940).

Kitson, F., *Low Intensity Operations* (Faber, London, 1971).

Klugmann, J., *History of the British Communist Party*, Vol. 1 (Lawrence & Wishart, London, 1968).

Laurie, P., *Scotland Yard* (Bodley Head, London, 1970).

Laurie, P., *Beneath the City Streets* (Penguin, Harmondsworth, 1972).

Leigh, L. H., *Police Powers in England & Wales* (Butterworth, London, 1975).

Madgwick, D. & T. Smythe, *The Invasion of Privacy* (Pitmans, London, 1974).

MacDermott, G., *The New Diplomacy* (Plume Press/Ward Lock, London, 1973).

McGuffin, J., *The Guinea Pigs* (Penguin, Harmondsworth, 1974).

Mather, T. C., *Public Order in the Age of the Chartists* (Manchester University Press, Manchester, 1959).

Marcuse, H., *Counterrevolution and Revolt* (Allen Lane, London, 1972).

Marshall, G., *Police and Government* (Methuen, London, 1965).

Miliband, R., *The State in Capitalist Society* (Weidenfeld and Nicolson, London, 1969).

Moylan, Sir J., *Scotland Yard* (Putnam, London, 1934).

Newsam, Sir F., *The Home Office* (Allen and Unwin, London, 1954).

O'Higgins, P., *Censorship in Britain* (Nelson, London, 1972).

Osborne, B., *Justices of the Peace, 1361–1848* (Sedgehill Press, 1960).

Page, B., D. Leitch, & P. Knightley, *Philby* (Penguin, Harmondsworth, 1969).

Payne, R., *Private Spies* (Barker, London, 1967).

Potter, J. D., *Scotland Yard* (Burke, London, 1972).

Pritt, D. N., *Law, Class and Society,* Books 1–4 (Lawrence and Wishart, London, 1971).

Radzinowicz, L., *A History of English Criminal Law*, Vols 1–4 (Stevens, London, 1948/1956/1956/1968).

Reith, C., *British Police and the Democratic Ideal* (O.U.P., London, 1943).

Reynolds, G. W. & A. Judge, *The Night the Police Went on Strike* (Weidenfeld and Nicolson, London, 1968).

Roper, H. Trevor, *The Philby Affair* (Kimber, London, 1968).

Rude, G., *Paris and London in the 18th Century* (Fontana, London, 1970).

Rule, J., *Private Lives and Public Surveillance* (Allen Lane, London, 1973).

Sampson, A., *Anatomy of Britain* (Hodder and Stoughton, London, 1971).

Scott, Sir H., *Scotland Yard* (Penguin, Harmondsworth, 1957).

Seth, R., *The Specials* (Gollancz, London, 1961).

Sillitoe, Sir P., *Cloak Without Dagger* (Cassells, London, 1955).

Smellie, K. B., *A Hundred Years of English Government* (Duckworth, London, 1937).

Smith, P. Slee, *Industrial Intelligence and Espionage* (London Business Books, London, 1970).

Strong, Sir K., *Intelligence at the Top* (Cassells, London, 1968).

Sweeney, G., *At Scotland Yard* (Grant Richards, London, 1904).

Symons, J., *The General Strike* (The Cresset Press, London, 1957).

Thomas, H., *Crisis in the Civil Service* (A. Blond, London, 1970).

Thompson, A., *Big Brother in Britain Today* (Joseph, London, 1970).

Thompson, E. P., *The Making of the English Working Class* (Penguin, Harmondsworth, 1968).

Thompson, E. P., (ed.), *Warwick University Ltd* (Penguin, Harmondsworth, 1970).

Thomson, Sir B., *Queer People* (Hodder and Stoughton, 1922).

Thomson, Sir B., *My Experiences at Scotland Yard* (Doubleday, Page and Co., U.S.A., 1923).

Thomson, Sir B., *The Story of Scotland Yard* (Grayson and Grayson, London, 1935).

Thomson, Sir B., *The Scene Changes* (Collins, London, 1939).

Troup, Sir E., *The Home Office* (Putnam, London, 1925).

Whittaker, B., *The Police* (Penguin, Harmondsworth, 1964).

Wilcox, A. F., *The Decision to Prosecute* (Butterworth, London, 1970).

Williams, D., *Not in the Public Interest* (Hutchinson, London, 1965).

Williams, D., *Keeping the Peace* (Hutchinson, London, 1967).

Williams, G. R., *The Hidden World of Scotland Yard* (Hutchinson, London, 1972).

Woodcock, G., *Anarchism* (Penguin, Harmondsworth, 1962).

Pamphlets

Big Business and Politics, Labour Research Department, 1974.

The Black Book on the Police, anon, 1972.

The Campbell Case (by N. D. Siederer), reprint from the Journal of Contemporary History, Vol. 9, no. 2, 1974.

European Military Institutions – a Reconnaissance, The Universities Service Study Group, Edinburgh University. 1970–71 Report.

The Greek Embassy Case (written and published by Andy Anderson), 1967.

The Labour Government v. The Dockers, Solidarity, 1965 (reprint).

Lessons of the General Strike (by Bob Dent), Millenium Press, 1973.

The New Technology of Repression, British Society for Social Responsibility in Science, 1974.

The RSGs (by N. Walter), Solidarity, 1963.

The Secret Police and You, The Campaign for the Limitation of Secret Police Powers, 1956.

A Year with the Secret Police, Campaign for the Limitation of Secret Police Powers, 1957.

The Security Industry in the United Kingdom, Cambridge University, Institute of Criminology, 1970.

The Sedition Act Explained (by I. Jennings), New Statesman, 1934.

Sources of Conflict in British Industry, Institute for the Study of Conflict, 1974.

The State (by P. Kropotkin), Freedom Press, 1969.

The Strange Case of Major Vernon, National Council for Civil Liberties, undated.

Study War No More (by Zoe Fairbairns), CND, 1974.

Resistance Shall Grow, anon, 1963.

Riot Control (by Major-General A. J. Deane-Drummond), Royal United Services Institute, 1975.

Whose Conspiracy? (by Geoff Robertson), National Council for Civil Liberties, 1974.

Government publications

Report of the Conference of Privy Councillors, Cmnd 9715, HMSO, 1956.

The Report of the Committee of Privy Councillors appointed to inquire into the interception of communications (The Birkett Report), Cmnd 283, HMSO, 1957.

Royal Commission on the Police, Cmnd 1728, HMSO, 1962.

Security Procedures in the Public Service (The Radcliffe Report), Cmnd 1681, HMSO, 1962.

Lord Denning's Report, Cmnd 2152, HMSO, 1963.

White Paper on the Central Organisation for Defence, Cmnd 2097, HMSO, 1964.

Departmental Committee on Section 2 of the Official Secrets Act 1911 (The Franks Report), Vols 1–3, Cmnd 5104, HMSO, 1972.

Report of the Committee on Privacy (The Younger Report), Cmnd 5012, HMSO, 1972.

Report to the Home Secretary from the Commissioner of Police for the Metropolis on the actions of the police officer concerned with the case of Kenneth Joseph Lennon, HMSO, July, 1974.

Report of the Commissioner of Police for the Metropolis, HMSO, 1973–75.

Report of Her Majesty's Chief Inspector of Constabulary, HMSO, 1973–75.

List of Abbreviations

ACTT	Association of Cinematograph and Television Technicians
AIL	Anti Internment League
BSIA	British Security Industry Association
BUI	British United Industrialists
CID	Criminal Investigation Department
CND	Campaign for Nuclear Disarmament
CO	Commissioner's Office
COS	Chiefs of Staff Committee
CRO	Criminal Records Office
DAC	Deputy Assistant Commissioner
DEP	Department of Employment and Productivity
DHSS	Department of Health and Social Security
DIC	Defence Intelligence Committee
DI5	*See* MI5
DIS	Defence Intelligence Staff
DMI	Directorate of Military Intelligence
D-Notice	Services, Press and Broadcasting Committee Notice
DORA	Defence of the Realm Act
DPP	Director of Public Prosecutions
FCO	Foreign and Commonwealth Office
GCHQ	Government Communications Headquarters
GLC	Greater London Council
GMC	General Medical Council
IB	Investigation Branch (Post Office)
IRA	Irish Republican Army
IRIS	Industrial Research and Information Services
IS	International Socialists
JIB	Joint Intelligence Bureau
JIC	Joint Intelligence Committee
JP	Justice of the Peace
MI5	Military Intelligence (internal)
MI6	Military Intelligence (external)
MOD	Ministry of Defence

NCCL	National Council for Civil Liberties
NID	National Intelligence Department
NSC	National Security Committee
NSP	National Security Plan
NUJ	National Union of Journalists
NUM	National Union of Mineworkers
NUWM	National Unemployed Workers' Movement
OSA	Official Secrets Act
PNCU	Police National Computer Unit
PUS	Permanent Under-Secretary
QC	Queen's Council
RCS	Regional Crime Squad
RSG	Regional Seat of Government
RUSI	Royal United Services Institute
SIS	Secret Intelligence Service (*see* MI6)
SLL	Socialist Labour League
SPG	Special Patrol Group
SWAPO	South-West African People's Organisation
TUC	Trades Union Congress

Subject Index *(See p. 318 for Name Index)*

Name Index